ABSOLUTE BEGINNER'S GUIDE

 TO

iPod and iTunes

Brad Miser

800 East 96th Street,
Indianapolis, Indiana 46240

Absolute Beginner's Guide to iPod and iTunes

International Standard Book Number: 0-7897-3177-0

Library of Congress Catalog Card Number: 2004104259

Printed in the United States of America

First Printing: June 2004

07   06   05   04   4   3

Trademarks

Warning and Disclaimer

Bulk Sales

Que Publishing offers excellent discounts on this book when ordered in quantity for bulk purchases or special sales. For more information, please contact

U.S. Corporate and Government Sales
1-800-382-3419
corpsales@pearsontechgroup.com

For sales outside of the U.S., please contact

International Sales
1-317-428-3341
international@pearsontechgroup.com

Associate Publisher
Greg Wiegand

Acquisitions Editor
Stephanie J. McComb

Development Editor
Kevin Howard

Managing Editor
Charlotte Clapp

Project Editor
Sheila Schroeder

Copy Editor
Bart Reed

Indexer
Ken Johnson

Proofreader
Cindy Long

Technical Editor
Brian Hubbard

User Reviewer
Rick Ehrhardt

Publishing Coordinator
Sharry Lee Gregory

Interior Designer
Dan Armstrong

Cover Designer
Anne Jones

Page Layout
Kelly Maish

Contents at a Glance

Table of Contents

About the Author

Brad Miser has written extensively about computers and related technology, with his favorite topics being anything that starts with a lowercase *i*, such as the iPod and iTunes. In addition to *Absolute Beginner's Guide to the iPod and iTunes*, Brad has written many other books, including *Special Edition Using Mac OS X, v10.3 Panther*; *Mac OS X and iLife: Using iTunes, iPhoto, iMovie, and iDVD*; *iDVD 3 Fast & Easy*; *Special Edition Using Mac OS X v10.2, Mac OS X and the Digital Lifestyle*; and *Using Mac OS 8.5*. He has also been an author, development editor, or technical editor on more than 50 other titles. He has been a featured speaker on various computer-related topics at Macworld Expo, at user group meetings, and in other venues.

Brad is the senior technical communicator for an Indianapolis-based software development company. Here, Brad is responsible for all product documentation, training materials, online help, and other communication materials. He also manages the customer support operations for the company and provides training and account management services to its customers. Previously, he was the lead engineering proposal specialist for an aircraft engine manufacturer, a development editor for a computer book publisher, and a civilian aviation test officer/engineer for the U.S. Army. Brad holds a Bachelor of Science degree in mechanical engineering from California Polytechnic State University at San Luis Obispo (1986) and has received advanced education in maintainability engineering, business, and other topics.

In addition to his passion for computers and technology, Brad likes to run and play racquetball; playing with home theater technology is also a favorite pastime.

Once a native of California, Brad now lives in Brownsburg, Indiana with his wife Amy; their three daughters, Jill, Emily, and Grace; and their guinea pig, Buddy.

Brad would love to hear about your experiences with this book (the good, the bad, and the ugly). You can write to him at bradmacosx@mac.com.

Dedication

I leave you, hoping that the lamp of liberty will burn in your bosoms until there shall no longer be a doubt that all men are created free and equal.

—*Abraham Lincoln*

Acknowledgments

To the following people on the *ABG iPod and iTunes* project team, my sincere appreciation for your hard work on this book:

Stephanie McComb, my acquisitions editor, who made this project possible and convinced the right people that this was a good idea and that I was the right one to write it. **Marta Justak** of Justak Literary Services, my agent, for getting me signed up for this project and providing advice and encouragement along the way. **Kevin Howard**, my development editor, who helped make the contents and organization of this book much better. **Rick Ehrhardt**, my user reviewer, who made the jump to an iPod and iTunes at just the right time and provided lots of invaluable feedback that made this book much better.

Brian Hubbard, my technical editor, who did a great job ensuring that the information in this book is both accurate and useful. **Bart Reed**, my copy editor, who corrected my many misspellings, poor grammar, and other problems. **Sheila Schroeder**, my project editor, who skillfully managed the hundreds of files that it took to make this book into something real. **Que's production and sales team** for printing the book and getting it into your hands.

Thanks to the following companies that provided some of the excellent iPod accessories that are covered in this book. **Dr. Bott "Distribution Macintosh Style,"** www.drbott.com, 9720 SW Hillman Court, Suite 840, Wilsonville, OR 97070. The team at **XtremeMac**, www.xtrememac.com, 15751 SW 41st Street, Suite 100, Fort Lauderdale, FL 33331. **TEN Technology**, www.tentechnology.com, 310-765-4834. **Griffin Technology**, www.griffintechnology.com, 615-399-7000. **Marware**, www.marware.com, 954-927-6031.

And now for some people who weren't on the project team, but who were essential to me personally. **Amy Miser**, my wonderful wife, for supporting me while I wrote this book; living with an author under tight deadlines isn't always lots of fun, but Amy does so with grace, understanding, and acceptance of my need to write. **Jill**, **Emily**, and **Grace Miser**, my delightful daughters, for helping me stay focused on what is important in life. While an iPod can play beautiful music, these precious people are beautiful music given form! (And, a special thanks to **Buddy** the guinea pig for his early-morning visits to cheer me up while I was working!)

We Want to Hear from You!

As the reader of this book, *you* are our most important critic and commentator. We value your opinion and want to know what we're doing right, what we could do better, what areas you'd like to see us publish in, and any other words of wisdom you're willing to pass our way.

As an associate publisher for Que Publishing, I welcome your comments. You can email or write me directly to let me know what you did or didn't like about this book—as well as what we can do to make our books better.

Please note that I cannot help you with technical problems related to the topic of this book. We do have a User Services group, however, where I will forward specific technical questions related to the book.

When you write, please be sure to include this book's title and author as well as your name, email address, and phone number. I will carefully review your comments and share them with the author and editors who worked on the book.

Email: feedback@quepublishing.com

Mail: Greg Wiegand
          Associate Publisher
          Que Publishing
          800 East 96th Street
          Indianapolis, IN 46240 USA

For more information about this book or another Que Publishing title, visit our Web site at www.quepublishing.com. Type the ISBN (excluding hyphens) or the title of a book in the Search field to find the page you're looking for.

INTRODUCTION

If you have been toying with the idea of getting into digital music.... If you have an iPod and aren't sure what to do with it.... If you wish you had a good way to stop messing around with a bunch of CDs when you want to listen to music.... If you've heard great things about iPods, have seen the commercials for the iTunes Music Store, and want to know what all the fuss is about, then welcome to the *Absolute Beginner's Guide to iPod and iTunes*!

Meet the Digital Music Triumvirate

In this book, you'll learn about three of the most amazing things to happen to music since the first time someone decided that banging a stick on a rock had an appealing sound. These are the iPod, iTunes, and the iTunes Music Store.

The iPod Rocks

Apple's iPod has taken the portable digital device market by storm—and for good reason. Because the iPod includes a hard drive with up to 40GB of space, it is possible for you to take your music collection wherever you go. The iPod's tools enable you to organize, customize, and listen to your music in many ways while you are on the move—in your car, at home, or working at your computer. With its tight integration with iTunes and the iTunes Music Store, managing your music is both fun and easy. Your trusty iPod can also be used as a portable hard drive (for example, you can use it to carry files from your home to your office), to capture sound, and to store pictures; there are numerous peripheral devices that expand its amazing capabilities even further. And, iPods are just plain cool (see Figure I.1).

If you have never used an iPod before, this book is perfect for you and will help you learn everything you need to know. If you have some experience with an iPod, this book will still help you take your iPod skills to the next level. (If you are already an iPod expert, well, you aren't likely to be picking up a book called *Absolute Beginner's Guide to iPod and iTunes* now are you!)

iTunes Jams

With iTunes, you can create, organize, and listen to your entire music library from your computer (see Figure I.2). iTunes enables you to build as large a Library as you have the space on your computer's hard drive to store it. Then, you can customize music playback through playlists and smart playlists as well as create custom audio CDs in a variety of formats. It also provides other useful features, such as custom labeling and information tools, the ability to share your music on a local network, an Equalizer, and more. Because Apple's iTunes Music Store is integrated into iTunes, you can easily purchase and add music to your Library from within the application. Moreover, iTunes is the best software tool available for the iPod.

FIGURE I.1

Whether you choose an iPod or an iPod mini, it will rock your world.

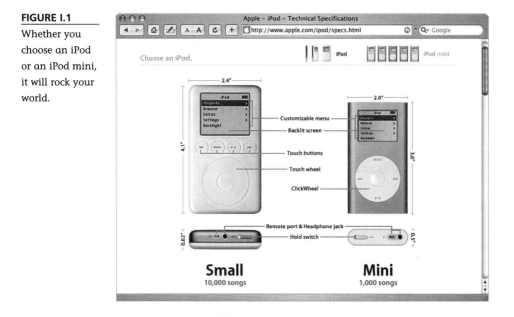

FIGURE I.2

iTunes will change the way you listen to music.

Just as with the iPod, if you have never used iTunes before, this book is perfect for you and will help you learn everything you need to know. If you have some experience, my hope is that you will learn how to get even more out of this outstanding program. Even if you have used iTunes quite a bit, you might manage to find some tidbits that will help your iTunes expertise grow.

iTunes Music Store

Using the iTunes Music Store, named as *Time* magazine's Invention of the Year for 2003, you can find, preview, and purchase music from a collection of hundreds of thousands of songs and download that music into your iTunes Music Library. Songs can be purchased individually or in albums, for $.99 per song (less when purchasing an entire album). Music you buy can be listened to, placed on a CD, and moved onto your iPod. Since its inception, the iTunes Music Store has rapidly become the most popular source of legal digital music on the Internet. After you have used it a time or two, you'll understand why.

Quick Guide to *Absolute Beginner's Guide to iPod and iTunes*

Absolute Beginner's Guide to iPod and iTunes provides all the information you need to get the most out of these amazing digital music tools. From the basics of listening to audio CDs with iTunes to the advanced customizing of music on an iPod and purchasing music online, this book equips you to use these awesome tools.

The book is organized into the following three major parts, each focusing on one of the three components of the iPod/iTunes/iTunes Music Store triumvirate:

- Part I: The iPod
- Part II: iTunes
- Part III: The iTunes Music Store

Within each part, the chapters generally start with the basics of the topic and get more advanced as you continue. Within the chapters, the information is presented in roughly the order in which you will typically perform the tasks being described.

Speaking of tasks, this book contains many step-by-step instructions—I hope your motto will be "learn by doing." You should be able to learn how to do a task fairly quickly and relatively painlessly by following the steps using your own music and your own tools. Although my writing is so utterly fascinating that you will likely want to read this book like a good novel, try to resist that urge because you will probably get better results if you actually work with the tools while you read this book.

Of course, you can read this book from start to finish in the order in which the chapters are presented. This will work fine if you have some experience with iTunes and have some music in your iTunes Library. However, because these tools are so well integrated, you can't really use the iPod or the iTunes Music Store effectively without knowing the basics of using iTunes first.

If you are totally new to these topics, I recommend that you get a jumpstart on iTunes by reading the core iTunes chapters first, which include Chapters 12, 13, 14, 15, 16, and 17. Then, you should read the core iPod chapters, which are Chapters 1, 2, 3, 4, and 5. From there, read Chapters 22 through 25 to get the scoop on working with the iTunes Music Store.

After you have finished these core "courses," you can read the rest of the chapters as they interest you. For example, when you are ready to burn your own CDs or DVDs, check out Chapter 19, "Burning Your Own CDs or DVDs." And when you want to explore the world of amazing iPod accessories, read Chapter 7, "Rocking Your World with iPod Accessories."

Going Both Ways

Because the iPod, iTunes, and the iTunes Music Store all work equally well on both Windows and Macintosh computers, this book covers these topics from both perspectives. So, you'll notice that some of the figures are screenshots taken on a Windows computer whereas others are taken on a Macintosh. Although the screens on these two computers look slightly different, they work very similarly, so seeing a screen on the Mac shouldn't cause a problem for you if you use a Windows computer, and vice versa. When there are significant differences, I explain them in the text.

Special Elements

As you read, you will see three special elements: Notes, Tips, and, only rarely, Cautions. Also, each chapter ends with a section titled "The Absolute Minimum." Explanations of each of these are provided for you here.

note

Notes look like this. They are designed to provide you with information that is related to the topic at hand but not absolutely essential to it. I hope you will find the Notes interesting, even if you don't find them useful immediately.

tip

Tips help you get something done more quickly and easily, or they tell you how to do a task that is related to what's being described at the moment. You might also find an explanation of an alternate way to get something done.

caution

If something you can do (and probably shouldn't) might end in a bad result, I warn you in a Caution. Fortunately, you won't find many of these throughout the book, but when you do see one, you might want to take a close look at it.

THE ABSOLUTE MINIMUM

Finally, each chapter ends with "The Absolute Minimum" section. The contents of this section vary a bit from chapter to chapter. Examples of this content include the following:

- A summary of the key points of the chapter.
- Additional tips related to the chapter's topic.
- References to sources of additional information.

So, now that you know all you need to about this book, it's time to strike up the band....

PART I

THE iPOD

1

TOURING THE IPOD

In less than two years of existence, Apple's iPod has become one of the most popular personal digital devices ever created. When initially released, the iPod's critics said it was too expensive when compared to other digital music players and that people would never spend the additional money to get the iPod's much superior functionality and style (even the critics couldn't deny the iPod's amazing attributes). As they often are, the critics were very much mistaken. People who love music love the iPod. Its combination of features and style, and because it's simply very, very cool, led it to quickly dominate sales in its category.

The Apple iPod: A Lot of Hype or Really Hip?

So, what's the iPod all about?

It's about being able to take your entire music collection with you and listen to anything you want when you want to listen to it. And, using iPod's companion iTunes software, you can create and carry customized collections of your music to make getting to the specific music you want to hear even easier and more fun.

The way your music sounds on an iPod is just amazing, too. You definitely don't have to compromise music quality for portability. With the iPod, you get the best of both. If you have never heard music on an iPod before, prepare to be amazed.

That's the bottom line, but it isn't the whole story. With the iPod, you can do much more, as you will learn through the rest of this part of this book. And because of the iPod's stylish design and ease of use, you will likely want to take it with you wherever you go.

So What Is an iPod Anyway?

The iPod is a small digital device that includes a hard drive (just like the one in your computer, only smaller), an operating system, a processor and other computer components, as well as an LCD screen, controls, and other system elements needed to deliver its amazing functionality. It also includes a rechargeable lithium battery to give you plenty of listening time, a Headphones port to which you attach audio devices (including headphones, powered speakers, and so on), and the Dock connector port to enable you to move music from a computer onto the iPod and recharge its battery.

The iPod's software enables you to manage and play digital audio files. You can also use its software to set a variety of preferences, in addition to using the iPod's other built-in tools.

Even with all this, iPods are quite small. The largest iPod is only 2.4 inches wide, 4.1 inches tall, .73 inches thick, and weighs a mere 6.2 ounces. This is roughly the size of a deck of playing cards. The smallest model, the iPod mini, comes in at a svelte 2 inches wide, 3.6 inches tall, .5 inches thick, and a mere 3.6 ounces. This is about the size of a deck of playing cards cut in half!

note

iPods can work with a variety of audio file formats, including AAC, MP3, Audible books, AIFF (Mac only), and WAV. Because you just listen to these formats on an iPod, you don't need to know that much about them to use one. However, you will want to understand these formats when you prepare music for an iPod using iTunes. If you can't wait to learn what these formats are all about, see "Audio File Formats You Might Encounter When You Use iTunes" on page **164**.

All iPod Models Aren't Equal, But They Are All Cool

iPods comes in three basic models: the iPod, the iPod mini, and the original iPod. All three of these models are definitely cool, and all perform the same basic function. However, each offers specific features and options. Let's take a quick look at each of these models.

The iPod

The third major generation of iPods was a substantial improvement over the first two generations and quickly made the much-beloved-but-now-obsolete original iPods go the way of other extinct digital devices. Among this generation's improvements are the addition of the Dock (to enable the device to be connected to a computer more easily), larger hard drives for more music storage, improved controls, better software, and more accessories (see Figure 1.1).

> **note**
>
> At press time, only the three models of iPods detailed in this chapter were available. However, Apple frequently updates the iPods to increase storage space and add new features. To get the scoop on the latest iPod models right now, go to http://www.apple.com/ipod.

FIGURE 1.1

The iPod will definitely rock your world.

Within the iPod family are currently three major versions, the biggest difference among them being the size of the hard drive they contain. However, there are also minor differences in accessories between the least expensive model and the other two. Here are the current members of the iPod clan (see Figure 1.2):

FIGURE 1.2

Pick an iPod, any iPod; you can't go wrong.

- **15GB**—The base iPod model isn't really basic. It offers a 15GB drive and includes the same great features as its bigger siblings. However, it includes fewer accessories than the other models. The most notable omission is the Dock. Even so, you can fit as many as 3,700 songs on this iPod. And that's a lot of music! The current list price of this model is $299.

- **20GB**—The middle model of iPod includes a 20GB hard drive and includes more accessories than the base model. Apple rates this model at 5,000 songs, and it includes a Dock, wired remote, and carrying case. This model lists for $399.

note

If you haven't purchased an iPod yet (what are you waiting for?), I recommend that you get at least the middle model. In addition to more room for music, you get the Dock and other accessories that are easily worth the price difference between the larger two models and the least expensive one.

■ **40GB**—The top-of-the-line iPod has a 40GB hard drive, rated at 10,000 songs. Because of this, it is slightly heavier (by 0.6 ounces) and larger (0.09 inches thicker) than the other models. It includes the same accessory set as the 20GB model and costs $499.

Small Is Beautiful: The iPod Mini

As if the iPod isn't small enough, Apple introduced an even smaller iPod, known as the *iPod mini*. These smaller iPods offer similar features to their bigger cousins and include a 4GB hard drive rated at 1,000 songs. Unlike the iPod, which comes only in its elegant white and silver finish, the iPod mini comes in five colors (see Figure 1.3). The iPod mini also has different controls than the iPod, but they work in a similar way.

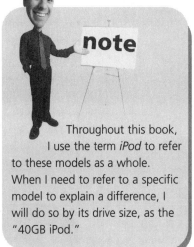

note

Throughout this book, I use the term *iPod* to refer to these models as a whole. When I need to refer to a specific model to explain a difference, I will do so by its drive size, as the "40GB iPod."

FIGURE 1.3

The difference between the various iPod mini models is only skin deep.

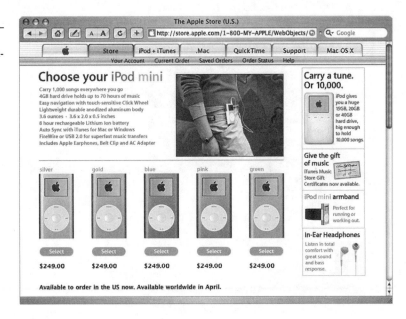

The One That Started It All: The Original iPod

The first generation of iPod offered many of the same features as its successors, although it had a smaller hard drive (the first iPod included a 5GB drive) and was larger and heavier than later generations (see Figure 1.4). It was also compatible only with Macintosh computers, and its software was a bit more limited, too. Although it is no longer being produced, this is the model that started it all, and for that we owe it a debt of gratitude (if one can owe anything to a device, that is).

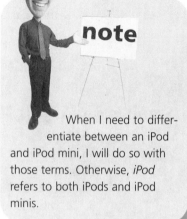

note

When I need to differentiate between an iPod and iPod mini, I will do so with those terms. Otherwise, *iPod* refers to both iPods and iPod minis.

FIGURE 1.4

The first, but not the best, iPod had a 5GB hard drive and paved the way for the later generations.

Because the original iPod hasn't been produced for a long time, it seems unlikely you will be using this model while you are reading this book (because the book assumes you are relatively new to the iPod world). To save some pages, I won't be covering the original iPod elsewhere in this book. Much of the information about iPods and iPod minis is also applicable to the original iPod, but there are some differences in its controls and software.

What You Can Do with an iPod

The iPod is definitely a great music player, but it is much more than that, as you will learn throughout this part of the book. For now, here are some of the great things you can do with an iPod:

- Take your entire music collection with you wherever you go.

- Play your music in many different ways, such as by album, artist, genre, song, playlist, and so on.

- Eliminate the need to carry CDs with you anywhere; using an adapter or an FM transmitter, your iPod can provide music in your home, car, or any other place you happen to be.

- View your calendar.

- Access contact information for your favorite people and companies for quick and easy reference.

- Keep track of the time and date.

- Listen to your favorite audio book.

- Have a portable hard drive for transferring information between computers or for backing up your files.

- Record sound.

- Store pictures from a digital camera.

note

Although the original iPod is obsolete in the sense that it is no longer in production, you might be able to find a used one for sale. If you can find a good deal on one, this can be a good way to enter the iPod market or to get a second iPod. The original iPods are still very useful; I have one myself and use it quite often.

note

Additional accessories are required to perform some of these tasks.

THE ABSOLUTE MINIMUM

The iPod just might be the neatest gadget ever. After you have tried one, you will likely find it to be indispensable, and you might wonder how you ever got along without it. Before we jump into configuring and using an iPod, consider the following two points:

- An iPod enables you to take all your music with you and listen to it anytime, anywhere.

- The iPod is actually a mini computer and includes a hard drive, an operating system, and other computer components.

- There are two types of iPods in production: iPods and iPod minis.

- No matter which iPod you have, you'll be amazed at all the amazing things it can do, from basic listening to being your own personal portable hard drive.

- The original iPod worked only with Macintosh computers, but soon Apple realized that there was no reason to keep Windows users out in the cold. Current iPod models work just as well for both platforms. Whether you use a Windows computer, a Mac, or both, your iPod will work great.

IN THIS CHAPTER

- Find out what cool stuff came with your iPod.

- Charge the iPod's battery.

- Install the iPod's software on your computer.

- Connect the iPod to your computer and transfer music from your computer to it.

- Use a Dock to connect an iPod to your computer.

2

GETTING STARTED WITH AN iPOD

Getting started with an iPod involves the following general steps:

1. Understand what is included with the iPod.

2. Charge the iPod's battery.

3. Install the iPod's software on your computer.

4. Connect the iPod to your computer and transfer music from your computer to the iPod.

5. Disconnect the iPod from your computer.

After you have performed these steps, you will be ready to learn how to use the iPod, which you'll start doing in the next chapter.

Exploring the iPod's Box

The iPod is so cool that even its box is stylish! In this section, you'll learn about the items included in that stylish box and how and where you use them. What you get with an iPod depends on the type and model of iPod you purchased. The following list tells you what comes with each type of iPod:

- **An iPod or iPod mini**—You probably didn't need this item listed or explained, but I like to be thorough!

- **Installation CD**—This CD contains the iTunes installer you will use to install the iPod's companion software on your computer.

- **Information manuals**—These include the *Quick Reference* and the *User's Guide*. (Because you have this book already, you might not find these to be very useful.)

- **Power Adapter**—You use this to charge an iPod's battery.

- **FireWire to Dock connector port cable (iPod only)**—You use this cable to connect the iPod's Dock connector port (or the Dock port on a Dock) to a FireWire port on your computer. You can also use it to connect the FireWire port on the power adapter to the iPod's Dock port.

- **USB 2.0 to Dock Connector Port cable (iPod mini only)**—You use this cable to connect the iPod mini's Dock connector port to a USB 2 port on your computer.

- **Earbud earphones**—You use these to listen to the iPod's output.

- **Six-pin to Four-pin FireWire adapter (iPod only)**—This adapter is used when the computer to which you are connecting an iPod uses a four-pin FireWire port.

note

Unless you have an iPod and an iPod mini and you use both Windows and Macintosh computers, you won't need to read all of this chapter. That is because its sections are based on specific options, such as using an iPod mini with a Mac or using an iPod with a Windows computer. As you read through sections, skip those that don't apply to you. (Of course, should you ever need them, they will be here waiting patiently for you.)

tip

As you are handling the iPod, it will turn on if you press any control. For now, turn it off again by pressing and then holding the **Play/Pause** button down until the iPod shuts off again.

- **Dock Port covers (iPod only)**—These plastic inserts can be placed in an iPod's Dock port to prevent it from being damaged by dirt or other debris.
- **Dock (some iPod models)**—Currently included with the 20GB and 40GB models, the Dock is a base unit into which you can place the iPod to connect it to your computer. The Dock eliminates the need to mess around with cables each time you connect your iPod to your computer.
- **iPod Remote (some iPod models)**—This remote is connected inline with the earbuds and enables you to control the iPod from its control panel. It is currently included with the 20GB and 40GB models.
- **Case (some models of the iPod)**—Some models include a carrying case with a belt clip.
- **Belt clip (iPod mini only)**—You can insert your iPod mini into this clip and then clip the clip to a belt to carry the iPod mini with you.

note

You can purchase a Dock separately if your iPod didn't include one. See Chapter 7, "Rocking Your World with iPod Accessories," for more information.

More sophisticated remotes are available for the iPod. See Chapter 7 for details.

Charging the iPod's Battery

Like all portable electronic devices, the iPod has an internal battery. Before you start using an iPod, you should charge its battery.

To charge an iPod using the power adapter, connect the FireWire to iPod Dock connector cable to the power adapter and to the iPod. Then plug the power adapter into a power outlet.

While the iPod is charging, a battery icon will appear on its display and the word "Charging" will appear at the top of the screen. According to Apple, the iPod's battery is charged to the 80% level in one hour and fully charged in four hours.

When the iPod is fully charged, the display will contain a "full" battery icon and the status message will be "Charged." Unplug the power adapter and then disconnect the cable from the power adapter and from the iPod.

tip

If you are going to connect the iPod to a Macintosh or to a Windows computer using a six-pin FireWire cable, you don't need to charge the iPod's battery because that is done automatically when you connect the iPod to your computer. If you use a four-pin cable, you have to charge the battery by using the power adapter.

Installing the iPod's Software (Including iTunes)

Included in the iPod's box is a software installation CD. On this CD is the iTunes application you will use to manage the music that you place on the iPod. You'll learn all about iTunes in Part II of this book, titled "iTunes." But for now, install the software by using the steps in the section that is appropriate for the type of computer you are using (Windows PC or a Mac).

Installing the iPod's Software on a Windows PC

If you have installed even one application from a CD, you won't have any trouble with the iPod CD, as the following steps will confirm:

1. Insert the **Installation CD** in your computer. The disc will be mounted on your computer, the software will begin to run, and the Choose Setup Language dialog box will appear.

2. Choose the language you want to use on the drop-down list and click **OK**. Because I am linguistically challenged and can only read English, that is the language I use throughout this book. They say music is the universal language (I think it is math myself) and so iTunes can use many different languages. You can choose the language that works best for you.

   After you click OK, the InstallShield Wizard window will appear, and you can watch the initial installation process. When that is complete, you will see the **iPod for Windows** dialog box (see Figure 2.1) or the **iPod mini for Windows** dialog box.

3. Click **Install**. The **iPod Serial Number** dialog box will appear.

note

If you'd rather, you can download and install a "fresh" copy of iTunes from the Internet. This is usually a good idea so you get the latest version. To get help doing that, see the section "Downloading and Installing iTunes on a Windows PC" on page **172**. Then come back here and complete the iPod software installation.

note

If you have trouble reading the serial number, you aren't alone. The text is very small!

FIGURE 2.1

You might see a slightly different window depending on the model of iPod you are using, but in any case, the Install button is the same.

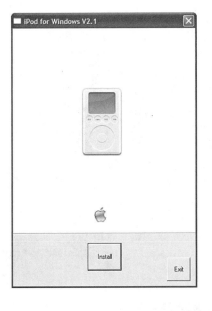

4. Enter your iPod's serial number, which can be found on the back of your iPod, and click **Next**. You will see the **Select Country or Region** dialog box.

5. Select the country or region that is most applicable to you and click **Next**. You will see the **Registration Information** dialog box.

6. Complete your registration information. Most of it is optional; however, you do have to provide at least a name and an email address. When you are done, click **Next**. You will see the second screen in the registration process.

7. Complete the fields about where you will use the iPod and what best describes what you do, if you'd like to. These are both optional. (Speaking of which, given how easily you can carry an iPod around with you, which is the whole point, how much sense does a question about where you will use it make?)

tip

If the country or region you want to choose isn't listed, check the **Show All** check box and hopefully it will be then.

note

A pet peeve of mine is forced registration like Apple requires with the iPod. One shouldn't have to register to make a product one has purchased work. Ah well, what can we do?

8. If you want to receive email from Apple, click the **Yes** radio button, or click **No** if you don't want to receive email.

9. Click **Next**. You will see the **iPod configuration** screen. This screen asks you to choose whether or not you want to configure your iPod now. In order to configure your iPod, it must be connected to your computer.

10. Click **Cancel** to skip the iPod configuration step for now (you'll learn how to do this later in this chapter). The installer will do its work, and you can watch its progress in the resulting windows. When the process is complete, you will see the **InstallShield Wizard for iTunes** window (see Figure 2.2).

> **tip**
>
> If you have already installed a newer version of iTunes than the one shown in the InstallShield Wizard for iTunes window, you can cancel out of the iTunes installation process here.

FIGURE 2.2

When you install the iPod software, you can also install iTunes.

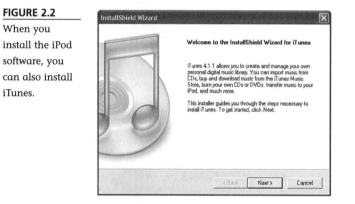

11. Read the information in the installer window and click **Next**.

12. If you have a lot of time and patience, read the license agreement; when you are done (if you are like me, you will realize it is incomprehensible and will just assume you aren't giving away your first born), click **Yes**.

13. In the resulting **Information** window, you can read information about iTunes, such as what it can do and what you need to install it. When you are done reading, click **Next**. You'll see the **iTunes for Windows Setup Type** dialog box.

14. Check the following options to make them active or uncheck them to make them inactive:

   - **Install desktop shortcuts**—This option places a shortcut to iTunes on your desktop. Unless you don't like desktop shortcuts for some reason, you should usually leave this option checked.

   - **Use iTunes as the default player for audio files**—This option causes iTunes to be used to play most audio files that you will access on the Internet, CDs, and so on. If you prefer to use another application, uncheck this check box. However, I recommend that you leave it checked; you can always change the default application to be something else after you have become comfortable with iTunes.

   - **Use QuickTime as the default player for media files**—If you choose this option, the QuickTime Player application will be used when you view video or other multimedia content. Just like the previous option, if you prefer to use a different application, uncheck this check box.

15. Click **Next**. You'll see the **Choose Destination Location** dialog box.

16. If you don't want to accept the default installation location (which is C:\Program Files\iTunes\), click the **Browse** button and choose the location you do want to use. Then click **Next**. You'll see a window advertising the iPod.

17. Click **Next**. As the installer starts to work, you will see the **Setup Status** window. This window provides you with information about the installation process.

    When the process is complete, you will see the **Installation Successful** window.

18. Click **Finish** to restart your computer and complete the installation process. When your computer restarts, iTunes will be ready for you and your iPod.

tip

If you choose to install iTunes from the iPod CD, you should update the application to ensure you are working with the most current version. For information about updating iTunes, see "Keeping iTunes Up to Date on a Windows PC Manually" on page **305**.

Installing the iPod's Software on a Macintosh

You can install the iPod's software on a Macintosh using the following steps:

1. Insert the **iPod** or **iPod mini CD** in your Mac. It will be mounted.

2. Using the Finder, open the **installation CD** so you can see its folders.

3. Open the **iPod Installer** folder.

4. If you are installing software for an iPod, open the **iPod installer package**. If you are installing software for an iPod mini, open the **iPod mini installer package**.

5. Allow the installer to check for the appropriate software by clicking **OK**. The install window will appear (see Figure 2.3).

FIGURE 2.3

This is the initial screen of the iPod installer.

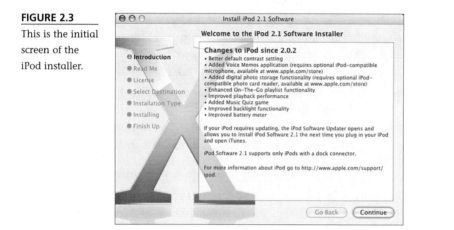

6. Click **Continue**. The installer will start and you will see the next screen in the process.

7. Read the information on each screen that appears and click **Continue** to move to the next screen.

8. When you get to the license agreement page, click **Agree**. You'll see the **Select a Destination** screen.

9. Choose the destination on which you want to install the iPod software. Typically, you should install the software on your active start-up drive. When you select a drive, it will be marked with a green arrow to show you the drive you have selected. In the lower part of the screen, you will see information about the drive on which you have elected to install the software.

10. Click **Continue**.

11. If prompted to do so, authenticate yourself as an administrator and click **OK**. The installer will run. When the process is complete, you will see the **installation complete** screen (see Figure 2.4).

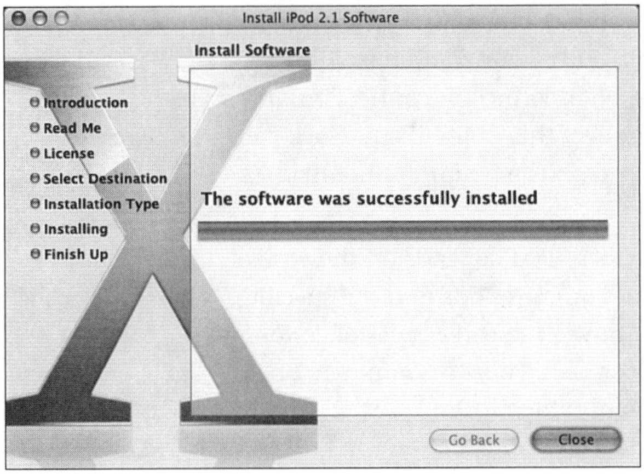

FIGURE 2.4

When you see this screen, you are done installing the iPod software on your Mac.

12. Click **Close**. The installer will quit. The iPod Updater application will launch. To enable you to update the iPod's software, you will need to connect the iPod to your computer. You'll learn how to do that in the next section.

13. For now, quit the iPod Update by choosing **iPod Updater**, **Quit**.

You also need to have iTunes installed on your computer. Because you are using a Mac and I have assumed that you are running Mac OS X, you probably already have a copy installed on your computer. You should update the version you have installed to make sure you are using the most current version of the application. For the steps to do this, see "Keeping iTunes Up to Date on a Macintosh" on page **305**.

If you don't have a copy of iTunes installed on your Mac already, you can install it from the iPod installation CD or by downloading a copy from the Internet. For help with those tasks, see "Installing and Configuring iTunes on a Macintosh" on page **178**.

Connecting and Configuring an iPod on Your Computer

In order to load music onto an iPod, you must connect the iPod to your computer so that the music files can be moved from your iTunes Library onto the iPod.

note

For Macs and Windows computers connecting to an iPod with a six-pin FireWire connector, connecting an iPod to the computer also charges the iPod's battery. Because of this, you should use six-pin FireWire whenever possible.

To do this, you connect one of the cables supplied with your iPod to your computer. All iPod cables have the Dock connector connection on one end. You connect this to the iPod's Dock connector port located on the bottom of the iPod (see Figure 2.5).

How you connect an iPod depends on the type of connections your computer has and the specific iPod model you have. The three types of connectors you use to connect iPods to computers are six-pin FireWire (all Macintoshes), USB 2, and four-pin FireWire (see Figure 2.6).

tip

If a Dock was included with your iPod, you connect the cables to the Dock and then insert your iPod into the Dock to connect it. See "Connecting an iPod to a Computer with a Dock" on page **32**.

Bottom of an iPod mini

FIGURE 2.5
You use the Dock connector port on the bottom of the iPod to connect it to a computer.

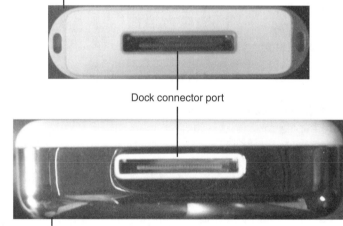

Dock connector port

Bottom of an iPod

FIGURE 2.6
These are the ports you might use to connect an iPod to your computer.

Six-pin FireWire   USB 2   Four-pin FireWire

Connecting an iPod to a Windows Computer

Connecting an iPod to a Windows computer requires that you decide on the type of connection you will be using. The following three options are possible:

■ **Six-pin FireWire**—If your computer includes a six-pin FireWire port, you can use that to connect it to the iPod. This has the advantage of also charging the iPod at the same time.

■ **USB 2**—If you have a computer that supports USB 2, you can use USB 2 to connect your iPod to the computer. USB 2 is slightly faster than FireWire, but your iPod won't also charge when it is connected to your computer in this way.

iPod minis include the cable you need to connect an iPod to a USB 2 port.

For other models, you will need to purchase the iPod Dock Connector to FireWire and USB 2.0 cable. This cable is actually two cables linked to a single iPod Dock Connector Port connector. You can connect the USB 2 cable to your computer and the FireWire connector to the iPod's power adapter. This enables you to charge the iPod while it is also connected to your computer. You can purchase the iPod Dock Connector to FireWire and USB 2.0 cable at the Apple Store (`http://store.apple.com/`).

■ **Four-pin FireWire**—If your computer includes a four-pin FireWire connector, you can use that to connect some models of the iPod by using the included six-pin to four-pin adapter. This method is not as desirable as the other two because it doesn't charge the iPod at the same time like six-pin FireWire does, and it is slightly slower than USB 2. You should use this option only if one of the others isn't available to you.

note

As soon as you connect an iPod to your computer, the iTunes application will open and will begin transferring music in your iTunes Library onto your iPod. Of course, if you don't have any music in your iTunes Library because you haven't added any to it yet, this won't do very much. You will need to build an iTunes Library before you can transfer any music onto your iPod. To get help with this, jump over to Part II of this book and read Chapters 12–17. After you have created an iTunes Library, you can transfer its music to your iPod.

caution

When you connect an iPod to a computer using USB 2, it is not charging and so uses battery power.

Assessing Your Windows Computer for an iPod

The first step to deciding which connection type to use is to determine which types are supported by your computer. There are a couple of ways you can do this.

Look at your computer to see which ports it includes. If it has at least one six-pin FireWire port available, you don't need to do anything else because this is the method you should use. Because a six-pin FireWire connection also charges the iPod when it is connected to your computer, this is the best option. If your computer doesn't support six-pin FireWire, consider adding a FireWire PCI card. These are relatively inexpensive at around $40 and require only a few minutes to install.

caution

You can't use a four-pin FireWire cable with an iPod mini even if you get an adapter for it. With a mini, you can only use six-pin FireWire or USB 2.

If you don't see a six-pin FireWire connector, locate the USB ports on your computer. Unfortunately, you can't tell by observation whether a USB port supports USB 2 or USB 1 because the ports are identical in appearance. Check the documentation that came with your computer to determine if it supports USB 2. If you can't find that information, contact your computer's manufacturer. If your computer does support USB 2, you are in good shape.

If your computer doesn't have a six-pin FireWire connector and doesn't support USB 2, look for a four-pin FireWire port. If it has one, you might be able to use a six-pin to four-pin FireWire adapter to connect your iPod to your computer.

If your computer doesn't have any FireWire ports and does not support USB 2, you'll have to add a PCI FireWire or USB 2 card to your computer before you can connect an iPod to it.

To use an iPod with a Windows computer, you must also be running Windows 2000 with Service Pack 4 or Windows XP Home or Professional.

Using Six-Pin FireWire to Connect an iPod to a Windows Computer

If your computer has a six-pin FireWire port, use the six-pin FireWire cable included with your iPod. Connect the Dock connector end to the Dock connector port on the iPod and the FireWire end to the FireWire port on your computer. The iPod will immediately be mounted on your computer. Skip to the section titled "Configuring an iPod on Your Computer" on page **30**.

Using USB 2 to Connect an iPod to a Windows Computer

If your computer supports USB 2, use the USB 2 cable included with an iPod mini or the accessory FireWire/USB 2 cable you purchased to connect an iPod to the computer. Use a USB 2 port that is on the computer itself rather than one that is on a keyboard, monitor, or other peripheral.

To use the USB 2 cable included with the iPod mini, plug the Dock connector end into the Dock connector port on the iPod and the USB 2 end into the USB port on your computer. The iPod will immediately be mounted on your computer. Skip to the section titled "Configuring an iPod on Your Computer" on page **30**. Make sure you insert the Dock connector end of the cable into the iPod's Dock connector port so that the icon on the connector is facing toward the front face of the iPod. If you attempt to force the connector in upside down, you can damage your iPod.

To use the iPod Dock Connector to FireWire and USB 2.0 cable, connect the Dock connector end to the Dock connector port on the iPod (this cable is not supported on a iPod mini). Then, connect the USB 2 cable to a USB port on your computer. Connect the FireWire end to the iPod power adapter and then plug the power adapter into a power outlet. The iPod will immediately be mounted on your computer. Skip to the section titled "Configuring an iPod on Your Computer" on page **30**.

Using Four-Pin FireWire to Connect an iPod to a Windows Computer

To use four-pin FireWire, you will need to have a four-pin to six-pin FireWire adapter (this is included with all iPods except the mini). Connect this adapter to the FireWire end of the iPod's FireWire cable. Next, connect the Dock connector end to the Dock connector port on the iPod. Then, plug the four-pin end of the adapter into your computer. The iPod will immediately be mounted on your computer. Move on to the section titled "Configuring an iPod on Your Computer" on page **30**.

Connecting an iPod to a Macintosh Computer

All Macintoshes produced in the past several years have at least one six-pin FireWire port. You can use the FireWire cable included with your iPod to connect it to your Mac. Connect the Dock

caution

Because the iPod will charge when it is connected to your Mac, you need to use a powered port, which is one located on the Mac itself. If you use a port on a FireWire hub or other FireWire device, it might or might not be powered.

connector end of the cable to Dock connector port on the iPod. Then plug the FireWire end of the cable into a FireWire port on your Mac.

Many Macs also support USB 2, but because the iPod will charge when you use a six-pin FireWire cable to connect it to your Mac, you should use FireWire instead of USB 2. However, if you don't have an available FireWire port, you can use the USB 2 cable included with an iPod mini or the iPod Dock Connector to FireWire and USB 2.0 cable to connect an iPod to your Mac. See the section titled "Using USB 2 to Connect an iPod to a Windows Computer" on page **29** for information about using USB 2 to connect an iPod to your computer.

Configuring an iPod on Your Computer

The first time you connect an iPod to your computer, the iPod will turn on and immediately be mounted on your computer, iTunes will open, and the iPod Setup Assistant will open (see Figure 2.7). Type a name for your iPod in the text box. You can use any name you'd like; this will be the name of your iPod when it is shown in the iTunes Source List. Check the **Automatically update my iPod** check box. Then click **Finish** (Windows) or **Done** (Mac). iTunes will update the iPod and will transfer all the music in your iTunes Library onto the iPod—if it can.

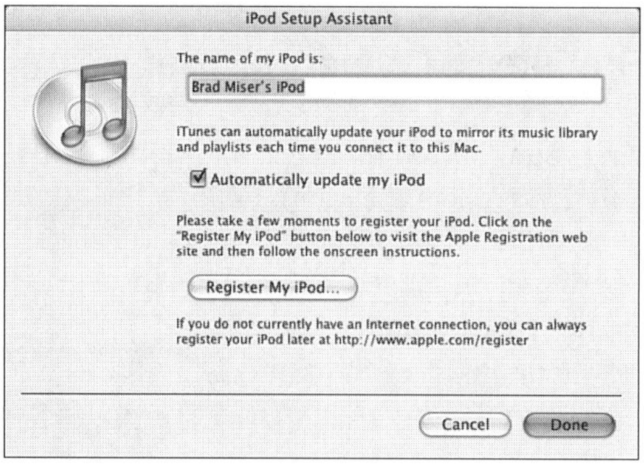

FIGURE 2.7

The trusty iPod Setup Assistant is ready to do its work.

While music is being transferred, the iPod icon on the iTunes Source List will flash red (see Figure 2.8). You'll also see information about the transfer in the iTunes Information area at the top of the iTunes window. If you are playing music while you transfer music to an iPod, you will see information about the music you are playing rather than information about the transfer.

iPod mini on Source List   Information area

FIGURE 2.8

If this book were
printed in color,
you would see
that the iPod
mini icon in the
iTunes Source
List is flashing
red to show that
music in the
selected playlist
is being moved
onto the iPod.

If all the music in your iTunes Library will fit on the iPod, the
process will complete without any further action
from you. When this process is complete, you will
hear a "whoosh" sound and you'll see the "iPod
update is complete" message in the information
area at the top of the iTunes window. The "OK to
disconnect" message will also be displayed on the
iPod's screen. When you see these messages, you
can disconnect your iPod from your computer.
Squeeze the buttons on each side of the Dock
connector end of the cable and remove the cable
from the iPod; the iPod will be ready to use. You
can leave the cable plugged into your computer
if you want to.

caution

While you have an iPod
connected to your com-
puter, you will see the
message "Do not discon-
nect" on the iPod's screen.
You should wait until the file transfer is complete or eject an iPod
before you disconnect it. You'll
learn more about this in the next
chapter.

If there is more music in your iTunes Library than can fit on the iPod, you will see a message telling you that the iPod doesn't have enough room for all your music (see Figure 2.9). In this case, iTunes will create a playlist of music that will fit on the iPod and then transfer this music to your iPod. This is fine for now; in later chapters, you'll learn how to choose which music is transferred onto your iPod. Click **OK** to close the message window.

FIGURE 2.9

Because I had more music than can be stored on an iPod mini, iTunes lets me know about it.

The iPod "Brad Miser's iPod mini" does not have enough space to hold all of the songs in your music library.

For your convenience, iTunes has created a new playlist named "Brad Miser's iPod mini Selection" which contains a selection of songs from your music library that will fit on this iPod. You may change the songs in this playlist at any time. Your iPod will be automatically updated with this playlist every time it is connected.

You can easily change which playlist(s) will be automatically updated to your iPod by selecting your iPod in the Source list on the left and clicking this button below.

OK

iTunes will move the playlist it created (whose name will be the name of your iPod plus the word "Selection") onto your iPod. When this process is complete, you will hear a "whoosh" sound and you'll see the "iPod update is complete" message in the information area at the top of the iTunes window. The "OK to disconnect" message will also be displayed on the iPod's screen. When you see these messages, you can disconnect your iPod from your computer. Squeeze the buttons on each side of the Dock connector end of the cable and remove the cable from the iPod; the iPod will be ready to use. You can leave the cable plugged into your computer if you want to.

note

A playlist is a collection of songs. You can use iTunes to create your own playlists and then listen to those playlists on an iPod. There are also a couple of playlists you can create and manage on the iPod itself. You'll learn about these later in this part of the book.

Connecting an iPod to a Computer with a Dock

If your iPod came with a Dock, you can connect the Dock to your computer instead of the iPod itself. When you want to transfer music to the iPod, you simply set it into the Dock. Using a Dock means that you don't need to mess around with cables (see Figure 2.10).

FIGURE 2.10

An iPod Dock eliminates the need to mess around with cables every time you connect your iPod to your computer.

To use a Dock, connect the Dock connector end of the cable you use to connect the iPod to your computer into the Dock connector port on the Dock instead of the port on the iPod. To connect the iPod to the computer, simply set it into the Dock. When the Dock can communicate with the iPod, you'll hear a tone. Other than that, using an iPod in a Dock is just like using one connected to a computer by a cable. When you connect the Dock connector end of the cable into the Dock connector port on the Dock, make sure the icon on the cable faces up. If you try to insert the cable in upside down, you can damage the connector.

When you want to disconnect your iPod from the computer, lift it out of the Dock. (You might have to place one hand on the Dock to keep it from lifting up when you lift the iPod out.) Before you pull an iPod out of a Dock, make sure the "OK to disconnect" message appears on the iPod's screen.

THE ABSOLUTE MINIMUM

Fortunately, a lot of the material in this chapter is only useful the first time you use your iPod. After all, installing software and connecting cables isn't all that thrilling. But it is necessary to do the thrilling stuff that starts in the next chapter. Before we leave this topic, consider the following points:

- You can install more than one iPod on the same computer. For example, you might be fortunate enough to have an iPod and an iPod mini. If you have more than one iPod, use a different name for each so you can keep them straight. You can even connect them to your computer at the same time if you have enough ports and cables available to do so.

- If your iPod didn't come with a Dock, you can purchase one separately. I strongly recommend that you do so because a Dock makes connecting and disconnecting an iPod much easier. You'll learn more about Docks in Chapter 7.

- The Dock includes a Line Out port. You can use this to connect the Dock to speakers or other audio device to play the iPod's music on that device. You'll learn more about this in Chapter 8, "Using an iPod with a Home Stereo or Car Stereo."

3

Using an iPod

The iPod is a well-designed device that is easy to control—once you understand its controls and how they work. Because the iPod is likely quite different from other devices you have used, it can take a little time to get totally comfortable controlling one. That's where this chapter comes in. Whether you have an iPod or an iPod mini, you'll learn about the iPod's controls and how to use them. You'll also come to know (and love) the iPod's menu structure and the major screens with which you will deal. You'll get into the details of using all these controls and screens in subsequent chapters.

In this chapter, you'll learn the specific controls on each type of iPod that you use to perform certain actions. Throughout the rest of this part of the book, I'll refer to the action in general and expect that you know which control to use for your model of iPod. For example, I'll explain where the Play button is on both types of iPods, but in later chapters, I'll just write that you should press the Play button without telling you where it is on each model.

Getting Ready to Play

In order to hear the music that is stored on your iPod, you must attach a sound output device to it. The most common one you might think of is the earbud headphones that were included in the package.

To use these, you connect the mini-jack on the earbud cable to the Headphones port located on the top of the iPod (see Figure 3.1). When you do so, you'll hear any sound coming from the iPod through the earbuds.

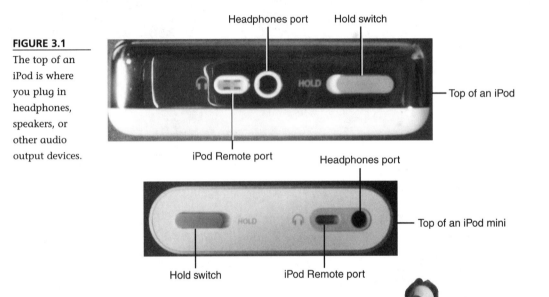

FIGURE 3.1

The top of an iPod is where you plug in headphones, speakers, or other audio output devices.

Although you are likely to use earbuds or other headphones with an iPod, those are certainly not the only audio output devices through which you can play an iPod's music. Following are some other devices you might want to use to play your iPod's music:

- **Powered speakers**—You can connect a set of powered speakers to the Headphones port to play your iPod's music on those speakers. For example, you can use any set of computer speakers to create a mini stereo system.

  If you connect a set of unamplified speakers, you aren't likely to hear very much if anything. The iPod doesn't put out enough power to drive a set of unpowered speakers.

note

On the top of the iPod, you'll also see the iPod Remote port in which you connect a remote control (you'll learn about these in later chapters). And, you'll also see the Hold switch, which you'll learn about later in this chapter.

■ **FM Transmitter**—You can connect an FM transmitter to the Headphones port to broadcast your iPod's output over FM. You can then tune into your iPod's music on an FM tuner, such as the one in your car or home stereo system. You'll learn about these devices in Chapter 7, "Rocking Your World with iPod Accessories."

■ **Home or Car Stereo**—You can use various cables and connectors to connect the Headphones port to an input port on a home stereo receiver, a car stereo, or boom box to play your iPod's music over one of these devices. You'll learn how to do this in Chapter 8, "Using an iPod with a Home Stereo or Car Stereo."

> **note**
>
> If you have an iPod, read the section "Controlling an iPod" on this page. If you have an iPod mini, skip to the section "Controlling an iPod Mini" on page **39**. If you have both, well, read both of these sections.

Controlling an iPod

The main controls on an iPod consist of the control buttons located just under the iPod's screen and the Scroll pad and Select button toward the bottom of the iPod's front face (see Figure 3.2).

Turning an iPod On

To turn an iPod on, press any **button**, the **Scroll pad**, or the **Select button**. You'll see the Apple logo on the iPod's screen, and after the iPod starts up, you'll see the main menu.

Choosing an iPod's Language

The first time you turn an iPod on, you'll immediately move to the Language selection screen that you use to choose the language in which your iPod will display information. To choose a language, slide a finger or thumb clockwise on the **Scroll pad** to move down the language list or counterclockwise to move up the list. When the language you want to use is highlighted, press the **Select button** to choose it. You will then move to the main menu. You only have to do this the first time you turn an iPod on or if you reset it.

> **note**
>
> In this section, you'll just get information about controls that are different between the two models. When you understand this, you can read about the menus and screens that are the same for the two models.

FIGURE 3.2

The controls on the iPod will become second nature to you after you use them a few times.

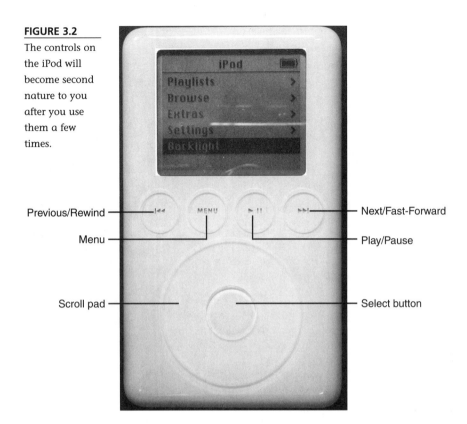

Previous/Rewind

Menu

Scroll pad

Next/Fast-Forward

Play/Pause

Select button

Making Selections on an iPod

The previous information about selecting a language gives you the general idea of how you control an iPod. Now, let's give you a very specific idea of how you move around your iPod to make it follow your commands.

The iPod is based on menus on which you make choices. To make a choice on a menu, you slide a finger or thumb clockwise on the **Scroll pad** to move down the current menu or counterclockwise to move up on the current menu. As you move up or down, a different command on the menu will be highlighted. When the command you want to use is highlighted, press the **Select button** to choose it. If the command is for another menu, that menu will appear. You can then move up and down that menu to choose another command. If the menu provides a list of songs, albums, or other categories, you can use the same process to select and play an item, such as a song.

To move back to a previous menu, you press the **Menu button**.

You'll learn the specific menus and screens you will use later in this chapter. For now, just understand how to move up and down the iPod's menu structure.

Changing Volume

When a song is playing, you control the iPod's volume by sliding a finger or thumb on the **Scroll pad** clockwise to increase the volume or counterclockwise to decrease it.

Controlling an iPod Mini

If you don't have an iPod mini, skip to the section titled "Looking at the iPod's Menus and Screens" on page **41**.

The main controls on an iPod mini are all located within the Click Wheel (see Figure 3.3).

Turning an iPod Mini On

To turn an iPod mini on, press the **Click Wheel** in any location or press the **Select button**. You'll see the Apple logo on the iPod mini's screen, and after the iPod mini starts up, you'll see the main menu.

note

In this section, you'll just get information about controls that are different between the two models. When you understand this, you can read about the menus and screens that are the same for the two models.

FIGURE 3.3
The controls on the iPod mini are all on the Click Wheel.

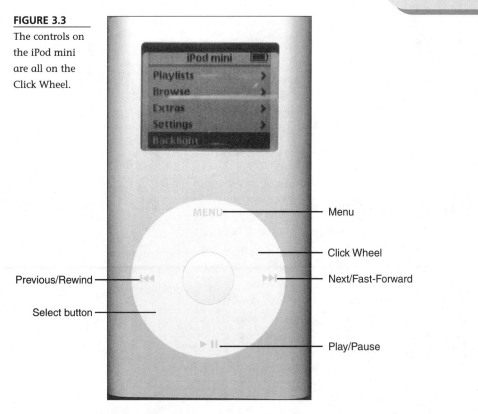

Menu

Click Wheel

Previous/Rewind ——— Next/Fast-Forward

Select button ——— Play/Pause

Choosing an iPod Mini's Language

The first time you turn an iPod mini on, you'll immediately move to the Language selection screen that you use to choose the language in which your iPod mini will display information. To choose a language, slide a finger or thumb clockwise on the **Click Wheel** to move down the language list or counterclockwise to move up the list. When the language you want to use is highlighted, press the **Select button** to choose it. You will then move to the main menu. You only have to do this the first time you turn an iPod mini on or if you reset it.

Making Selections on an iPod Mini

The previous paragraph about selecting a language gives you the general idea of how you control an iPod mini. Now, let's give you a very specific idea of how you move around your iPod mini to make it follow your commands.

The iPod mini is based on menus on which you make choices. To make a choice on a menu, you slide a finger or thumb clockwise on the **Click Wheel** to move down the current menu or counterclockwise to move up on the current menu. As you move up or down, a different command on the menu will be highlighted. When the command you want to use is highlighted, press the **Select button** to choose it. If the command is for another menu, that menu will appear. You can then move up and down that menu to choose another command. If the menu provides a list of songs, albums, or other categories, you can use the same process to select and play an item, such as a song.

To move back to a previous menu, you press the **Menu button**.

You'll learn the specific menus and screens you will use later in this chapter. For now, just understand how to move up and down the iPod mini's menu structure.

Using the iPod Mini's Click Wheel

The iPod mini's Click Wheel is kind of cool because it contains both the wheel that you use to move up and down the menus and the various buttons you use to control the iPod mini. These buttons are located at each 90-degree point around the **Click Wheel**. To use a button, you simply press down on its icon on the wheel. The button will click and the action it represents will happen.

Why it is called a Click Wheel, I don't know. The wheel doesn't move, your finger or thumb moves around the wheel. Perhaps Apple should have called it the Click Pad to be more similar to the iPod.

Because there isn't a clear delineation between locations on the wheel, you don't have to be precise when you press a button. Press down close to the button's label on the wheel and you will likely get the expected action.

Changing Volume

When a song is playing, you control the iPod's volume by sliding a finger or thumb on the **Click Wheel** clockwise to increase the volume or counterclockwise to decrease it.

Looking at the iPod's Menus and Screens

Now that you have an idea of how to move around your iPod, let's get a good understanding of its menus and screens.

Although the controls you use to move around menus and screens are slightly different on the two models, the steps you use to move around are the same. Here they are:

1. Slide your finger or thumb clockwise on the **Scroll pad** (iPod) or **Click Wheel** (iPod mini) to move down a menu or counterclockwise to move up a menu. As you move your digit, different menu options will be highlighted on the screen to show that they are selected.

2. When you want to use a menu command, highlight it and press the **Select button**. That command will be active and the screen will change to reflect what you have done. For example, if you selected another menu, that menu will appear on the screen. If you select a song, the Now Playing screen will appear and that song will start to play.

3. To move back to a previous screen, press the **Menu button**. You'll move back to the screen you were on before the current one. Each time you press the Menu button, you'll move back one screen until you get back to the Main menu.

The Main Menu

The iPod's Main menu provides the major (dare I say main?) commands available to you (see Figure 3.4).

tip

You can change the contents of various menus, as you will learn later in this part of the book. The menus I describe here are the iPod's and iPod mini's default menus.

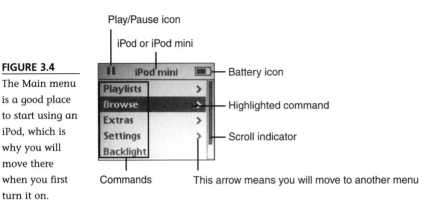

FIGURE 3.4

The Main menu is a good place to start using an iPod, which is why you will move there when you first turn it on.

The Main menu commands are the following:

- Playlists
- Browse
- Extras
- Settings
- Backlight
- Now Playing

All these commands take you to their respective menus, except for the Backlight and Now Playing commands. The Backlight command turns the iPod's Backlight on (more on this later). The Now Playing command, which appears only when you have selected and are playing music, takes you to the Now Playing screen (more on this later, too).

When a menu choice leads to another menu, a right-facing arrow will appear along the right edge of the screen for that choice. If you don't see an arrow for a command, that command will cause an action to happen instead.

When there are more options on a menu than can be listed on the screen, you will see the Scroll bar; the dark part of the bar represents how much of the menu you are seeing on the screen out of the total menu, which is represented by the full bar. (Remember that to scroll up and down a menu, you use the Scroll Pad or Click Wheel.)

note

That clicking sound you hear is the iPod's way of providing additional feedback to you each time you move to a different menu option. Oh, by the way, the technical term for this feature is the Clicker.

The Playlists Menu and Screens

The Playlists command takes you to the Playlists menu, which lists the playlists that are stored on your iPod. (If you haven't read Part II of this book, titled "iTunes," playlists are collections of music that you create in iTunes.) On the Playlists menu, you will see each playlist you have created in iTunes. Because each playlist represents a "menu" of the songs in that playlist, when you select it, you will see the songs menu that lists each song in the playlist. You'll learn how to work with the Playlists menu and screens in detail in Chapter 4, "Listening to Music on an iPod."

note

There is one playlist on the iPod that you won't find in iTunes because it wasn't created there. That is the On-the-Go playlist. You can create this playlist from music that is stored on the iPod. You'll learn how to use this in Chapter 4.

The Browse Menu and Screens

The Browse command takes you to the Browse menu. This menu enables you to browse the music stored on your iPod by Artists, Albums, Songs, Genres, or Composers. When you select one of these options, you will move to a menu that lists each category within the category you selected. For example, when you browse by Artists, you'll see a list of all the artists with which music on your iPod is associated. You'll get the scoop on browsing in Chapter 4.

The Extras Menu and Screens

The Extras command takes you to the Extras menu. On this menu, you will find various options that are related only because they are on the same menu. These commands enable you to access the iPod's non-music features, such as the Clock, Calendar, and so on. You'll learn about these extras in Chapter 9, "Using the iPod's Calendar, Contact Manager, and Other Non-Music Tools."

The Settings Menu and Screens

The Settings command is like the Preferences command in most computer programs. It enables you to configure various aspects of your iPod, such as the contrast of the screen, the Clicker settings, and so on. You'll use this command to configure the Backlight, as you'll learn later in this chapter, and we'll get into it in detail in Chapter 6, "Configuring an iPod to Suit Your Preferences."

The Backlight Command

This option turns the iPod's Backlight on if it is off or off if it is on. See the section titled "Using the iPod's Backlight" below to learn more about the iPod's Backlight.

The Now Playing Menu

The Now Playing command appears on the Main menu only when you have selected and played music. When you choose this command, you move to the Now Playing screen, which shows you the song that is currently playing (see Figure 3.5). This is an important screen because you can control various aspects of how music is playing from this screen, such as the volume level. You'll explore the Now Playing screen in Chapter 4.

FIGURE 3.5

The Now Playing screen shows you the music currently playing on an iPod.

Using the iPod's Backlight

The Backlight lights up the iPod's or iPod mini's screen so you can see it in dark conditions. (The iPod's Backlight also causes its buttons to glow.) You can turn the Backlight on or off manually and you can configure it to turn off automatically after a specific period of time.

Turning the Backlight On

To turn the Backlight on, move to the **Main menu**, select **Backlight**, and click the **Select button**. The Backlight will come on and your iPod's world will be a lot brighter.

After the current backlight time passes, the Backlight will turn off automatically.

caution

The Backlight uses quite a bit of power. To maximize the play time you get between recharges, you should use the Backlight only when you really need it or you should set the automatic settings to have it on only briefly.

Configuring the Backlight

If you don't want to have to manually turn the Backlight on, you can set the iPod to turn it on briefly each time you press a button. This is very useful because you can always see what you are doing no matter what lighting conditions you are in. You can also have the backlight on at all times, but I don't recommend that option because of the drain on the iPod's battery.

You can configure your iPod's Backlight settings by performing the following steps:

1. Choose **Main menu**, **Settings**. You'll see the Settings screen.

2. Choose **Backlight Timer**. You'll see the Backlight Timer screen (see Figure 3.6).

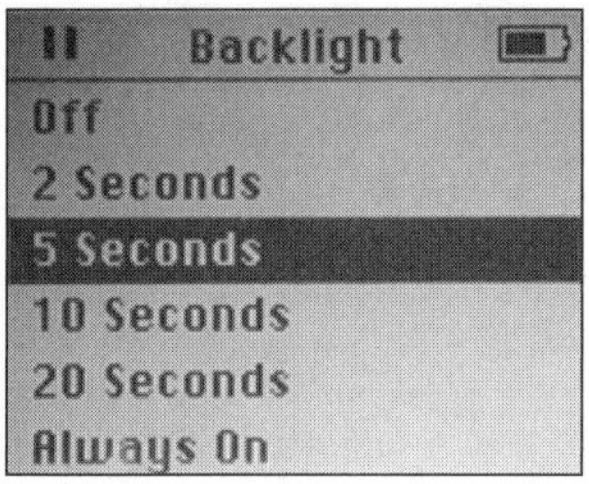

FIGURE 3.6

You use the Backlight Timer menu to configure your iPod's Backlight.

II	Backlight	▬
Off		
2 Seconds		
5 Seconds		
10 Seconds		
20 Seconds		
Always On		

3. If you want the backlight to come on each time you press a control, choose the amount of time you want it to remain on. Your options are 2, 5, 10, and 20 seconds.

4. If you want the backlight to come on only when you choose the Backlight command on the Main menu, choose **Off**.

5. If you want the backlight on all of the time, choose **Always On**.

6. Press **Menu** twice to move back to the Main menu.

note

To enable me to write and you to read fewer words, I've used some shorthand to indicate iPod menu selections. For example, when you see "choose **Main menu**, **Settings**," this means to move to the iPod's Main menu and then to the Settings menu by highlighting the Settings command and pressing the Select button. When you see "Choose **Backlight Timer**," that means to highlight the Backlight Timer command and click the Select button.

tip

For battery conservation, I don't recommend the 10- or 20-second settings. Try the 5-second setting because it provides a decent length of illumination time, but won't be quite so hard on your battery.

Putting an iPod on Hold

In Figure 3.1, you can see the Hold switch. This switch disables all the controls on an iPod so that you don't inadvertently press a button, such as if you carry your iPod in your pocket.

To disable the iPod's controls, slide the **Hold switch** to the right on an iPod or to the left on an iPod mini (these directions assume you are looking at the iPod's face with its top pointing up). When you do so, the area underneath the switch that was exposed when you slid it will be orange to indicate that the iPod is in the Hold mode. You'll also see the Lock icon on the iPod's screen (see Figure 3.7).

To reenable the iPod's controls, slide the **Hold switch** to the left on an iPod or to the right on an iPod mini (these directions assume you are looking at the iPod's face with its top pointing up). The orange area of the Hold switch and the Lock icon on the iPod screen will disappear and you can again control your iPod.

tip

If your iPod isn't responding to your attempts to control it, check the Hold switch to make sure it isn't active. It is amazing how easy it is to forget that you put your iPod in Hold mode and then wonder why you can't control it.

Lock icon

FIGURE 3.7

When you see the Lock icon, the Hold switch is active and you can't use any of the iPod's controls.

> ▶ 🔒 Now Playing   🔋
> 3 of 1834
> **She Loves You**
> **The Beatles**
> 1
> 1:07   -1:20

Turning an iPod Off

To turn an iPod off, press and hold the **Play/Pause button** for a second or two. The iPod screen will turn off. You can turn the iPod off from any screen, whether or not music is playing.

note

If you aren't playing music, iPods will turn themselves off after a period of inactivity in order to conserve their battery.

THE ABSOLUTE MINIMUM

iPods and iPod minis are great devices that do all sorts of cool things. Like any other piece of technology, iPod controls can require a bit of getting used to before using one becomes second nature to you. Fortunately, as you have seen in this chapter, the iPod's design does make sense, and after you gain an understanding of how the menus and screens are laid out, you won't have any trouble learning to use them in detail, which is where we are headed next. For now, review the following list to see where you've been:

- To hear music on your iPod, you need to attach an output device to it, such as headphones or powered speakers.

- You use the iPod's Scroll pad buttons to control it. For example, press any button or the pad to turn it on. Use the Scroll pad to choose a command on a menu and the Select button to activate it.

- You control an iPod mini in similar ways, except that an iPod mini doesn't have buttons because its main controls are located on its Click Wheel.

- iPods have a menu structure that enables you to access its various screens and commands; in this chapter, you saw an overview of these.

- You won't always be using an iPod in bright conditions; its Backlight helps you see the screen better.

- You use the Hold switch to prevent unintentionally activating commands.

- To turn an iPod off, press and hold the Play button down until its screen turns off.

IN THIS CHAPTER

- Pick some music, any music.
- Control your music like a pro.
- Create and listen to an On-The-Go playlist.
- Check your battery.
- Make your iPod obey you from a distance.

4

LISTENING TO MUSIC ON AN iPOD

In this chapter, you'll learn how to listen to and control your iPod tunes. Like any other device on which you listen to music, listening to music on an iPod is a two-step process. You first select the music to which you want to listen. Then you play and control that music.

As you rock on, jazz up, classical out, etc., you'll also find some other tasks useful, such as creating and using an On-The-Go playlist, rating your tunes, and monitoring your battery.

Selecting Music to Which You Want to Listen

The iPod is cool, but it isn't psychic. You need to tell it what music you want to listen to. There are two primary ways you do this: You can use playlists or you can browse all the music stored on the iPod.

Selecting Music with Playlists

When you transfer music from your iTunes Library to an iPod, the playlists you have created and that are shown in the iTunes Source List come over, too. You can select music to listen to by choosing a playlist using the following steps:

1. Choose **Main menu**, **Playlists**. You'll move to the Playlists menu (see Figure 4.1).

> **note**
>
> In order to play music on an iPod, you must have some stored on it. You do this by loading music into your iTunes Library and then transferring that music to the iPod. For help with the first part, see Chapters 12 through 17. For help with the second part, see Chapter 2, "Getting Started with an iPod."

FIGURE 4.1

Almost all the playlists you see on an iPod's Playlists menu should look familiar to you because they are the same playlists that appear in your iTunes Library.

Playlists screen

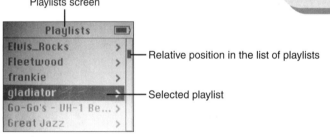

Relative position in the list of playlists

Selected playlist

2. Highlight the playlist you want to listen to and press the **Select button**. The songs in that playlist will be shown (see Figure 4.2).

> **tip**
>
> Remember that you can scroll up or down any menu, including the Playlists menu, by using the Scroll pad or Click Wheel.

3. If you want to play the entire playlist, press the **Play/Pause button**. If you want to start with a specific song, highlight it and press the **Select button**. The Now Playing screen will appear, and the first song in the playlist or the one you highlighted will begin playing (see Figure 4.3).

4. Use the techniques you'll learn throughout this chapter to control the tunes.

> **tip**
>
> If you want to play the entire playlist and don't want to see the songs it includes, you can just select the playlist and press the Play/Pause button (in other words, step 3 is optional). The Now Playing screen will appear, and the first song in the playlist will begin to play.

Playlist title

FIGURE 4.2
This playlist is called "gladiator" because it contains the *Gladiator* soundtrack. Here, you see the list of songs in the playlist.

gladiator

Progeny
The Wheat
The Battle
Earth
Sorrow
To Zucchabar

FIGURE 4.3
One of the songs from the selected playlist is now playing.

Now Playing

1 of 17

Progeny
Hans Zimmer and Lis...
Gladiator Soundtrack

0:30   -1:43

Browsing Your iPod's Music

Choosing music with playlists is great, and you might often find that method to be the one you end up using most because it gets you to specific music quickly. However, some music stored on your iPod might not be in a playlist, you might want to listen to all the music by a specific artist, and so on. In these cases, you can browse the music stored on your iPod to choose the music to which you want to listen. You can browse your music by the following categories:

- Artists
- Albums
- Songs
- Genres
- Composers

To browse your iPod's music, do the following steps:

1. Choose **Main menu**, **Browse**. You'll see the Browse menu, which contains the categories listed previously (see Figure 4.4).

2. Highlight the category by which you want to browse your music, such as Artists to browse by artist, and press the **Select button**. You will see the menu that shows you all the music that is associated with the category you selected in step 1. For example, if you choose Artists, you will see all the artists whose music is stored on your iPod (see Figure 4.5).

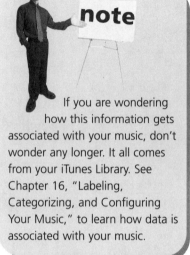

note

If you are wondering how this information gets associated with your music, don't wonder any longer. It all comes from your iTunes Library. See Chapter 16, "Labeling, Categorizing, and Configuring Your Music," to learn how data is associated with your music.

Browse menu

FIGURE 4.4

The Browse menu enables you to browse your music by various categories.

▶	Browse	🔋
Artists		**>**
Albums		>
Songs		>
Genres		>
Composers		>

Selected category

FIGURE 4.5

When you browse by a category, such as Artists, you will see all the music on your iPod that is associated with that category.

▶	Artists	🔋
All		**>**
101 Strings		>
Al Green		>
The Alan Parsons ...		>
America		>
Amistad		>

3. Browse the resulting list of music that appears until you find a category in which you are interested; then press the **Select button**. You will see the list of contents of the category you selected. For example, when I was browsing by artist and chose B.B. King, the list of my B.B. King music was displayed (see Figure 4.6).

tip

If you choose the All option on any of the category screens, all your music for that category will be shown on the next screen.

FIGURE 4.6

This screen shows all the music on this iPod by B.B. King.

4. To move down to the next level of detail, select an item on the current list and click the **Select button**. The resulting screen will show you the contents of what you selected. For example, I selected the B.B. King album called "Spotlight on Lucille" and saw that album's contents (see Figure 4.7).

tip

You can start playing music at any time by making a selection and pressing the Play/Pause button. The entire contents of what you select will begin to play. For example, if you select the name of an artist on the Artists list, all the music by that artist will start playing, beginning with the first song on the first album. You don't have to drill down to lower levels of detail as these steps show.

FIGURE 4.7

Here, I am looking at the contents of a specific album by B.B. King.

5. To play everything shown on the screen, starting at the top, press the **Play/Pause button**. To start with a specific song, select it and press the **Play/Pause button**. The Now Playing screen will appear, and the first song or the song you selected will start to play (see Figure 4.8).

FIGURE 4.8

I drilled down to a specific album and pressed the Play/Pause button to hear it.

▶ Now Playing 🔋
1 of 12
Slidin' And Glidin'
B.B. King
Spotlight On Lucille

2:17   -1:42

Although the previous steps used the Artists category as an example, you can browse and select music in any of the other categories in just the same way.

Controlling Your Music

OK, so now you have selected music and started to play it. What's next? Learn to control it of course.

After you have selected and started to play music using these steps, you can use the techniques you'll learn throughout this chapter to control the tunes.

Playing the Basic Way

Here are the basic controls you can use:

■ **Play/Pause button**—When music is paused, pressing this button causes it to play again. When music is playing, pressing this button causes the music to pause.

■ **Previous/Rewind button**—If you press this button once quickly, you will jump back to the start of the song. If you press this button twice quickly, you will jump back to the start of the previous song. If you press and hold this button down, the music will rewind; release the button when you get to the point at which you want it to start playing again.

No, an iPod doesn't have a Stop button. But, thanks for asking.

■ **Next/Fast-forward button**—Press this button once and you will jump to the start of the next song. Press this button down and hold it, and you will fast-forward the song; release the button when you get to the point in the song where you want to be.

■ **Scroll pad/Click Wheel**—When the Now Playing screen is shown, drag a digit clockwise to increase the volume or counterclockwise to decrease the volume. When you touch the Scroll pad or Click Wheel, the Volume bar will appear on the screen to visually indicate the current volume level; the shaded part of the bar represents the current volume level (see Figure 4.9). As you change the volume, the shaded area will expand or contract, depending on whether you increased or decreased the volume. When you release the pad or Wheel, the Volume bar will disappear.

> **tip**
>
> As you control your music, you can use the information at the bottom of the Now Playing screen to see where you are. You'll learn all about this screen shortly.
>
> You can rewind or fast-forward music whether it is playing or not.

FIGURE 4.9

When you touch the Scroll pad or Click Wheel, the Volume bar appears, and you can drag on the pad/Wheel to change the volume level.

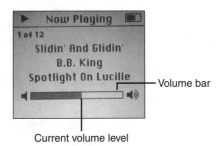

Volume bar

Current volume level

You can only change the volume using the Scroll pad or Click Wheel when the Now Playing screen is shown. That is why the Now Playing option is listed on the Main menu. You can quickly jump to this screen to change the volume when you need to.

Playing the iPod Way

The basics of listening to music are cool. Now let's take a look at some of the cool iPod playback features that aren't so obvious.

You can move around menus while music is playing just like you can when it isn't. As you choose other menus, the music will continue to play until you pause it or choose different music and play that instead.

> **tip**
>
> Remember that you move "up" the menu structure by pressing the Menu button.

The Now Playing screen provides lots of information about the music that is currently playing or paused (see Figure 4.10).

Number of song out of total selected

FIGURE 4.10

The Now Playing screen is packed with features, some of which might not be obvious to you.

Song title

Artist

Album title

Played portion

Elapsed time   Time remaining

Timeline bar

At the top of the screen, you see information about the number of the current song out of the total you selected. For example, if you are playing the first song in a playlist containing 50 songs, this will be 1 of 50. This information helps you know where you are in the selected source.

In the center of the screen, you will see information about the song currently selected, including song title, artist, and album. If any of this information is too long to be shown on one line, it will begin scrolling across the screen a second or two after a song starts playing.

tip

If you selected All in any category and then played it, the display will tell you how many songs are stored on your iPod.

At the bottom of the screen, you will see the Timeline bar. In the normal mode, this gives you a visual indication of the song's length and how much of the song you have played so far (represented by the shaded part of the bar). Under the left edge of the bar, you will see the amount of time the current song has been playing. At the right end of the bar, you will see the time remaining to play (this is a negative number and counts down to zero as the song plays).

If you click the **Select button** one time, the Timeline bar changes to indicate that you can now rewind or fast-forward using the Scroll pad or Click Wheel (see Figure 4.11). When the Timeline bar is in this mode, you can drag the **Scroll pad** or **Click Wheel** clockwise to fast-forward or counterclockwise to rewind the music. As you drag, the Current Location marker moves to its new location and the time information is updated. When you release the Scroll pad or Click Wheel, the Timeline bar will return to its normal mode in a second or so.

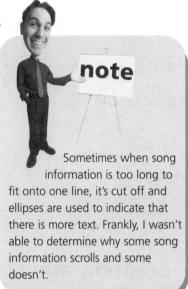

note

Sometimes when song information is too long to fit onto one line, it's cut off and ellipses are used to indicate that there is more text. Frankly, I wasn't able to determine why some song information scrolls and some doesn't.

If you click the **Select button** twice, the Timeline bar is replaced by the Rating display. If the song currently playing has been rated, you will see the number of stars for that song (see Figure 4.12). If the song hasn't been rated, you see five dots instead (see Figure 4.13). You can rate the current song by dragging the **Scroll pad** or **Click Wheel** clockwise to give the song more stars or counterclockwise to reduce the number of stars. A second or so after you stop touching the Scroll pad or Click Wheel, the Timeline bar will return to its normal mode.

FIGURE 4.11
When the Timeline bar looks like this, you can rewind or fast-forward using the Scroll pad or Click Wheel.

Current Location marker

FIGURE 4.12
You can rate your music in iTunes and display the rating on your iPod.

FIGURE 4.13

You can rate your iPod music by choosing one of the dots shown here.

> **II   Now Playing   🔋**
> **1 of 12**
> **Slidin' And Glidin'**
> **B.B. King**
> **Spotlight On Lucille**
> ● ● ● ● ●

The neat thing about this is that the next time you connect your iPod to your computer, the rating information you set on the iPod is carried over to that music in your iTunes Library. So, you need to rate a song in only one place.

Creating and Using an iPod On-The-Go Playlist

Working with playlists that you create in iTunes is very useful, but you can also create a single playlist on the iPod and listen to that playlist as much as you'd like. This enables you to create a playlist when you are away from your computer in order to listen to a specific collection of music.

To add a song to your On-The-Go playlist, view a list, such as the list of songs on an album, on which the song is listed. Highlight the song you want to add and hold the **Select button** down until the highlighting on the song flashes. Continue adding songs using the same process until you have selected a group of songs.

To see the contents of your On-The-Go playlist, choose **Main menu**, **Playlists**, **On-The-Go**. You will see the contents of the On-The-Go playlist that you have created. You can play this playlist just like any other playlist on your iPod.

When you connect your iPod to your computer, the On-The-Go playlist will be transferred into iTunes and will be available on the iTunes Source List.

note

You can rate your music in iTunes. For more information on why and how you do this, see Chapter 16 for details.

tip

When you are viewing a playlist, including the On-The-Go playlist, that contains the song that is currently playing, it is marked with a speaker icon.

When the On-The-Go playlist is empty and you select it, you will see an informational message about how to add songs to it. This can be handy if you forget and you don't have this book with you (which I know is unlikely to ever happen).

If you want to clear the On-The-Go playlist, choose **Main menu**, **Playlists**, **On-The-Go**, **Clear Playlist**, **Clear Playlist** (no, that isn't a mistake, you choose this command twice, but each is on a different screen). All the songs that were in the playlist will be removed, and it will become empty again. (The songs that were in that playlist are not removed from your iPod; the playlist is just cleared of those songs.)

Monitoring an iPod's Battery

Even though the iPod's battery lasts a long time, it will eventually run out of juice and your music can come to a crashing halt. To prevent this, keep an eye on your iPod's Battery icon (see Figure 4.14). As your battery drains, the shaded part of the battery will decrease to indicate how much power you have left. When 1/4 or less is shaded, you should think about recharging your iPod. (For more information about the iPod's battery, see Chapter 11, "Maintaining an iPod and Solving Problems.")

> **note**
>
> As far as I know, you can't remove just a single song from the On-The-Go playlist; you have to remove all of them or none of them. Also, you can't use the same techniques to change playlists that you created in iTunes. This works only for the On-The-Go playlist.

FIGURE 4.14
Is this iPod mini's battery half full or half empty? You make the call.

Battery icon

```
▶ Now Playing 🔋
2 of 2
Jumpin' At The Woodsid
     Count Basie

0:12              -2:53
```

Adding and Using Apple's iPod Remote

Some iPod models include Apple's iPod Remote. This clever gadget is a control that you plug into the iPod's Headphones port and Remote port and then plug your headphones or speakers into it. When you do this, you can use the controls on the remote to control your iPod (see Figure 4.15). This is particularly useful when you are carrying your iPod in a belt case or in another way such that its controls aren't easily accessible. Because the remote is on a wire, you can place it in an accessible location using its clip, such as on your clothing.

Headphones port (on top)

FIGURE 4.15
The iPod
Remote even
has a clip that
you can use to
attach it to your
clothes for easy
access.

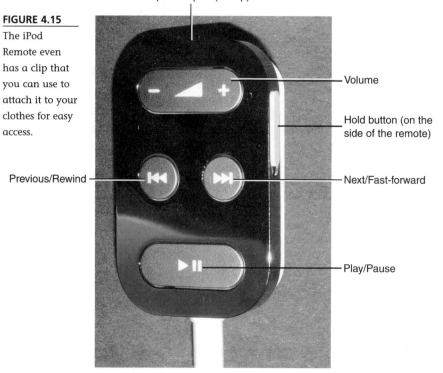

Volume

Hold button (on the
side of the remote)

Previous/Rewind

Next/Fast-forward

Play/Pause

The controls on the remote work just like those on the
iPod itself. One exception to this is that you can use
the Volume control on the remote to change the
volume regardless of what screen is currently being
displayed. The other is that you don't have a Scroll
pad or Click Wheel on the remote, so you will
choose your music using the iPod's controls and
then control its playback using the remote.

note

If you do carry your
iPod in a case or other way,
I strongly recommend that you get
a remote to make controlling the
iPod much easier.

THE ABSOLUTE MINIMUM

Now you know just about everything you need to listen to music on your iPod. It isn't that difficult because the iPod's controls are very well designed. Not to get controlling on you, but here are few more control points for your consideration:

■ The first step to listening to music is to choose the music you want to listen to. You do this by choosing playlists or browsing your iPod's music.

■ After you have selected music, you can use the pretty-obvious playback controls to control it. You also learned some useful but not so obvious ways to control it, too.

■ After you have used it for a bit, you'll find that you can easily control the iPod or the iPod mini with a single thumb. Often, the best way to hold an iPod is to set it in your palm and use your thumb to control it. It doesn't take long until you can navigate like a pro.

■ When you use the Scroll pad or Click Wheel to move around the iPod's screens or to control music, don't think you have to drag on it slowly or in small increments. You can move quite rapidly by dragging your finger or thumb quickly. You can move even faster by moving your digit in complete circles.

■ You can use the On-the-Go playlist to create a playlist on the iPod.

■ As you play your music, keep an eye on your iPod's battery so you don't run out of power.

■ Apple's iPod Remote is really cool, and if you have it, use it. However, other kinds of remotes are available as well. For more information on the Apple iPod Remote and other remotes, see Chapter 7, "Rocking Your World with iPod Accessories."

5

BUILDING AN IPOD'S MUSIC LIBRARY

The first time you connected your iPod to your computer, all the music in your iTunes Library was transferred to your iPod automatically—that is, all the music that would *fit* within the iPod's disk space limitations. If your iPod has enough disk space to hold all your iTunes music, then everything is just fine. However, as you build your iTunes Library, there may come a day when this isn't true anymore and you can't just let everything run on automatic to keep your iPod's music library current. That's where this chapter comes in. Here, you'll learn how to take control over the music stored on your iPod, even if your iPod's disk is large enough to hold all your iTunes music.

Creating an iTunes Music Library

As your learned back in Chapter 2, "Getting Started with an iPod," and read in each of the following two chapters, you manage the music that you store on your iPod within the iTunes application. The iTunes Library and the playlists you create within iTunes are the sources of music that you listen to with an iPod. The two general steps to creating these music sources are to build your iTunes Library and to create iTunes playlists.

Building an iTunes Music Library

You can get music for your iTunes Library from three main sources: your audio CDs, the iTunes Music Store, and the Internet. Although the specific steps you use to add music from these various sources to your Library are a bit different, the end result is the same. Your iTunes Library will contain all the music in your collection.

I don't provide the details of building and managing an iTunes Library here because Part II of this book is dedicated to iTunes and provides all the information you need to use this excellent application. The chapters that specifically focus on building your Library are Chapter 15, "Building, Browsing, Searching, and Playing Your iTunes Music Library," and Chapter 16, "Labeling, Categorizing, and Configuring Your Music," but you'll also want to read Chapters 12 through 14 to install and learn to use iTunes.

Creating iTunes Playlists

From the earlier chapters in this part of the book, you learned that the playlists stored within iTunes are transferred to your iPod so that you can listen to them. You create and manage these playlists within iTunes. Chapter 17, "Creating, Configuring, and Using Playlists," provides an in-depth look at playlists and gives you all the information you need to create and manage your playlists.

note

Throughout this chapter, I assume that you have a good working knowledge of iTunes, hopefully from reading Part II, "iTunes." If you haven't read Part II of this book yet, you need to at least read Chapter 12, "Touring iTunes," and Chapter 13, "Getting Started with iTunes," so you understand the very basics of the application. However, the process of managing your iPod's music library will be much better if you have read Chapters 12 through 17 before reading through the rest of this chapter.

note

Remember that there is one special playlist, called the *On-The-Go playlist*, that you can create on the iPod.

Assessing the Size of Your iTunes Library and How Much Disk Space Your iPod Has

In order to determine how you are going to manage the music on your iPod, you need to understand how large your music collection is and how much storage space is available on your iPod. This information will determine the way in which you build and maintain your iPod music library.

Determining the Size of Your iTunes Library

You can determine how much storage space you need in order to move your entire music collection in just a few steps. Open **iTunes**. Choose **Library** in the Source List. With the Browser open, select **All** in the Genre or Artist column. The iTunes window will show all the music you have placed in your Library. Look at the **Source Information** area at the bottom of the iTunes window (see Figure 5.1). Here, you will see the number of songs, the total playing time, and the disk space required to store all the music in your Library. The number you should be most interested in is the disk space required because that is what you use to determine if all your music can fit onto your iPod's disk.

FIGURE 5.1

At this point in time, my Library required 9.27GB of disk space.

Source Information

Determining How Much Storage Space You Have on an iPod

You have two ways to determine how large the disk is in your iPod.

One is to refer to the documentation that came with your iPod, or perhaps you can simply remember the size of iPod you purchased. At press time, the possibilities were about 4GB for an iPod mini and 15GB, 20GB, or 40GB for an iPod. This method is easy and provides a pretty good estimate of the room on your iPod's disk.

If you can't remember or want to determine the iPod's available disk space more accurately, you can get this information directly from the iPod itself. To do this, choose **Main menu**, **Settings**, **About**. On the resulting About menu, you'll see the capacity of your iPod's disk (see Figure 5.2).

> **note**
>
> Apple has periodically updated the iPod with larger and larger disks. The original iPod had a 5GB disk and was the only model available when it was released. Now, you can choose a size that best fits your needs and budget.

FIGURE 5.2

This iPod mini has a disk capacity of 3.7GB.

About	
BRAD'S IPOD	
Songs	508
Capacity	3.7 GB
Available	1.5 GB
Version	1.0

The capacity shown on the About menu is the amount of storage space available for your music. Some space is required to store the files needed for the iPod to function. This is the reason that the capacity you see will always be slightly less than the rated size of the iPod's disk.

> **tip**
>
> You can also get information about the status of the iPod's disk by connecting it to your computer and selecting it on the Source list. The Source Information area will provide information about the iPod's disk, including used space and free space.

Understanding and Configuring iPod Synchronization Options

After you know how much space you need to store all your music (the size of your iTunes Library) and how much space is available on your iPod (its disk capacity), you can choose how you want to build and manage your iPod's music library.

Understanding Your Synchronization Options

Three basic options are available for managing the
library of music on your iPod:

- **Automatically Update All Songs and
  Playlists**—When you use this method, the
  entire process is automatic; iTunes makes
  sure your iPod's music library is an exact
  copy of your iTunes Library each time you
  connect your iPod to your computer.

- **Automatically Update Selected
  Playlists Only**—When you use this
  method, iTunes still manages the update
  process for you, but it updates only the
  specific playlists you select.

- **Manually Manage Songs and
  Playlists**—When you use this method, you
  manually move songs and playlists onto
  your iPod.

If you don't want
iTunes to open automati-
cally when you connect an iPod to
your computer (why you might
not want this to happen, I don't
know), open the iPod Preferences
dialog box and uncheck the
"Open iTunes when attached"
check box.

When you first connected your iPod to your computer,
an automatic method was used to move songs onto your iPod. However, if there
were more songs in your iTunes Library than could be stored on your iPod, some
slight of hand was done by iTunes so that you wouldn't have to get into the details
of this process before listening to music on your iPod. In that case, iTunes created a
playlist containing a selection of your music that
would fit on your iPod, and iTunes moved that music
to your iPod so you can listen to it.

After the first time, you need to choose the synchronization method you want to use. Finding the right
method for you is a matter of preference, but I can
provide some general guidelines for you.

If all the music in your iTunes Library will fit onto
your iPod (the space required for your iTunes
Library is less than your iPod's disk capacity), I recommend you use the option Automatically Update
All Songs and Playlists. This option is the easiest
because it requires literally no work on your part.
Each time you connect your iPod to your computer,
the update process is performed automatically, and
you will have your complete music collection
available on your iPod.

Even if you have
enough space on your
iPod for all your iTunes music, you
can still choose one of the other
update options if they suit your
preferences better.

If the size of your iTunes Library is larger than the disk capacity of your iPod, managing the music library on your iPod is slightly more difficult.

If you take full advantage of iTunes playlists to create collections of music to which you listen, using the option Automatically Update Selected Playlists Only is a good choice. After you choose the playlists you want to be updated, iTunes handles the process of keeping them up to date for you so you don't have to think about it each time you connect your iPod to your computer. Of course, you need to make sure you create and can select playlists that contain the music you want to be able to listen to on your iPod. This can require some effort, but because playlists are so useful, you will likely do that work anyway so you can listen to them on your computer.

Finally, if you don't use a lot of playlists or you simply want to choose the specific music you want to place on your iPod, you can use the manual method to do so.

After you have determined how you want to manage your iPod's music library, you need to configure iTunes to implement your decision.

Understanding How iTunes Updates Playlists on the iPod

When iTunes updates a playlist on your iPod, it takes a "snapshot" of that playlist and places it on the iPod. If you change the playlist in some way, the next time you update your iPod, the previous "snapshot" is replaced by the new playlist.

For example, suppose you have a smart playlist that is dynamic and plays the 50 songs you have played most. As you listen to songs in iTunes, the contents of that playlist change to reflect the

caution

If you use the same iPod with more than one computer, you need to be careful before selecting one of the automatic methods. When you use an automatic method, iTunes will copy its Library onto the iPod. When it does this, it will also remove any songs on the iPod that aren't in its Library so that the music on the iPod is an exact copy of the music in the iTunes Library. If you share the iPod on more than one computer, you should not use the Automatically Update All Songs and Playlists method if you have different music in the iTunes Library on each computer.

tip

By default, when iTunes performs an update, it moves all the songs from each affected source onto the iPod. If you don't want specific songs to be moved onto an iPod, open the iPod Preferences dialog box and check the "Only update checked songs" check box. If a song's Selected check box is not checked, it won't be included in the music moved onto an iPod during an update.

songs you have listened to. When that playlist is moved to the iPod, it contains the songs as they were in the playlist when you performed the update. The playlist on the iPod will remain unchanged until you perform the next update. At that time, if the contents of the playlist have changed, the revised playlist will replace the one currently stored on the iPod.

The same principle applies when you make changes to a playlist manually, too. For example, if you sort a playlist to change the order in which songs play, that order will be reflected in the playlist when you update it onto your iPod. If you change the order of the songs in the playlist again in iTunes, the next time you update the iPod, the songs will play in the new order on the iPod.

> **caution**
>
> Whichever update method you choose, make sure that the "OK to disconnect" message is showing on your iPod's screen before you disconnect it from your computer. It is also safe to disconnect your iPod when the large battery charging icon or battery charged icon appears on the iPod's screen.

When iTunes moves a playlist from its Library onto an iPod, it moves only the songs in that playlist onto the iPod. This can sometimes be confusing. For example, if you purchase an album by a specific artist and then include only some of the songs on that album in a playlist that gets moved to an iPod, only those songs by that artist in the playlist get moved onto the iPod. As an example, this can be confusing the first time you browse your iPod by artist and can't figure out why a song you know you have by that artist is not on your iPod.

Configuring iTunes to Automatically Update All Songs and Playlists

Choosing the "fully automatic" method is automatic in itself in that this is the default option. However, should you ever need to choose this option, you can do so with the following steps:

1. Connect your **iPod** to your **computer** (remember Chapter 2!). iTunes will open automatically and the iPod will appear on the Source List.

2. Select the iPod on the Source List and click the **iPod Options** button (see Figure 5.3). You'll see the iPod Preferences dialog box.

3. Click the **Automatically update all songs and playlists** radio button (see Figure 5.4).

Selected iPod

FIGURE 5.3
FIGURE 5.3

To choose an update method, select the iPod and click the **iPod Options** button.

iPod Options

FIGURE 5.4

The iPod Preferences dialog box enables you to configure the update process for your iPod.

4. Click **OK**. The dialog box will close, and the automatic update will be performed. The next time you connect your iPod to your computer, iTunes will attempt to update its library automatically. As long as there is enough space on your iPod, you won't need to do anything else.

caution

If your iTunes Library is too large for your iPod's disk space, you will have to use one of the other methods to update it or live with the "Selection" playlist that iTunes creates for you. (More on this later in this chapter.)

Every time you connect your iPod to your computer, the update will be performed. You will see the update information in the Information area of the iTunes window, and the iPod icon will flash red. When the process is complete, you will see the "iPod update is complete" message in the Information area, and the "OK to disconnect" message will be displayed on the iPod's screen. Then, it is safe to disconnect your iPod from your computer.

If you use the "fully automatic" method when your iPod doesn't have enough space to store all your iTunes Library, iTunes creates a special playlist called *nameofyouripod* Selection, where *nameofyouripod* is the name you gave your iPod when you configured it. This playlist contains a selection of music from your iTunes Library that will fit on your iPod. If you don't change the update option, iTunes will update this playlist (and only this playlist) each time you connect your iPod to your computer. (It actually changes the update mode to "Automatically update selected playlists only" and chooses the *nameofyouripod* Selection playlist on the playlists list in the iPod Preferences dialog box.) You can use this playlist just like the others in your iTunes Source List, such as adding songs to it, removing songs from it, changing their order, and so on.

caution

If you disconnect your iPod during the update process, you can damage its data.

Configuring iTunes to Automatically Update Selected Playlists

To have iTunes automatically update selected playlists only, use the following steps:

1. In iTunes, create the **playlists** you want to place on your iPod.

2. Connect your **iPod** to your **computer**. It will appear on the Source List and an update determined by the current update option (such as fully automatic) will be performed.

3. Select the **iPod** for which you want to set an update option and click the **iPod Options** button. The iPod Preferences dialog box will appear.

note

When you change the update method, you will see a warning prompt telling you that the current music on the iPod will be replaced by the new update method. This should be what you expect, so just click OK to clear the prompt.

4. Click the **Automatically update selected playlists only** radio button (see Figure 5.5). Just below this button, you will see a list of all the playlists configured in your iTunes Library. Next to each is a check box. If that check box is checked, that playlist will be updated automatically. If that check box is not checked, that playlist will be ignored.

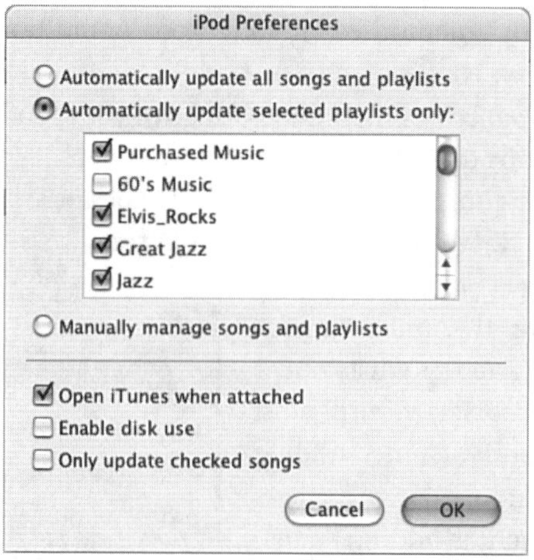

FIGURE 5.5

You can choose the playlists that are updated automatically by checking their check boxes.

5. Click **OK**. The dialog box will close and the playlists you selected will be updated on your iPod. The next time you connect your iPod to your computer, the playlists you selected will be updated automatically.

Configuring iTunes So You Manually Manage Songs and Playlists

When you choose this option, you manually place songs and playlists on your iPod. To choose this option, do the following steps:

1. Connect your **iPod** to your **computer**. It will appear on the Source List and an update determined by the current update option (such as fully automatic) will be performed.

2. Select the **iPod** for which you want to set an update option and click the **iPod Options** button. The iPod Preferences dialog box will appear.

> **note**
>
> If you use the Automatically update selected playlists only option, smart playlists are even more useful because their content can be dynamic (see Chapter 17). For example, you can create a playlist that automatically contains all the new music in your iTunes Library. If you choose to have this playlist updated automatically, each time you connect your iPod to your computer, that playlist will be updated, so your newest music will always be placed on your iPod.

3. Click the **Manually manage songs and playlists** radio button. You will see a prompt explaining that with this option, you must manually unmount the iPod before disconnecting it; read the information and click **OK** to close the prompt. (I'll explain what this means in a later section.)

4. Click **OK**. The dialog box will close. An expansion triangle will appear next to the iPod on the Source List, and all the playlists stored on it will be shown under its icon. You can then manually add or remove songs or playlists (the steps to do this appear in a later section).

Updating Specific Songs and Playlists Automatically

If you chose the Automatically update selected playlists only option, the playlists you selected are updated on your iPod each time you connect it to your computer. To change the contents of your iPod's music library, change the contents of the playlists that you have selected to update. When you connect the iPod to your computer, those playlists will be updated. For example, for playlists, you can add songs, remove songs, and so on. The next time you connect your iPod to your computer, the changes you made will be reflected on the iPod's version of that playlist.

Every time you connect your iPod to your computer, the update will be performed. You will see the update information in the Information area of the iTunes window, and the iPod icon will flash red. When the process is complete, you will see the "iPod update is complete" message in the Information area, and the "OK to disconnect" message will be displayed on the iPod's screen. Then, it is safe to disconnect your iPod from your computer.

note

Smart playlists can change over time automatically. These playlists will automatically change on your iPod each time you connect it to your computer. This is great way to keep the music on your iPod fresh.

Manually Updating an iPod

If you choose the manual option, you must manually move songs and playlists onto the iPod. To do this, use the following steps:

1. Connect your **iPod** to your **computer**.

2. Select the iPod you want to update. If it isn't expanded already, click the **Expansion triangle** next to the iPod on the Source List. In the iTunes Content pane, you will see all the songs in the iPod's music library. Under the iPod's icon on the Source List, you will see the playlists it contains (see Figure 5.6).

iPod's Expansion triangle   Songs on the selected iPod

FIGURE 5.6

When you configure an iPod for manual updating, you can expand it on the Source List to see the playlists it contains.

3. To add a **playlist** to the iPod, drag it onto the Source List and drop it on the **iPod icon** (see Figure 5.7). When you are over the iPod, the plus sign will appear next to the pointer to show you that you can release the mouse button. When you do so, the playlist and the songs it contains will be moved onto the iPod.

note

As songs are moved onto the iPod, you will see information about the process in the iTunes Information area at the top of the iTunes window.

FIGURE 5.7

When you drag a playlist into an iPod, it and the songs it contains will be moved into the iPod's library.

4. To remove a playlist from the iPod, select it by clicking it in the list of playlists under the iPod and pressing the **Delete** key. You will see a prompt asking you to confirm that you want to delete the playlist.

5. Click **OK**. The playlist will be deleted from the iPod.

6. To add songs to the iPod, select the **source** containing those songs, such as the Library. The contents of that source will be shown in the Content pane. Drag the **songs** you want to add from the Content pane and drop them on the iPod's icon. The songs you selected will be copied into the iPod's music library.

note

When you remove a playlist from an iPod, you only remove the playlist, not the songs it contains. You can still play those songs by browsing for them.

7. To remove **songs** from the iPod, select **them** in the Content pane and press the **Delete** key. These songs will be deleted from the iPod. They will also be deleted from any playlists on the iPod containing them.

8. When you are done updating the **iPod**, unmount it by selecting **its icon** and clicking the **Eject** button (see Figure 5.8). After the iPod has been successfully unmounted, it will disappear from the Source List and you will see the "OK to disconnect" message on its screen.

tip

If you don't want to be bothered by the confirmation prompts, check the Do not ask me again check box.

Update complete message

FIGURE 5.8

Before you disconnect an iPod that you have manually updated, you must eject it.

Eject button

9. Disconnect your **iPod** from your **computer**.

You must eject an iPod that you manually update before disconnecting it because iTunes doesn't know when it should shut down any processes it is using that are related to the iPod. Because it is, in effect, a hard disk, the iPod must not be in use when you disconnect it; otherwise, its data can be damaged. When the update process is handled by iTunes automatically, it "ejects" the iPod for you. When you do the update manually, you need to tell iTunes that you are done so that it can prepare the iPod to be disconnected safely.

caution

Don't disconnect your iPod from your computer unless the "OK to disconnect" message is displayed on its screen. If you do so, you can damage its data. It is also safe to disconnect your iPod when the large battery charging icon or battery charged icon appears on the iPod's screen.

THE ABSOLUTE MINIMUM

Managing the music on your iPod is essential if you are to be able to listen to the music you want to when the mood strikes you. Fortunately, maintaining your iPod's music library isn't all that hard. As you build and maintain that library, keep the following points in mind:

- You use the iTunes application to create the music library on your iPod.
- You can determine the amount of used and free space on the iPod's hard disk in a number of ways, including by using the iPod's About command.
- There are three ways to synchronize the music in your iTunes Library and on your iPod.
- When you use the "fully automatic" option, the synchronization is done for you automatically, and your iPod will be updated with your current iTunes Library each time you connect the iPod to your computer.
- You can also choose to have only specific playlists updated automatically.
- You can manage the music on your iPod manually as well.
- If you have more than one iPod, such as an iPod and an iPod mini, you can choose different update options for each. For example, you might want to use the "Automatically update selected playlists only" option for the iPod mini and the "fully automatic" option for the iPod.

6

CONFIGURING AN IPOD TO SUIT YOUR PREFERENCES

Back in Chapter 3, "Connecting an iPod to Your Computer," you learned how to configure an iPod's Backlight using the Settings menu. As you no doubt noticed, there are more options available on the Settings menu than just the Backlight. In this chapter, you'll learn about many of these settings that you can use to customize an iPod to suit your personal preferences.

Configuring Music Playback

Several of the iPod's settings relate to the way in which music plays. These include Shuffle, Repeat, and Sound Check.

Shuffling Music

You can use the iPod's Shuffle feature to have songs play in a random order. To shuffle music, use the following steps:

1. Choose **Main menu**, **Settings**. You'll see the Settings menu.

2. Highlight the **Shuffle** command (see Figure 6.1).

FIGURE 6.1

You can use the Shuffle setting to have an iPod play your music in a random order.

3. If you want the songs within a selected browse category or playlist to play in a random order, press the **Select** button once. The Shuffle setting will become Songs. This causes the iPod to shuffle the songs within a music source when you play it.

4. If you want the iPod to select random albums when you select a browse category or playlist, press the **Select button** twice. The Shuffle setting will become Albums. This causes the iPod to select an album randomly, play all the songs on the album, choose another album randomly, and repeat this pattern until you turn Shuffle off again.

5. Select the **music** you want to play in a randomized fashion and play **it**. On the Now Playing screen, you'll see the Shuffle indicator to remind you that you are in Shuffle mode (see Figure 6.2).

note

The Shuffle feature works on any source of music you select, including playlists or any of the Browse categories, such as Artists, Albums, Genre, and so on. When you use the Songs mode, all the songs will be selected and play in a random fashion.

FIGURE 6.2

The Shuffle indi-
cator reminds
you that you are
playing in the
Shuffle mode.

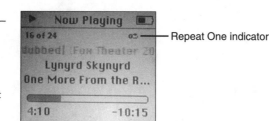

Shuffle indicator

6. To disable the Shuffle feature, press the **Select button** until you see Off next to the Shuffle setting. Your music will again play in a linear fashion.

Repeating Music

The Repeat feature enables you to repeat an individual song as many times as you'd like or to repeat all the songs in a selected music source as many times as you can stand.

To repeat the same song ad infinitum, choose **Main menu**, **Settings**. Highlight **Repeat** and press the **Select** button once so that One is displayed next to the Repeat setting. Select the **song** you want to hear and play it. It will play and then play again until you pause the iPod or choose a different song. While the song plays, the Repeat One indicator will appear on the Now Playing screen (see Figure 6.3).

note

Like the Shuffle feature, the Repeat feature works with any music source you select, including playlists or any of the Browse categories.

FIGURE 6.3

You can make
the same song
play over and
over until you
just can't take it
anymore.

Repeat One indicator

If you want to repeat all the songs within a selected music source, choose **Main menu**, **Settings**. Highlight **Repeat** and press the **Select button** twice so that All is displayed next to the Repeat setting. Select the **music source** (such as a playlist) you want to hear and play **it**. It will play and then repeat until you pause the iPod or choose a different music source. While the music source plays, the Repeat All indicator will appear on the Now Playing screen (see Figure 6.4).

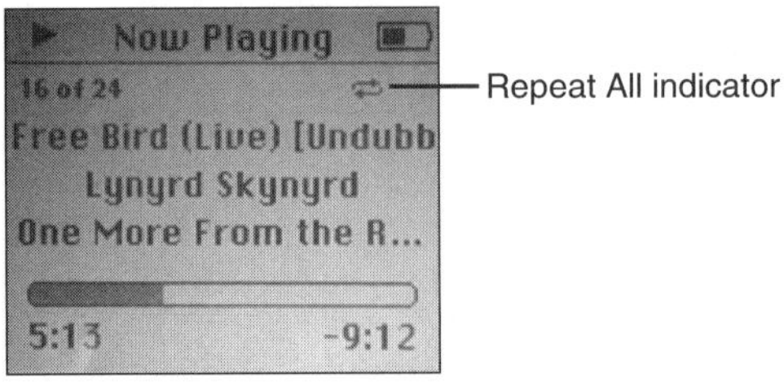

FIGURE 6.4

You can use the Repeat All mode to repeat all the songs in a selected music source, such as a playlist.

Repeat All indicator

To turn Repeat off, choose **Main menu**, **Settings**. Highlight **Repeat** and press the **Select button** until Off is displayed next to the Repeat setting. Music will again play one time through and then stop.

Using Sound Check

iTunes' Sound Check feature causes songs to play back at the same relative volume level—if you have ever been jolted out of your chair because of one song's volume level being much higher than the next one, you know why this is a good thing. Using the iPod's Sound Check setting, you can cause the iPod to use the volume levels set by iTunes when Sound Check is on.

To use **Sound Check**, make sure it is on in iTunes. Then, connect **your iPod** to **your computer** so the iPod's music will be updated, or you can perform a manual update if that is how you have configured iTunes for your iPod. After the update is complete, on the iPod choose **Main menu**, **Settings**. On the Settings menu, highlight **Sound Check** and press the **Select button**. The Sound Check setting will become On to show you that it is in use. When you play music back, it will play at the same relative volume level.

To return the volume level to the "normal" state, choose **Main menu**, **Settings**. Highlight **Sound Check** and press the **Select button** so that Off appears as the Sound Check setting.

Using the iPod's Equalizer

The iPod also has a built-in Equalizer that you can use to improve (improve being a relative term, of course) the music to which you listen. The iPod includes a number of presets designed to enhance specific kinds of music and other audio sources. To use the iPod Equalizer, do the following steps:

The current state of the Equalizer is shown next to its setting on the Settings menu. For example, when the Equalizer is turned off, "Off" will appear next to the EQ setting.

1. Choose **Main menu**, **Settings**.

2. Highlight the **EQ** setting and press the **Select button**. You'll see the EQ menu (see Figure 6.5). On this menu, you will see all the presets that are available to you. The list is pretty long, so you will need to scroll down to see all your options. The presets include those designed for specific styles of music, such as Acoustic, Classical, Jazz, and so on, as well as for situations in which you might be using your iPod to play music, such as on Small Speakers.

note

If you have created your own presets on the iTunes Equalizer, they won't be available on your iPod. The iPod includes a set of presets, and those are all that you can use. Fortunately, the list of presets is quite large, so this isn't much of a limitation.

FIGURE 6.5

Choose an Equalizer preset on the EQ menu to activate it.

▶	EQ	🔋
Bass Booster		
Bass Reducer		
Classical		
Dance		
Deep		
Electronic		

3. Highlight the **preset** you want to use and press the **Select button**. You'll return to the Settings menu, and the preset you selected will be shown next to the Equalizer setting (see Figure 6.6). When you play music, the Equalizer will adjust the volume levels of various frequencies to enhance certain frequencies and to reduce the levels of others.

tip

If you want to see a visual representation of the effect of the Equalizer preset you are using, view the Equalizer in iTunes with the same preset selected. See Chapter 18, "Equalizing Your Music," to learn how to do this.

FIGURE 6.6

If you like bass, try the Bass Booster Equalizer preset.

▶	Settings	🔋
Shuffle		Off
Repeat		All
Backlight Timer		>
EQ – Bass Booster		>
Sound Check		Off
Contrast		>

Setting Up Your Main Menu Preferences

You can configure the commands on the iPod's Main menu to customize it to suit your preferences. For example, suppose you frequently browse your music by artist. You can add the Browse by Artist command to the Main menu so that you don't have to drill down through the Browse menu to get to this category you use frequently. To configure your Main menu, do the following steps:

1. Choose **Main menu**, **Settings**. The Settings menu will appear.

2. Highlight **Main Menu** and press the **Select button**. You'll see the Main Menu menu (see Figure 6.7). On this menu, each command is listed along with its current Main menu state. If "On" is listed next to a command, it appears on the Main menu. If "Off" is listed to a command, it doesn't appear on the Main menu.

FIGURE 6.7

You can add items to the Main menu by turning them on or remove them by turning them off.

▶	Main Menu	🔋
Playlists		On
Browse		On
Artists		On
Albums		On
Songs		Off
Genres		Off

3. To add a **command** to the Main menu, highlight it and press the **Select button** so that "On" is listed next to that command. That command will then appear on the Main menu.

4. To remove a **command** from the Main menu, highlight it and press the **Select** button so that "Off" is listed next to that command. That command will not appear on the Main menu.

5. Repeats step 3 or 4 for each command until you have set all the commands you want on the Main menu to "On" and all those you don't want to appear on the Main menu to "Off." When you view the Main menu, your command preferences will be in effect (see Figure 6.8).

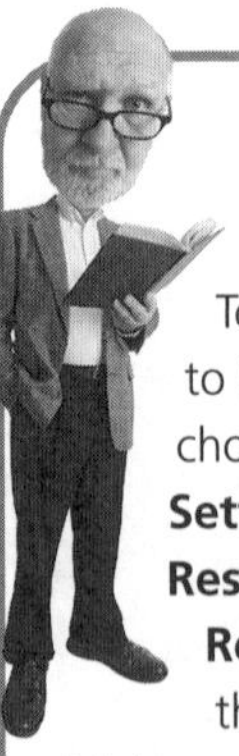

tip

To return the Main menu to its default commands, choose **Main menu**, **Settings**, **Main Menu**, **Reset Main Menu**. Select **Reset** again to confirm the command. The iPod's Main menu will be just like it was when you first powered it up.

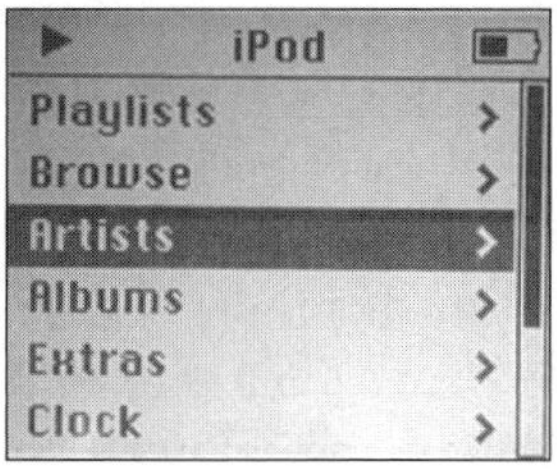

FIGURE 6.8

Using the Main menu settings, I customized the Main menu on this iPod (notice that I can use the Artists command on the Main menu to more quickly browse this iPod's music by artist).

Setting the Screen's Contrast

You can adjust the contrast of the iPod's screen so that you find it easier to read. To do this, choose **Main menu**, **Settings**, **Contrast**. You'll see the Contrast menu, which consists of the Contrast slider (see Figure 6.9). Drag the **Scroll pad** or **Click Wheel** clockwise to increase the contrast (which makes the text and background darker) or counterclockwise to decrease the contrast, making the text lighter. As you drag, the shaded part of the Contrast bar indicates the current relative contrast level. When you think you have a setting that suits you, move to other menus to see if the setting is correct for your eyes and viewing conditions. Otherwise, continue to adjust it until it is correct.

tip

You can reset an iPod's contrast to the default setting by pressing and holding the **Menu** button for about 4 seconds.

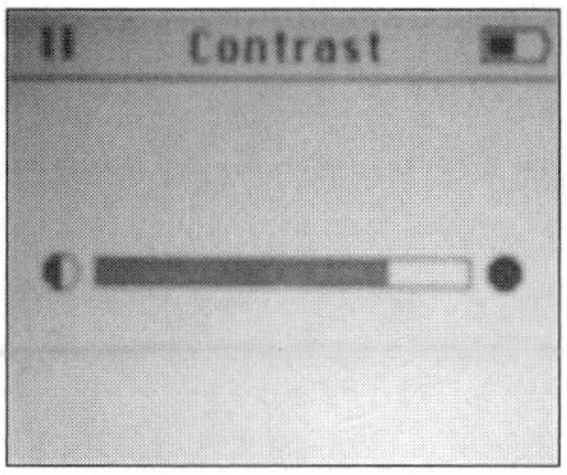

FIGURE 6.9

Increasing the contrast of the iPod's screen can make it easier to read.

Setting the Sleep Timer

You can configure your iPod to turn itself off automatically after a specific period of time passes. To do this, use the following steps:

1. Choose **Main menu**, **Extras**, **Clock**, **Sleep Timer**. You'll see the Sleep menu, which consists of a list of sleep time periods, from Off (meaning that the Sleep Timer is turned off) to 120 Minutes (meaning that the iPod will shut off in 2 hours).

2. Choose the **Sleep Timer setting** you want by highlighting **it** and pressing the **Select button**.

When you have the sleep timer on and view the Now Playing screen, the current amount of time until the iPod sleeps is shown at the top of the screen (see Figure 6.10). When the counter gets to zero, the iPod will turn itself off. This happens regardless of whether you happen to be listening to music at the time or not. So, if your iPod suddenly shuts off and you don't first see a "battery low" warning, this is likely the reason.

FIGURE 6.10

This iPod will turn itself off in 29 minutes.

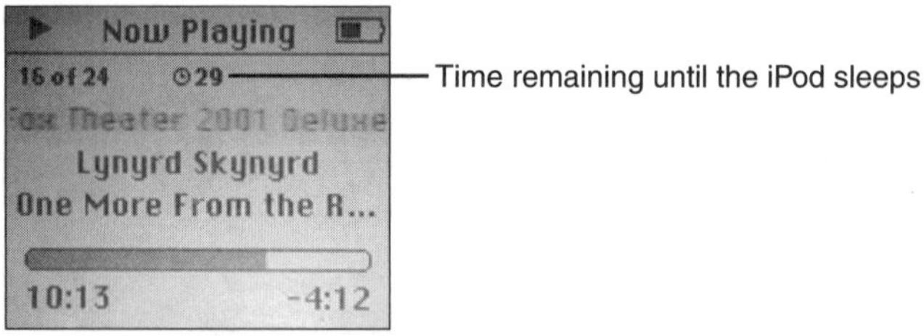

Time remaining until the iPod sleeps

Configuring the Clicker

As you select various menu options, your iPod "clicks" to give you audible feedback. If you don't like this, you can turn it off by choosing **Main menu**, **Settings**. Then highlight the **Clicker** option and press the **Select button** so that its setting becomes Off. Your iPod will start running in silent mode.

To make your iPod click again, highlight the **Clicker** option and press the **Select button** so that its setting becomes On. Your iPod will happily click away as you move around its menus.

Working with the iPod's Language

When you first turned your iPod on, you selected the language in which you wanted it to communicate with you. In most cases, you will never need to change that initial setting. However, you can if you do need to for some reason.

To choose a different language, choose **Main menu**, **Settings**, **Language**. You'll see the Language menu (see Figure 6.11). Highlight the **language** you want your iPod to use and press the **Select button**. The menus will change and use the language you selected.

tip

If you accidentally select a language that you can't read, you can use the information in the next section to reset the language even if you can't read the iPod's menus.

FIGURE 6.11
If I were multilingual, one of these settings might be useful, but since I am language limited, they aren't.

```
 ||    Language    ▭
 Italiano
 Nederlands
 Norsk
 Suomi
 Svenska
 한글
```

Returning an iPod to That Factory-Fresh Feeling

On occasion, all your work configuring your iPod might not be what you intended. Fortunately, you can return the iPod settings to their default values with a single menu command.

To do this, choose **Main menu**, **Settings**, **Reset All Settings**. You'll see the Reset All menu. Highlight **Reset** and press the **Select** button. Your iPod's menus and all other settings will be returned to their default condition.

tip

If you have set your iPod to use a language that you can't read, you can reset it by choosing the Settings command, which is the fourth command on the Main menu (by default), and then choosing the last command on the Settings menu (which is the Reset All Settings command). On the resulting menu, choose the second command and press the **Select** button to reset the iPod. Of course, if you have customized the Main menu, the Settings command might or might not be the fourth one down. When you customize the Main menu, it is a good idea to remember where that command is, just in case.

The Absolute Minimum

In this chapter, you've explored many of the options on the Settings menu and you've learned quite a number of ways to make your iPod suit your personal preferences. Check out the following list to review what you have learned and to pick up a few more pointers:

- Use the Shuffle, Repeat, Sound Check, and Equalizer to configure how music plays on your iPod.

- You can determine which commands appear on the Main menu by using the Main menu settings.

- Use the Contrast setting to set the contrast of the iPod's screen.

- Use the Sleep Timer to have your iPod go to sleep automatically.

- If you don't like the clicking sound that the iPod makes when you press a button, you can turn it off.

- Your iPod is multilingual; use the Language settings to determine which language your iPod uses.

- You can restore your iPod to its factory settings with the Reset All Settings command.

- The About command on the Settings menu provides important information about your iPod, including its name, disk capacity, available space, the software version installed on it, its model, and serial number.

- The Date & Time settings enable you to configure and work with your iPod's clock. You'll learn about those settings in Chapter 9, "Using the iPod's Calendar, Contact Manager, and Other Non-Music Tools."

- You use the Contacts setting to choose how contacts on your iPod are displayed. You'll learn about that in Chapter 9, too.

- The Legal setting takes you to the oh-so-useful Legal screen, which contains lots of legalese that you can read should you have absolutely nothing else to do.

IN THIS CHAPTER

- Control your iPod via remote control.
- Power and charge your iPod in your car.
- Connect your iPod to other devices.
- Broadcast your iPod's music via FM radio.
- Carry your iPod with style.

7

ROCKING YOUR WORLD WITH iPOD ACCESSORIES

The iPod is one of the coolest devices there is; part of this coolness is that it is such a versatile and adaptable device. Because of this, and due to the iPod's popularity, a large number of accessory devices are available for your iPod or iPod mini. The sheer quantity and variety of iPod accessories is amazing. There is no way I can cover all the iPod accessories that are available in one chapter (that would take a book in its own right!). So, what I have done is to select and review some of the best and most useful iPod accessories. You can use this information to start to build your own iPod toolkit.

Controlling Your iPod Remotely

The iPod's controls are well designed, but that doesn't mean that they are always easily accessible. Sometimes, you want to be able to use its controls when your iPod isn't in a position where you can easily reach, or even see, its controls. For example, when you are wearing an iPod in a case on your belt, you can't see its controls. Or, if you use an iPod in your car, you might not want to be looking for its controls instead of looking at the road ahead. In those situations, a remote control can be a great help.

naviPod by TEN Technology

The naviPod adds an IR remote control to your iPod (see Figure 7.1). The package includes the remote receiver, the transmitter, and a handy stand that keeps your iPod upright so that it can better receive the control's transmissions.

FIGURE 7.1

The naviPod is a great way to control your iPod from a distance.

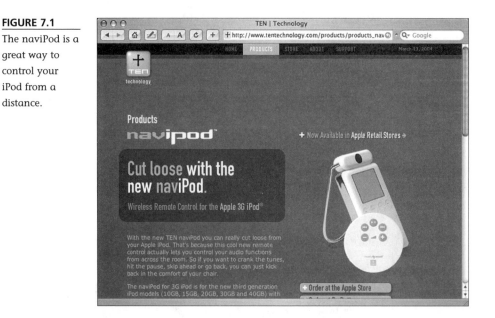

Installing the naviPod is a breeze. You simply plug the receiver into the Headphones and Remote ports on the top of your iPod; the receiver includes a Headphones port in which you can plug an output device, such as speakers or headphones. After you remove a battery protector from the handheld control/transmitter, you are ready to go. The handheld control replicates the playback controls on the iPod (everything except the Menu and Select buttons) and includes Volume buttons.

As long as you have the control in the line-of-sight of the receiver, you can control your iPod remotely. The unit's range and performance is similar to IR remote controls for your television or other devices.

The naviPod is a must-have accessory if you use your iPod with a home stereo or car stereo.

Web Site: www.tentechnology.com

List Price: $49.95

Pros: Easy installation; works extremely well; enables you to effectively control your iPod from a distance; highly recommended; works with iPod and iPod mini.

Cons: None.

note

My only suggestion for the naviPod, and it is a minor one indeed, is that the control doesn't include some way to attach it to your clothing. It would be nice if it included a clip so that you could carry it around with you more easily.

iPod Remote & Earphones by Apple Computer

This package includes a wired remote control (see Figure 7.2). You connect the remote's cable into the Headphones and Remote ports on the iPod. Then, you connect an output device, such as headphones, into the Headphones port on the control. The control includes Play/Pause, Fast-forward, and Rewind buttons along with a Volume control. It also includes a clip that you can use to attach it to your clothing.

FIGURE 7.2

Apple's wired remote is very useful when you are wearing your iPod.

Installing the remote is no harder than connecting headphones is. You simply plug it in, connect an output device, and clip the remote in a convenient location.

This control is ideal when you are wearing your iPod in a case because you usually can't see its controls very well. You can place your iPod in its case and then clip the remote to a convenient location so you can easily control the iPod.

Web Site: store.apple.com

List Price: $39

Pros: Simple installation; clipping on the remote makes it easy to use; the remote's buttons are easy to understand and use; the Volume control is better than using the Scroll pad or Click Wheel on the iPod to change volume; works with the iPod and iPod mini.

Cons: When using this unit, you have a lot of cable to manage because its wire is fairly long, and when you add headphones, you get even more cable to deal with.

Powering and Charging an iPod When You Aren't at Your Computer

It is very likely that you will want to use your iPod while you are traveling in a car. If you travel for long distances, you can drain the iPod's battery, and there go your tunes. The devices in this section enable you to power and charge your iPod while you are in your car.

Auto Charger for All iPod Models by Dr. Bott LLC

This device enables you to power and charge your iPod from a standard 12-volt power outlet, like those in all cars (see Figure 7.3). Using the device is simplicity itself; simply connect its Dock connector to the Dock connector on your iPod and plug the power adapter end into a power outlet in your vehicle. When the unit (and thus your iPod) is receiving power, its LED glows to let you know.

Web Site: www.drbott.com

List Price: $29.95

Pros: Easy way to power and charge your iPod while in your vehicle; works with the iPod and iPod mini.

Cons: None.

PowerPod iPod Auto Charger by Griffin Technology

The PowerPod is another device to power and charge your iPod from any 12-volt power outlet (see Figure 7.4). The power adapter and included Dock Connector to FireWire cable are separate. To use the unit, you connect the Dock connector end of the cable to your iPod and the FireWire end to the power adapter. Plug the power adapter into an available power outlet and power up.

Web Site: www.griffintechnology.com

List Price: $24.99

Pros: Great way to power and charge your iPod from any standard power outlet; works with the iPod and iPod mini; low cost.

Cons: Cable being separate from the power adapter makes you manage two things instead of just one.

FIGURE 7.3

Simple but effective, the Auto Charger enables you to power and charge your iPod while on the move.

FIGURE 7.4

The PowerPod provides iPod power on the move and is stylish too.

Connecting an iPod to a Computer and to Other Audio Devices

Your iPod is designed to connect not only to your computer, but to other devices as well. The gadgets in this section are designed to facilitate those connections.

iPod Dock and iPod mini Dock by Apple Computer

Included with some iPod models but also available separately, Docks take the hassle out of dealing with cables when you connect your iPod or iPod mini to a computer (see Figure 7.5). You connect the Dock to the cable instead of your iPod. When you want to connect your iPod to your computer, you simply drop it in the Dock. The connection is made more easily and quickly than using a cable alone. Docks also make a great way to store and display your iPod, not to mention making it possible to route the cables so you can keep them out of sight.

FIGURE 7.5

If you are an iPod mini owner, don't worry because there is a Dock for iPod minis, too.

Docks also include a Line Out port that you can use to send the iPod's output to any powered audio device, such as powered speakers, the amplifier for your home stereo, and so on.

I highly recommend that you get at least one Dock if you don't have one already. The convenience is well worth the cost; the added Line Out port is very useful, too. If you use your iPod with more than one computer, consider adding a Dock to each computer you use regularly.

Web Site: www.apple.com

List Price: $39 (iPod or iPod mini)

> **tip**
>
> You can use a Dock without it being connected to a computer. For example, you can connect the Dock to the iPod power adapter to use it as a standalone charging station. To use the Line Out port, you don't need to have anything connected to the Dock's Dock Connector port.

Pros: Makes connecting your iPod or iPod mini to a computer much easier and faster; enables you to keep the cable out of the way; provides a better way to store and display your iPod.

Cons: It can be more difficult than it should be to place an iPod in the Dock correctly, especially with the iPod mini Dock.

PocketDock by Sendstation

This simple device enables you to use any standard six-pin FireWire cable with any iPod with a Dock connector (see Figure 7.6).

FIGURE 7.6

One of the great things about a PocketDock is that it enables you to connect accessories designed for the Original iPod to iPods with a Dock Connector port.

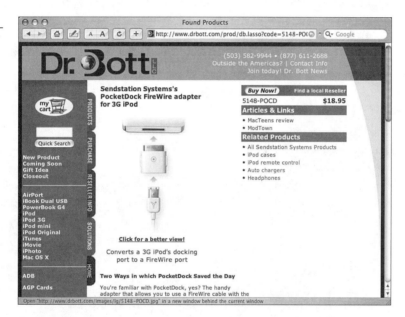

Web Site: www.drbott.com

List Price: $18.95

Pros: Comes in handy when you don't have the cable you need with a Dock connector or if you have accessories designed for the Original iPod; works with the iPod and iPod mini.

Cons: None.

iPod Connection Kits

The iPod's versatility enables you to use it with your computer and just about any audio device, including home stereo systems, boom boxes, and car stereos. To be able to connect your iPod to a variety of devices, you should get one of the iPod

Connection Kits that are offered by a number of man-ufacturers. These kits include a variety of cables and other items you need to connect your iPod to various devices. The best of these kits are covered in "Choosing an iPod Connection Kit" on page **106**.

Creating Your Own iPod Radio Station

Using cables to connect your iPod to a home or car stereo is fine, but dealing with cables can be a has-sle. You can broadcast your iPod's music over FM instead. Then, use any FM receiver to listen to the iPod's output.

iTrip by Griffin Technology

The iTrip transforms your iPod into an FM radio station (see Figure 7.7). Installing the unit onto your iPod is as easy as connecting it to the Headphones and Remote ports on top of the iPod. Then you run the iTrip installer from the included CD.

> **note**
>
> The hardest part of using any FM transmitter is that you have to find an FM fre-quency that is not being used by a radio station. In urban areas, this can be difficult to do. Even if a frequency doesn't have a radio station on it, it can be close enough to a frequency being used so that you get bleed over, which causes interference and static. This is a bigger problem when you use a transmitter in a car because you move around and the reception status can change constantly.

FIGURE 7.7
The iTrip might be as close to a perfect blend of form and func-tion as is possible.

After you have installed the iTrip's software, a playlist called iTrip Stations will be installed in your iTunes Library. You then update your iPod so that this playlist is moved into the iPod's music library.

To select the frequency on which you want to broadcast your iPod's music, you browse the iTrip Stations playlist and then choose the frequency you want to use. After you press the Play button, the iTrip will be set to use the frequency you selected. The iTrip's LED indicates when the selected frequency has been started on the iPod by first blinking rapidly; when this happens, you pause the iPod and the LED blinks three times slowly to let you know that frequency has been selected.

After that, you tune your FM radio to the frequency you selected and play the iPod to listen to its music.

My main qualm about this unit is that it takes some time to get used to how to know when the frequency you have selected is being used—you have to look for a series of LED blinks to let you know this. And, it would be nice if there were some way to use a remote at the same time you are using the iTrip.

Other than those quibbles, this is an excellent device, and its range of available FM frequencies can't be beat by any other transmitter. Because it doesn't require cables, it is definitely the cleanest and easiest unit to manage.

Web Site: www.griffintechnology.com

List Price: $35

Pros: Unit attaches firmly to the iPod; provides an astounding range of radio stations to use (basically you can use any available station); very stylish; no cables to deal with; the iPod and transmitter become one unit; powered by the iPod, so you have no additional batteries to deal with; works with the iPod and iPod mini.

Cons: Fills the Remote and Headphones ports, so you can't use the iTrip and a remote control at the same time; requires more complex steps to select the radio station to use.

note

FM transmitters broadcast with relatively low power. This means that the transmitter must be relatively close to the radio's antenna to get good reception. This can be problematic in a car if the antenna is at the back end of the vehicle while the iPod is at the front end.

TuneCast FM Transmitter for iPod by Belkin

The Belkin TuneCast FM Transmitter for iPod is another device that you can use to play your iPod's output over any FM radio (see Figure 7.8). To install the unit, you connect its cable to the Headphones port on the iPod and install batteries in the transmitter.

FIGURE 7.8
The TuneCast Transmitter also enables you to broadcast your iPod's tunes over the FM airways.

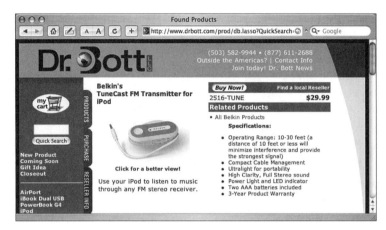

You select the frequency to use by using the slide switch located on the unit's body, making frequency selection extremely easy. There are only four possibilities, however, which is the unit's largest drawback. Unless one of these four happens to be unused in your area, you won't be able to use this unit at all.

After that, turn the transmitter on, set your FM radio to the selected frequency, and play the iPod.

Web Site: www.drbott.com

List Price: $29.99

Pros: Selection of a frequency is extremely simple; connects only to the Headphones port, so it can be used with a wired or wireless remote control; works with the iPod and iPod mini.

Cons: Limited set of frequencies; requires separate batteries; a cable connects the unit to the iPod, making the unit somewhat cumbersome.

Carrying an iPod

The iPod is designed to go with you to provide music wherever you are. However, to do this well, you need to use some sort of carrying case to hold your iPod. This accessory type offers the most variety, so choosing a case can be a bit difficult. In this section, you'll learn about some of cases available to you.

> **tip**
>
> Adding the wired remote makes using an iPod while it is in any of these cases more convenient.

SportSuit Basic by Marware

Marware is a leading provider of iPod cases, and its SportSuit series enables you understand why (see Figure 7.9). The SportSuit Basic case offers a durable neoprene exterior that helps protect an iPod from moisture and other elements. The case enables you to access the iPod's controls, screen, and ports so that you can do everything you need to while the iPod is in its case (except place it in a Dock). The SportSuit features a belt clip—you can remove the clip and replace it with other clips available from the manufacturer.

note

Many of the cases described in this section are available for both iPods and iPod minis.

FIGURE 7.9

The SportSuit Basic protects your iPod while enabling you to clip it to a belt or other clothing.

Web Site: www.marware.com

List Price: $24.95

Pros: Good protection for your iPod; provides access to the iPod display and controls; belt clip makes it easy to carry your iPod with you; other clip options are available.

Cons: None.

SportSuit Convertible by Marware

The SportSuit Convertible is a "big brother" to the SportSuit Basic (see Figure 7.10). In addition to all of that case's features, the Convertible also sports a cover to fully enclose and protect your iPod. (The Convertible gets its name because you can easily remove the cover when you don't need the extra protection it offers.) You also get an armband so that you can wear your iPod on your arm while exercising or in other situations.

FIGURE 7.10

The Convertible adds a cover and other features to the SportSuit Basic case.

Web Site: www.marware.com

List Price: $39.95

Pros: With its cover installed, the Convertible offers maximum protection for your iPod; cover can be removed easily; when the cover is removed, the Convertible provides good access to the iPod display and controls; belt clip makes it easy to carry your iPod with you; armband is included; other clip options are available; available in many colors.

Cons: None.

Deluxe iPod Case by XtremeMac

XtremeMac's Deluxe iPod Case provides good protection for your iPod and features a swivel belt clip design to make attaching or removing the iPod from your belt fast and easy (see Figure 7.11). The design of the clip attaching system prevents the iPod from being ejected from the clip unless it has been rotated to 90 degrees (if you have ever used a cell phone whose clip doesn't require this, you understand why this is good). The case's cover is permanently attached to the case; you access the iPod by flipping the cover up (it is held down by Velcro). When you do, there is nothing between the iPod and your fingers to interfere with controlling the unit.

Web Site: www.xtrememac.com

List Price: $29.95

Pros: Swivel clip design makes attaching and removing your iPod to and from your belt fast and easy; cover design prevents damage to iPod screen from rubbing contact; Headphones and Remote ports always accessible; quick flip of the cover provides access to Dock Connector port and iPod controls and display; available in black or camel tweed.

Cons: Cover design makes the use of devices that attach to the top of the iPod, such as the iTrip, cumbersome.

note

Some iPod models include a basic carrying case that has a belt clip. The base consists of two sides held together by elastic. You slide the iPod in between the sides to hold it in place. Unfortunately, the sides are solid, so you can't control or even see your iPod while it is in the case. Plus, because of the way you slide your iPod into it, you can easily scratch your iPod's screen. Apple should be ashamed of including such a lousy case when the iPods with which it includes the case are relatively expensive. Better to lower the price of the iPod by a few dollars and lose the worthless case. My advice, if you have one of these cases, is to toss it and get one of those described in this section.

iPod Mini Armband by Apple Computer

If you prefer to wear your iPod mini on your arm, you can use the iPod mini Armband (see Figure 7.12). This band features a neoprene wrap that goes around your arm and adjusts via a Velcro strap. You then snap the iPod mini into the armband's holder. This type of holder can be more comfortable to wear than those that use a belt clip.

tip

The Marware Mini SportSuite Convertible also enables you to wear your iPod mini, and it provides protection for the iPod at the same time.

FIGURE 7.11
The Deluxe iPod Case has a permanently attached cover that flips up for quick access to the iPod.

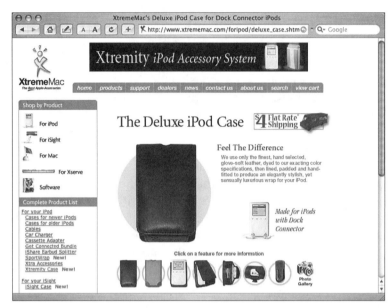

FIGURE 7.12
The iPod mini Armband enables you to wear your iPod on your sleeve, right next to your emotions.

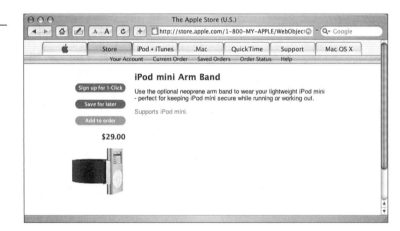

Web Site: `store.apple.com`

List Price: $29

Pros: Holds the iPod mini firmly in a convenient location for exercise or other activity; neoprene helps protect the iPod mini from moisture coming through the band.

Cons: Wide band is stiff and cumbersome to use and somewhat uncomfortable to wear; doesn't protect the iPod mini from any elements or inadvertent contact.

note

The iPod mini includes a plastic belt clip that you can use to wear the mini. Like the iPod mini Armband, this clip doesn't protect the iPod mini in any way, but at least you can easily carry it with you.

THE ABSOLUTE MINIMUM

This chapter covered some of the best and most useful iPod accessories available, but it was by no means comprehensive. To see more cool iPod accessories, check out the following sources of iPod goodies:

- **Dr. Bott LLC, located at** `www.drbott.com`—In addition to its own products, Dr. Bott carries a broad range of iPod products from other manufacturers, nicely organized by iPod type. You can also find a number of products for Macintosh computers here.

- **Griffin Technology, located at** `www.griffintechnology.com`—Griffin's iPod devices work very well and are perhaps the most stylish of them all. If you are a Mac user, check out Griffin's excellent Mac accessories too.

- **Marware, Inc., located at** `www.marware.com`—When it comes to iPod cases, Marware has what you need.

- **XtremeMac, located at** `www.xtrememac.com`—Don't let its name fool you, XtremeMac carries a number of excellent iPod accessories, including some of the most innovative cases available.

- **The Apple Store, located at** `www.apple.com`—Apple carries a complete line of its own iPod accessories, along with those from many other manufacturers.

IN THIS CHAPTER

- Get a connection kit for your iPod.
- Listen to your iPod with a home stereo.
- Listen to your iPod with a car stereo.

8

USING AN iPOD WITH A HOME STEREO OR CAR STEREO

One of the cool things about an iPod is how versatile it is. You can use one to play music just about anywhere and in just about any situation. In fact, the iPod can be the one constant in your musical universe. Wherever you go, you can take your trusty iPod along to provide the soundtrack for your life. That's so because you can interface an iPod with other devices in order to play your iPod's music through those devices. In this chapter, we'll take a look at two of the most common music components with which you might want to listen to your iPod's music: your home sound system or your car stereo.

Choosing an iPod Connection Kit

One of the best accessories you can get for your iPod is a connection kit. These kits typically include a number of cables and devices that provide you with lots of flexibility in connecting your iPod to other audio devices. With such a connection kit, you will be prepared to use your iPod with just about any other audio device.

Read the following sections to learn about some of the iPod connection kits that are available.

Apple's iPod Stereo Connection Kit

The Apple iPod Stereo Connection Kit enables you to connect an iPod to a home sound system. It includes the following components (see Figure 8.1):

- Stereo Mini-jack to RCA cable
- FireWire to Dock connector cable
- Power adapter
- Dock base
- Dock covers

note

You can assemble all the components you need to connect your iPod to an audio device separately. For example, you can purchase a stereo mini-jack to RCA adapter to connect an iPod to audio RCA ports. However, you'll find that purchasing a connection kit is easier and will provide you with more flexibility than purchasing individual components. A kit is also likely to be less expensive than if you purchase all the items separately.

FIGURE 8.1

Apple's iPod Stereo Connection Kit with Monster Cable includes everything you need to connect an iPod to a home stereo system.

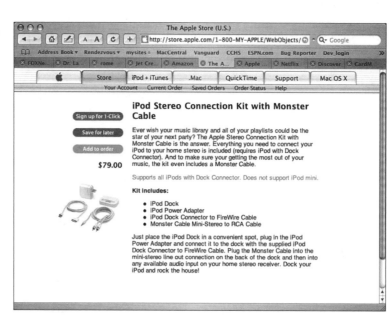

Notice that this kit includes several items that might have been included with your iPod, those being the Dock, power adapter, and the FireWire to Dock connector cable. These are indeed the same components that you might already have. The only thing unique to this kit is the Stereo Mini-jack to RCA cable.

To use this kit, you connect the Dock to your stereo and then place an iPod in the Dock when you want to listen to it over the stereo (you'll see the details of this in a later section in this chapter). Because everything you need is included, you can quickly and easily connect your iPod to a home stereo. The included power adapter and Dock mean that you don't need to mess around with cables when you want to listen to your iPod's music. You simply place your iPod in the Dock, and its music is instantly accessible.

> **note**
>
> The Dock covers included in the Apple kit are designed to enable its Dock to be used with a variety of iPod models. You install the correct Dock cover for your iPod on the Dock base to create a functional Dock.

However, this kit is somewhat limited when compared to other kits described in this chapter because it doesn't provide components you can use to connect an iPod to a car stereo as well.

Web Site: www.apple.com

List Price: $79

Pros: High quality Monster cable; includes Dock and the accessories you need to power the iPod when using it with a home stereo.

Cons: No auto stereo components; no iPod mini support; expensive.

XtremeMac's Get Connected iPod Audio Kit

XtremeMac is an excellent company that provides all sorts of iPod accessories. The XtremeMac Get Connected iPod Audio Kit provides a broad range of tools to enable you to use an iPod with both a home stereo and a car stereo. Its components include the following (see Figure 8.2):

- Cassette adapter
- iPod car charger
- iShare earbud splitter
- Mini-jack to RCA cable
- Seven-foot audio cable extension
- Mini-jack to mini-jack cable

> **note**
>
> You can use a cassette adapter to play an iPod's output through the cassette player in a car stereo. More on this later in this chapter.

FIGURE 8.2

XtremeMac produces some excellent iPod accessories, including the Get Connected iPod Audio Kit.

Web Site: www.xtrememac.com

List Price: $49.95

Pros: Extremely versatile kit that includes what you need to use your iPod in just about any situation; excellent value because of the number and type of components; supports both iPods and iPod minis; good quality cables.

Cons: No FM support.

Dr. Bott iPod Universal Connection Kit

Dr. Bott is another excellent source of iPod accessory items. The Dr. Bott iPod Universal Connection Kit includes a wide variety of components that you can use to connect your iPod to both home and car stereos. Its components include the following (see Figure 8.3):

> **note**
>
> A splitter cable has a stereo mini-jack connector on one end and two stereo mini-jack ports on the other. You can share an iPod's output using such a cable because it enables you to connect two headphones to one iPod.

- Cassette adapter
- iPod auto charger
- Mini-jack to RCA cable
- Six-foot audio cable extension
- Mini-jack to mini-jack cable
- iPod carrying pouch

Web Site: www.drbott.com

List Price: $47.95

Pros: Great versatility and includes what you need to use an iPod with home and car stereos; great value because of the variety of components it includes; supports iPods and iPod minis.

Cons: No FM support; cable quality not as good as the Apple or XtremeMac kits.

> **tip**
>
> There is nothing unique about the Headphones port on the iPod. You don't need special iPod cables to use this port; any standard mini-jack cables will work.
>
> Similarly, there is nothing iPod specific about cassette adapters. You can use any standard cassette adapter to connect an iPod to the cassette player in a car stereo.

FIGURE 8.3

Dr. Bott provides many cool iPod accessories, including the Universal Connection Kit II.

Dr. Bott iPod Connection Kit with FM Stereo Transmitter

This kit is very similar to the Dr. Bott iPod Universal Connection Kit, except that it replaces the cassette adapter with an FM transmitter so that you can broadcast your iPod's output and receive it via FM radio. This package includes the following items (see Figure 8.4):

- FM transmitter
- iPod auto charger
- Mini-jack to RCA cable
- Six-foot audio cable extension
- Mini-jack to mini-jack cable
- iPod carrying pouch

Web Site: www.drbott.com

List Price: $49.99

Pros: Great versatility and includes what you need to use an iPod with home and car stereos; the included FM transmitter is a good way to play iPod music over other components; great value because of the variety of components it includes; supports iPods and iPod minis.

Cons: Cable quality not as good as the Apple or XtremeMac kits.

FIGURE 8.4

Dr. Bott does it again; this time you get an FM transmitter instead of a cassette adapter.

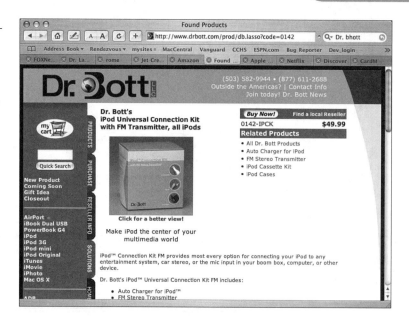

Using an iPod with a Home Stereo

You can connect your iPod to your home stereo and then listen to your iPod's music over that stereo. There are two fundamental ways you can do this: using wires or by using an FM transmitter.

Hard Wiring an iPod to a Home Stereo

You can connect your iPod to your stereo system using cables that are very similar to those you use to connect other audio components, such as a lowly CD changer. After you have connected the iPod to your amplifier/receiver, you can listen to it just like that CD changer.

The only challenge to this is choosing and connecting the proper cables to get the output of your iPod connected to the input of your receiver. Fortunately, this isn't all that challenging. You just need a cable that connects the Headphones port on your iPod to an audio input port on your home stereo receiver. In most cases, you need a cable that has a stereo mini-jack on one end and two RCA connectors on the other end. The mini-jack goes into the Headphones port on your iPod, while the RCA connectors go into the audio input ports on your home stereo's amplifier/receiver.

note

Although this section is focused on connecting an iPod to a home stereo receiver, the same techniques enable you to connect an iPod to other audio devices, such as boom boxes.

If you choose any of the kits described earlier in this chapter, you have everything you need to connect your iPod to a home stereo. If not, you will need to purchase the components you need separately.

There are two basic ways to connect an iPod to a home stereo using wires: You can connect the iPod directly to the cables or you can use a Dock. Each method has its pros and cons.

Connecting an iPod to a Home Stereo

To connect an iPod to a stereo receiver, simply plug the mini-jack end of a Mini-jack to RCA cable into the iPod's Headphones port. Then connect the RCA connectors to the audio input ports on the receiver. Figure 8.5 shows a diagram of a typical connection scheme.

tip

You can use any input port on a receiver to accept an iPod's input. For example, you can connect the cable to the CD ports, Aux input ports, and so on. Any ports that include a left and right channel will work.

FIGURE 8.5
Connecting an
iPod to a home
stereo isn't hard.

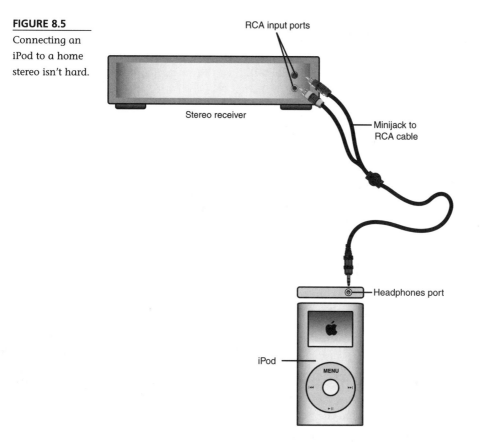

RCA input ports

Stereo receiver

Minijack to
RCA cable

Headphones port

iPod

MENU

Pros: Easy setup; inexpensive.

Cons: Somewhat messy because you need to
have a cable connected to the receiver, whose
input ports typically aren't accessible, so you
leave the cable connected and "loose"; you need
a separate power adapter and cable to charge
the iPod while using it with the stereo.

Using a Dock to Connect an iPod to a Home Stereo

The best way to connect an iPod to a home
stereo is to first use a Mini-jack to RCA cable to
connect a Dock to the stereo and then use the
FireWire cable to connect the Dock to the power
adapter (see Figure 8.6). Then, you can connect the
iPod to the stereo by simply placing it in the Dock. When connected, your iPod also
charges, so you don't have to worry about running out of battery power.

> **tip**
>
> If you also want to power
> the iPod while it is con-
> nected to the receiver, con-
> nect the Dock connector
> port to the Dock connector
> end of the Firewire cable.
> Then connect the FireWire
> end of that cable to the power
> adapter and plug the adapter into
> a wall outlet.

FIGURE 8.6

Using a Dock to connect an iPod to a home stereo enables you to connect the iPod by simply dropping into the Dock.

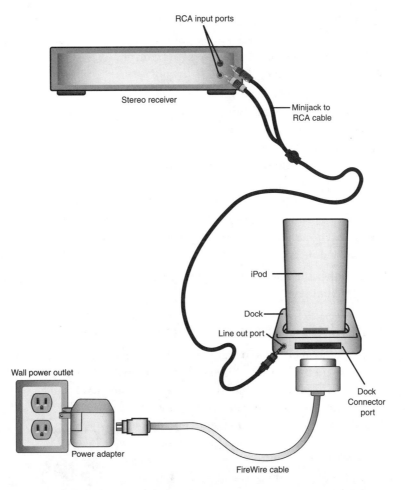

Pros: Easy setup; clean installation because you don't have loose wires—once it's set up, you only need to have the Dock exposed; easiest to use because you connect the iPod to the stereo by placing it in the Dock.

Cons: Relatively expensive because to be practical, you need to have a Dock and power adapter dedicated to this purpose, which means buying at least one more Dock and power adapter or purchasing Apple's Connection Kit.

Broadcasting iPod Music Over FM

You can use an FM transmitter to broadcast your iPod's music on standard FM radio frequencies. Then, you can tune in the frequency on which you are broadcasting on any receiver, such as the tuner in your stereo system's receiver, to listen to your music.

Choosing an FM Transmitter

In order to broadcast an iPod's output over FM, you need an FM transmitter. For help choosing, configuring, and using an FM transmitter, see "Creating Your Own iPod Radio Station" on page **96**.

Broadcasting iPod Music

Depending on the type of FM transmitter you use, setting up an iPod and FM transmitter so you can tune in your iPod's music requires from little to no work. You simply plug the transmitter into your iPod's Headphones port and play your iPod. Then, you set the tuner you are going to use to listen to the same frequency over which you are broadcasting your iPod's output. (For more detailed information about FM transmitters, see "Creating Your Own iPod Radio Station" on page **96**.

Pros: Easy to use an iPod with any audio device that can receive FM; simple setup and use; no messy wires.

Cons: Subject to interference; it can be difficult to find an unused FM station in a metropolitan area.

Playing an iPod Over a Home Stereo System

After you have installed or connected the components necessary to send your iPod's output to a home receiver, listening to your iPod's music is as simple as simple gets (however simple that is). On the receiver, select the iPod source, such as an Aux input or the FM tuner tuned to the frequency on which you are broadcasting your iPod's output. Then use the iPod controls to play the music and use the receiver's controls to set the volume level.

Typically, you should leave the iPod's volume set at a mid-range point when using it with a home receiver. That prevents any distortion that might occur when the iPod is using its maximum output level.

Using an iPod in this way is no different than other sources, such as a standard CD player.

tip

For the most convenience, use a remote control to control your iPod. These devices are covered in "Controlling Your iPod Remotely" on page **90**.

Using an iPod with a Car Stereo

Being able to take all your music with you on an iPod is cool everywhere, but no place more so than in your car. Forget trying to carry CDs with you (if you are like me, you never have the one you really want to listen to anyway). Just grab your iPod and you are ready for the open road.

Getting Sound from an iPod to a Car Stereo

There are two basic ways to get the output from your iPod to your car stereo: use a cassette adapter or use an FM transmitter.

Connecting an iPod to Your Car Stereo with a Cassette Adapter

A couple of the connection kits described earlier in this chapter are especially useful because they include a cassette adapter. These devices look like a standard cassette, but they also have a wire coming from them that ends in a mini-jack. You connect this plug into the iPod's Headphones port.

You then insert the cassette into a standard cassette player that is installed in many cars and use the car stereo's controls to play it.

When that is done, you can control the music from the iPod, just as if you were listening to it with headphones.

Connecting an iPod to Your Car Stereo via FM

You can also use an FM transmitter to broadcast your iPod's output. Then, you use your car's tuner to tune into the frequency you are broadcasting on. At that point, you can play your iPod and listen to its output over your car radio.

For more information about choosing, configuring, and using an FM transmitter, see "Controlling Your iPod Remotely" on page **90**.

note

Some car stereos have RCA input jacks. If yours does, you can use any Mini-jack to RCA cable to connect your iPod to your car's stereo in the same way that you can connect it to your home stereo.

note

Cassette adapters are convenient, but don't be surprised if the sound quality doesn't seem as good as you get when you listen to a CD or an FM radio station. These adapters often cause music to sound a bit muted. If this bothers you, try an FM transmitter instead.

The hardest part of using FM while you are in your car is finding an unused frequency. See "The Absolute Minimum" at the end of this chapter for some hints.

Powering and Charging an iPod While You Are on the Road

You can also power and charge your iPod while you are on the road by obtaining and using an auto power adapter. These devices plug into the 12-volt power outlet that is available in all cars (in the old days, this used to be where the cigarette lighter was installed). There are many of these devices available, and as you learned earlier in this chapter, some connection kits include them. For more information about other auto power adapters, see "Powering and Charging an iPod When You Aren't at Your Computer" on page **92**.

Mounting an iPod in Your Car

Finding a good spot to place your iPod in your car is probably the most difficult part of using an iPod in a car. You need the iPod within arm's reach, but you don't want it sliding around or falling off the dash. So, you want it close to you, but you want it held firmly too. Let's see, what is designed to keep something in place, but needs to be close enough to reach? Yep, you got it. A cup holder. It is likely that you have one or more of these near your radio and within your arm's reach. The odds are that one of these is the best place to keep your iPod while you are driving.

You can just drop the iPod in a cup holder. Depending on the size and configuration of the cup holder and the size of your iPod, this might work just fine. However, in most cases, you should put your iPod in a holder or case before doing this to protect it from scratches and to keep it from bouncing around. For more information about cases, see "Carrying an iPod with Style" on page **98**.

tip

Combined with a good frequency, broadcasting your iPod's music over FM results in the best sound quality. In fact, it might be so good that it will sound much better than it does when you use headphones.

caution

If you use wires, such as a power and cassette adapter, make sure you route them such that they don't interfere with any of your car's controls. It is easy to get them wrapped around something without knowing it until you are in a bad spot.

caution

If the cup holder you use is in plain sight from outside the car, make sure you remove your iPod and put it out of sight before you leave your vehicle. An iPod in plain sight will tempt any thief who happens by your car.

If you want to have the ultimate in carrying an iPod in a car, check out the Belkin TuneDok Car Holder for iPod (see Figure 8.7). This outstanding gadget holds your iPod securely, enables you to change its height for better visibility, has wire clips to keep your wires out of the way, and works in almost any type of cup holder. The $29.95 investment is well worth it if you use an iPod in your car regularly (or even infrequently).

FIGURE 8.7

This clever device makes any cup holder the perfect place for your iPod.

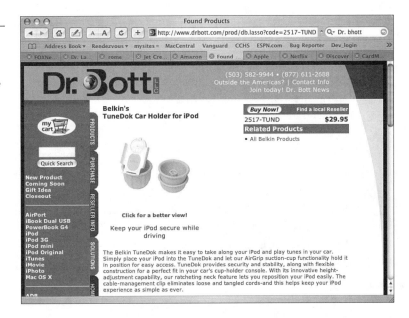

If you want to use an iPod mini in your car, it is a bit more difficult to hold it securely. The cup holder method is still your best bet, but it is likely you will need to add something else to keep it from moving around.

Controlling an iPod While You Are on the Road

If there is one dangerous topic in this book, this is it. Playing around with an iPod while you are driving is not a good idea. It is very easy to get focused on the iPod instead of where you are going, and your day can suddenly be ruined. To practice safe iPodding while you are on the road, consider the following tips:

caution

Take the information in this section seriously. Listening to music is not worth risking your life or property, not to mention the lives of others who share the road with you (myself included!).

- Choose the music to which you are going to listen while you are stopped. The iPod's screen is just not large enough to be able to see it clearly and look around you at the same time. Choosing music is at least a one-hand and two-eye operation. That doesn't leave much left for driving. So fire up your iPod, connect it to the radio with a cassette adapter or configure the FM transmitter, choose your music source and play it, place your iPod in its holder, and then drive.

- Consider creating playlists for driving. You can make these long enough so that you never have to change the music that is playing while you drive.

- If you must fiddle with your music while you drive, at least use a remote control. You can't change the music source with these devices, but you can change the volume, skip to the next song, and so on. Check out "Controlling Your iPod Remotely" on page **90** for information about some remotes that are available to you.

- Remember that you don't need to change the volume on the iPod itself. Set it at a mid-level and leave it alone. Use your car radio's controls instead.

- Keep your iPod secure, as explained in the previous section. Nothing is more distracting than the thought of your precious iPod flying around the car as you drive. If that does happen, remember that fixing you and your car (plus other people) will cost a lot more than a new iPod would!

- Remember the road rule of the day: Road first, music last.

THE ABSOLUTE MINIMUM

Using an iPod with a home or car stereo is easy to do and lets you listen to your iPod's music in many situations. Perhaps the best way to do this is to use an FM transmitter so you can tune in your iPod's music on your car radio or receiver's tuner. If you do this, check out the following pointers:

- Don't worry about other people being able to listen to your music when you use an FM transmitter. These devices have very limited range. If you are in a vehicle, someone might be able to pick up your iPod station if their vehicle is right next to yours; however, as soon as you separate even a few feet, they will lose the signal.

- Because you move around a lot when you drive, finding a good (meaning never used) FM frequency to use while you are on the road can be a challenge, especially if you are in a large metropolitan area. If a frequency isn't being used directly, it still might suffer bleed over from stations on other frequencies. If you choose a frequency that is being used or has bleed over, your iPod's music might be interrupted occasionally. For best results, select a station that you think is unused and listen to it for a while as you drive around. (Yes, you will feel kind of silly listening to static, but hey, it will help in the long run.)

- When you find a good candidate for unused frequency, set one of your radio's buttons to that frequency so that you can easily return to it. If you use an FM transmitter in more than one car, you might want to set it on the radio in each one.

- Don't be terribly surprised if you still have occasional static while using FM, even if you find a good unused station. Hopefully, you will be able to find a station where this is a rare occurrence, but it is likely to happen once in a while. If you can't find a frequency/transmitter combination that works satisfactorily, try using wires or the cassette adapter method instead.

- Remember that as you move among different areas, there are different radio frequencies being used. You might have to use different frequencies in the different areas in which you drive.

IN THIS CHAPTER

- Use your iPod like it is a $2 watch.

- Keep your appointments by placing calendar events on your iPod calendar.

- Take your contact information with you wherever you go.

- Store text gems on your iPod so you can read them at your leisure.

9

USING THE iPOD'S CALENDAR, CONTACT MANAGER, AND OTHER NON-MUSIC TOOLS

The iPod is all about music, but it also can do a number of other useful things that might not be obvious to you. These "other things" include providing an alarm clock, displaying a calendar, showing contact information, displaying text notes, and even playing games. Although none of these features alone would make the iPod great, they are nice extras, which is, I suppose, why they are located on the Extras menu.

Keeping Track of Time with the iPod Clock

You can use your iPod to keep track of time and as a basic, but perfectly functional, alarm clock. This is handy when you travel because you don't need to carry a separate clock with you. Or, if you are like me and don't wear a watch, an iPod can help you keep track of time.

Configuring the Time on an iPod

Before you use the iPod as a clock, you need to configure its time and date. Use the following steps to do this:

1. Choose **Main menu**, **Extras**, **Clock**, **Date & Time**. You'll see the Date & Time menu (see Figure 9.1).

FIGURE 9.1
You use the iPod's Date & Time menu to configure your iPod's clock.

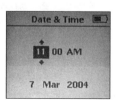

2. Choose **Set Time Zone**. You'll see the Time Zone menu.

3. Scroll on the list of time zones until you see the time zone you are in.

4. Highlight your time zone and press the **Select button**. The iPod's time zone will be set to the one you selected, and you will return to the Date & Time menu.

5. Choose **Set Date & Time**. You'll see the Date & Time menu again, except that this time it will be in the set date and time mode (see Figure 9.2). The hour will be highlighted.

FIGURE 9.2
You use this screen to set the time and date on your iPod.

6. Use the **Scroll pad** or **Click Wheel** to increase or decrease the hour until the correct hour is displayed.

7. Press the **Fast-forward button** so that the minute display is highlighted.

8. Use the **Scroll pad** or **Click Wheel** to increase or decrease the hour until the correct minute is displayed.

9. Press the **Fast-forward button** so that the AM/PM indicator display is highlighted.

10. Use the **Scroll pad** or **Click Wheel** to change the AM/PM to the correct value.

11. Continue using the **Fast-forward button** and **Scroll pad** or **Click Wheel** to set the correct date, month, and year.

12. Press the **Select button**. The date and time you selected will be set, and you will return to the Date & Time menu.

13. Highlight the **Time** setting. The default value is to use a 12-hour clock.

14. To use a 24-hour clock, press the **Select button**. The Time setting will become 24-hour, and a 24-hour clock will be used.

15. To display the time in the menu title area, highlight **Time in Title** and press the **Select button**. The Time in Title setting will become On, and the time will be displayed in the title bar—instead of the menu title (see Figure 9.3).

FIGURE 9.3

Placing the time in the title bar makes using an iPod as a clock much more convenient.

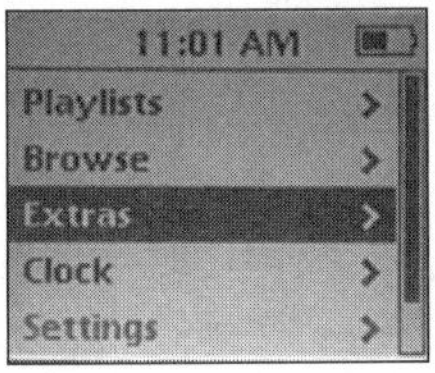

16. Press the **Menu button** to return to the Clock menu.

Displaying the Time on an iPod

There are a couple of ways to display the time and date on an iPod:

■ Choose **Main menu**, **Extras**, **Clock**. You'll see the Clock display (see Figure 9.4). In the title area, you'll see the current date. Just below the title, you'll see the current time.

FIGURE 9.4

Who says an iPod can't do everything that a $2 watch can do?

■ If you turn the Time in Title setting to On (as described in step 15 in the previous list of steps), the time will be displayed in the title area of every screen a second or two after you move to a new screen. When you first move to a screen, you will see the title, but after that small amount of time passes, the title will be replaced by the current time. The Sleep Timer feature of the iPod clock is explained in "Setting the Sleep Timer" on page **86**.

tip

For faster access to the Clock display, add the Clock command to the Main menu. See "Setting Up Your Main Menu Preferences" on page **84**.

Setting and Controlling an Alarm

You can also use the iPod's alarm clock to wake you up or remind you of an important time. To set an alarm, perform the following steps:

1. Choose **Main menu**, **Extras**, **Clock**, **Alarm Clock**. You'll see the Alarm Clock screen (see Figure 9.5). By default, the alarm is turned off, which is indicated by the Off setting.

FIGURE 9.5

You use this screen to set your iPod's alarm.

2. Highlight **Alarm** and press the **Select button**. The Alarm setting will become On, and the alarm will be active. The time at which the alarm is currently set to go off is shown next to the Time option on the Alarm Clock menu.

3. Highlight **Time** and press the **Select button**. You'll see the set alarm time screen.

tip

Even though you set the alarm by the minute, you can get to any time quickly by rapidly dragging around the Scroll pad or Click Wheel in full circles.

4. Use the **Scroll pad** or **Click Wheel** to choose the time you want the alarm to sound. Drag clockwise to increase the time or counterclockwise to decrease it.

5. When the correct alarm time is set, press the **Select button**. You'll return to the Alarm Clock menu.

6. Highlight **Sound**. By default, the alarm sound setting will be Beep, which you can hear even if you don't have earphones or speakers connected to the iPod. If you choose a different sound, you have to have speakers or headphones attached to the iPod to hear the alarm.

7. If you want to have a playlist start playing instead, press the **Select button**. You'll see a list of playlists on your iPod.

8. Highlight the playlist you want to use as the alarm sound and press the **Select button**. You'll return to the Alarm Clock menu, and the name of the selected list will be shown as the Sound setting.

9. Press the **Menu button**. You'll return to the Clock display. A bell icon will appear on the right side of the time to indicate that the alarm is set.

When the appointed time comes along, your iPod will turn on and play the beep sound or the selected playlist. Unless you are an incredibly light sleeper, don't expect the Beep sound to wake you up. It isn't very loud, and it doesn't play very long. You'll have better luck if you connect your iPod to speakers and use a playlist instead.

Planning Your Days with the iPod Calendar

You can use an iPod to display a calendar, and you can add events on a calendar application, such as Outlook or iCal, to the iPod calendar so that you can view those events. The iPod's calendar isn't designed as a replacement for a PDA or other full-featured calendar. Its purpose is only to enable you to view your calendar. For example, you can't add or delete events from the iPod calendar without using a computer.

Setting Up Your iPod Calendar

To start using your calendar, you need to add information to it. Because of space limitations, I have included coverage of the most popular calendar applications on each platform. You can use similar steps to add calendar information from other applications to an iPod. The iPod's Calendar feature is quite limited, but even so, it can be useful.

Moving Calendar Information from Outlook to an iPod (Windows)

To move calendar events from Outlook to your iPod, perform the following steps:

1. Open your Outlook calendar.

2. Select an event you want to move to your iPod calendar.

3. Choose **File**, **Save As**.

4. In the resulting Save As dialog box, move to the folder in which you want to store the events, choose **iCalendar Format** or **vCalendar Format** on the **Save as type** drop-down list, and click **Save**. The event will be exported from Outlook in the format you selected.

5. Repeat steps 2 through 4 until you have saved all the events you want to move onto your iPod. Unfortunately, repeating events are not moved. You have to move each event individually.

6. Connect your iPod to your computer. For this process to work, your iPod must be configured so it can be used as a hard disk. See Chapter 10, "Taking the iPod Further," for details.

7. Open the folder in which you saved the events you exported in step 4.

8. Open the **My Computer** folder in another window and then open the **iPod** so that you see the folders it contains (see Figure 9.6).

FIGURE 9.6

To add calendar events to your iPod, place them in the Calendars folder.

9. Drag the calendar events from the folder you opened in step 7 and place them in the **Calendars** folder on the iPod. When you do this, the events will be added to your iPod's calendar.

Moving Calendar Information to an iPod Using iSync and iCal (Mac)

Synchronizing your iCal calendar on your iPod is very straightforward, and you can even configure this to happen each time you connect your iPod to your Mac. Follow these steps:

1. Connect your iPod to your Mac and open the **iSync** application.

2. If you have never used iSync to synchronize your iPod before, choose **Devices**, **Add Device**.

3. Click the **Scan button**. You will see the iPod in the window.

4. Double-click the **iPod's icon**, and the iSync options dialog box will appear (see Figure 9.7).

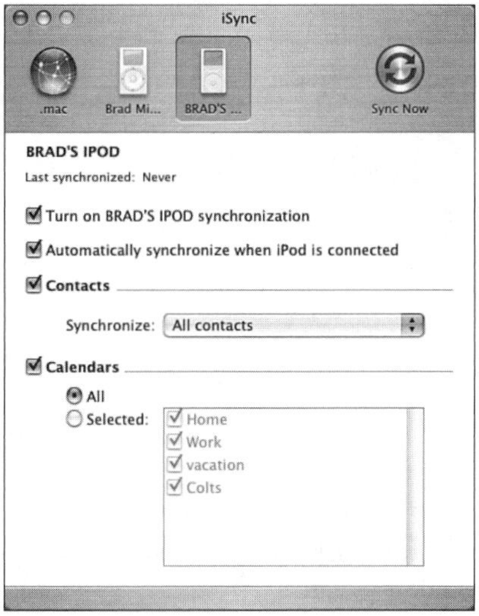

FIGURE 9.7

You can configure iSync to automatically move all your iCal events and Address Book contacts to your iPod.

5. Check the **Turn on *ipodname* synchronization** check box, where *ipodname* is the name of your iPod.

6. Check the **Automatically synchronize when iPod is connected** check box.

7. Check the **Contacts** check box and choose the specific contacts you want to move to your iPod on the **Synchronize** menu. For example, to have all your contacts synchronized, choose **All contacts**. If you want only a specific group of contacts to be moved, select that group instead.

8. Check the **Calendars** check box and choose the calendars you want to be moved to your iPod. Choose all your calendars by clicking the **All** radio button or choose specific calendars by clicking the **Selected** radio button and then checking the check box next to each calendar you want to place on your iPod.

9. Click the **Sync Now** button. The information you selected will be moved onto your iPod.

You only need to do these steps the first time you synch your iPod with iCal and your Address Book. If you configure automatic synchronization, this information will be updated each time you connect your iPod to your Mac.

Viewing Your iPod Calendar

To view your iPod calendar, do the following steps:

1. Choose **Main menu**, **Extras**, **Calendars**. You'll see the Calendars menu (see Figure 9.8).

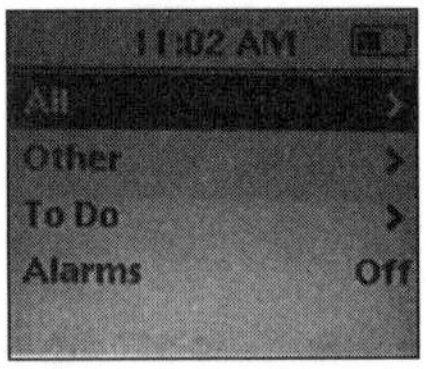

FIGURE 9.8

Choose a calendar to view it.

2. Highlight the calendar you want to view and press the **Select button**. If you want to see all the calendar events, choose **All**. You'll see the Calendar display (see Figure 9.9). The current date is highlighted. Dates with one or more events scheduled are marked with a black box.

Date with event

FIGURE 9.9

Dates with an event are marked with a black box in the lower-right corner of the date box.

3. To get details for an event, use the **Scroll pad** or **Click Wheel** to move to the date in which you are interested. As you move away from the current date, its box will take on a lighter shade and the currently selected date will be highlighted in the darker shade.

4. When the date in which you are interested is highlighted, press the **Select button**. The events for that date will be listed.

5. To see the detailed information for an event, highlight it and press the **Select button**. You'll see the detailed information for that event (see Figure 9.10).

FIGURE 9.10

Here, I am viewing the detail for an event on my iPod's calendar.

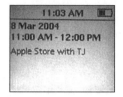

11:03 AM
8 Mar 2004
11:00 AM - 12:00 PM
Apple Store with TJ

6. Use the **Menu button** to move back to the list of events or back to the calendar.

The iPod calendar also picks up event alarms for the events you place on it. To configure the event alarm, open the **Calendars** menu and scroll until you see the **Alarms** option. Set this to **Beep** to hear the beep sound for an event alarm, **Silent** to see a silent alarm, or **Off** to turn the event alarm off.

To delete an event from your iPod, remove the event file from the Calendars folder on the iPod if you are using a file-based method (such as with Outlook). If you are using iCal, just remove the event from the iCal calendar and synchronize.

tip

If you are looking at an event several months prior to or after the current date, the easiest way to get back to the current date is to use the Menu button to move up to the Calendars menu again and then select the calendar.

Using an iPod to Keep an Address Book

The iPod's Contact Manager is analogous to the calendar, except that it is probably more useful because you mostly just refer to contact information rather than needing to manage it as you typically do with a calendar. Storing contacts on an iPod makes accessing phone numbers, email addresses, and other information fast and easy.

Configuring Your iPod Contacts

As with the calendar, the first step you need to do is to move contact information from your computer to the iPod. You can do this manually if you use a Windows computer or automatically if you use a Mac. After that, you can configure how contact information is displayed on your iPod.

Moving Contact Information from Outlook to an iPod (Windows)

Exporting contacts from Outlook is done with the same steps you use to export calendar information. The one difference is that you choose the vCard file format for contacts. The vCard file format is a standard format used for virtual cards that can be exported from or imported into most contact managers, including Outlook and Address Book.

After you have exported contact information from Outlook, the steps to import those contacts onto your iPod are very similar as well. Instead of using the Calendars folder on the iPod, you place contacts in the Contacts folder.

See "Moving Calendar Information from Outlook to an iPod (Windows)" on page **126** for the detailed steps to export information from Outlook and then import it to the iPod.

Moving Contact Information to an iPod Using iSync and Address Book (Mac)

Use the steps in the section "Moving Calendar Information to an iPod Using iSync and iCal (Mac)" on page **127** to move your contact information onto an iPod.

Configuring How Contacts Appear

When it comes to displaying contact information on an iPod, you have two options. To select an option, choose **Main menu**, **Settings**, **Contacts**. You'll see the Contacts preferences screen. This screen has two options. Use the **Sort** option to choose how contacts are sorted on the screen. Use the **Display** option to display how contacts are displayed on the screen. In both cases, your choices are First Last, which lists the first name followed by the last name, and Last First, which places the last name first and the first name last.

To select an option, choose the setting and press the **Select button** to toggle the option.

Viewing Your Contacts

To view your contacts, perform the following steps:

1. Choose **Main menu**, **Extras**, **Contacts**. You'll see the list of contacts sorted by your sort preference (see Figure 9.11).

2. To view a contact's detailed information, highlight the contact in which you are interested and press the **Select button**. You'll see a screen showing all the information for that contact (see Figure 9.12).

tip

To remove a contact from your iPod, remove the contact's vCard file from the Contacts folder on the iPod's hard drive. Or, remove the contact from the Address Book application and synchronize.

FIGURE 9.11

This screen displays a list of contacts stored on your iPod.

FIGURE 9.12

The 555 prefix should always tip you off to a bogus phone number.

3. Scroll down the screen to see all the information for the contact.

Using the iPod to Store and Display Text

You can also store and display text files on your iPod. For example, you might want to store instructions to perform a task that you have trouble remembering how to do or the directions to a location on your iPod for easy reference.

Creating Notes for an iPod

To create a note on an iPod, use any word processor or other application that can create a text file (filename extension should be .txt). Create the text you want to store on the iPod and save it as a TXT file.

Moving Notes to an iPod

Connect your iPod to your computer and place the text file you created in the **Notes** folder on the iPod's hard drive. (To do this, you need to configure your iPod so it can be used as a hard drive.)

Reading Notes on an iPod

After you have placed text files in the Notes folder, you can read them by choosing **Main menu**, **Extras**, **Notes**. You'll see the Notes screen, which contains a list of all the text files in the Notes folder on your iPod. To read a note, highlight it and press the **Select button**. You'll see the note's text on the screen (see Figure 9.13). Scroll down the screen to read all of the text if you need to.

note

In case you are wondering, there isn't a typo in the word *isn't* in the figure. The iPod didn't display the apostrophes in this note. I have heard that it does display them fine in some cases.

FIGURE 9.13

Hopefully, you'll put your iPod's Notes feature to better use than I did.

NOTE.TXT

If this were a real note, it might have useful information. But since it isnt, it doesnt.

The Absolute Minimum

Although the features in this chapter aren't a good reason to buy and use an iPod, they are a nice bonus that you can take advantage of without too much work on your part. Check out this list of features:

- You can use your iPod as a clock and even as an alarm clock. This is probably the most useful extra feature, at least in my book (which you happen to be reading right now).

- You can store calendar events on your iPod's calendar to make it a handy way to keep track of where you are supposed to be and when you are supposed to be there.

- Forget carrying around a paper list of contact information; store the names, addresses, email addresses, and phone numbers of people you need to contact on your iPod, and they will be with you whenever your iPod is.

■ Although the iPod's screen is too small to make reading long sections of text pleasant, you can store short text notes on your iPod and read them while you are on the move.

■ Lest you think these extra features are all work and no play, check out **Main menu**, **Extras**, **Games**. Sure, none of these iPod games will challenge Halo on the Xbox for the Best Game Ever title, but they might help you kill a few minutes of time.

In This Chapter

- Use your iPod as a portable FireWire or USB 2 hard drive.
- Use an iPod with more than one computer.
- Record your voice or other sounds with an iPod.
- Store images from a digital camera on your iPod and then transfer those images to a computer.

10

Taking the iPod Further

The iPod is one amazing device, isn't it! It excels as a music player, and with the accessories you learned about in Chapter 7, "Rocking Your World with iPod Accessories," you can do even more. As you learned in Chapter 8, "Using an iPod with a Home Stereo or Car Stereo," the iPod can also replace your home and auto CD player. In Chapter 9, "Using the iPod's Calendar, Contact Manager, and Other Non-Music Tools," you learned how to use the iPod to manage time, calendar, and contact information. This chapter extends your education in iPod utility and includes four more uses for your trusty iPod, including using the iPod as a hard drive, using it with more than one computer, using it to record sound, and using it to store digital images.

Using an iPod as a Portable FireWire/USB 2 Hard Drive

Here's some news for you: The iPod is a fully functional, portable FireWire/USB 2 hard drive. In addition to using the iPod's hard drive to store music, you can also use it just like any other hard drive you connect to your computer. Because you use FireWire or USB 2 to connect it, an iPod has speedy performance, too.

note

Just like any other drive you might use, you can work on files while they are stored on an iPod.

The uses for an iPod as a hard drive are almost endless; following are a few examples:

- **A transport drive**—Have files you want to move from one computer to another? No problem. Connect your iPod to one computer, copy files to it, connect it to the second computer, and copy files from the iPod onto that computer.

- **Extra storage space**—Need a few extra GB of disk space? No problem. Connect your iPod and you have it.

- **Temporary backup drive**—Have some important files you want to back up? Place them on an iPod and there you go.

Enabling an iPod to Be Used as a Hard Drive

To be able to use an iPod as a hard drive, you need to configure it within iTunes by using the following steps:

1. Connect your iPod to your computer. iTunes will open, and your iPod will be shown in the Source List.

2. Select the iPod and click the **iPod Options** button. You'll see the iPod Preferences dialog box (see Figure 10.1).

3. Check the **Enable disk use** check box. You'll see a warning prompt that explains that if you enable disk use, you'll have to manually unmount the iPod before disconnecting it.

4. Click **OK** to close the warning prompt.

5. Click **OK** to close the iPod Preferences dialog box.

note

If you don't enable an iPod to be used as a disk, you won't be able to see it from your computer's desktop. Only within iTunes will you be able to see the iPod when it is connected to your computer.

FIGURE 10.1

You use the iPod Preferences dialog box to enable your iPod to act as a hard drive.

Using an iPod as a Hard Drive

After you have enabled this functionality, you can use an iPod as a disk by performing the following steps:

1. Connect your iPod to your computer. iTunes will open, and if you have configured automatic updating, the iPod will be updated.

2. On your computer's desktop, open a new window and select the iPod, which will be listed just like other hard drives in your system (see Figures 10.2 and 10.3).

tip

The iPod includes three folders by default (Calendars, Contacts, and Notes). You can create other folders on the iPod just as you can other disks with which you work.

FIGURE 10.2

In the My Computer folder, you will see your iPod, which is listed in the Devices with Removable Storage section.

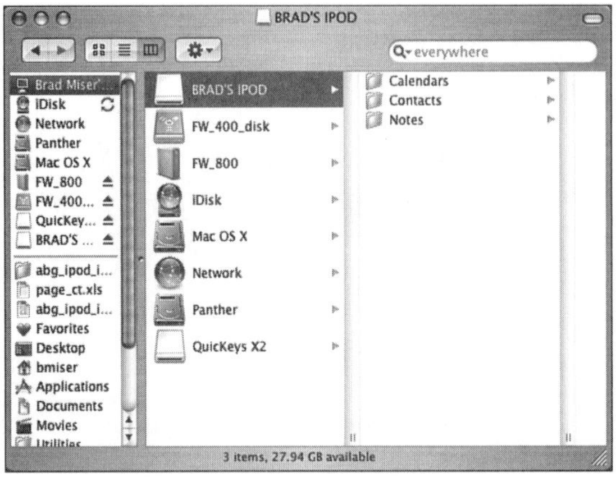

FIGURE 10.3

In the Mac's Finder, an iPod looks and works like other drives too.

3. To copy files onto the iPod, drag them from other locations on your computer and drop them onto the iPod.

4. When you are done moving files to or from the iPod, eject it. You can do this from the computer's desktop by selecting the **iPod** and choosing the **Eject** command or from within iTunes by selecting the **iPod** on the Source List and clicking the **Eject** button. The iPod will be unmounted, and you can disconnect it from your computer.

Using an iPod with More Than One Computer

Because the iPod is so very portable, you might use it with more than one computer. And because iTunes is free, there is no reason you can't install it on every computer you use.

Using an iPod with more than one computer only presents one minor complication: When you configure an iPod to be automatically updated, you link it to the iTunes Library on the machine you configured the update on. When you connect the iPod to another machine that

caution

When you have enabled an iPod to be used as a disk, you must manually eject it before disconnecting it from your computer. If you don't, you can damage the data stored on it. To let you know this, the "Do not disconnect" message will appear on the iPod's screen until it is safe for you to disconnect it.

tip

If you want to move music to the iPod from more than one iTunes Library, use the Manual update option. This option doesn't link the iPod to any Library, so you can move songs from multiple Libraries onto the iPod.

also has automatic updating set, you will see a warning prompt that explains that the iPod is linked to another iTunes Library (see Figure 10.4).

FIGURE 10.4

This warning prompt explains that the iPod is already linked to another iTunes Library.

If you click Yes in this prompt, the music currently on the iPod will be replaced by the music stored on the computer to which the iPod is connected and the link will be changed to the current iTunes Library. If you don't want to replace the iPod's music, click No.

Because you can link the iPod to only one computer at a time, you might want to use the iPod to move music from the "nonlinked" computer to the one that is linked with your iPod. If you have music on one computer that you want to store in the Library on another computer, do the following steps:

1. Mount the iPod as a disk on the computer that has the music you want to move to another computer.

2. Create a folder on the iPod called "Music to Move" or something similar.

3. Copy the music you want to move into the folder you created in step 2.

4. Connect the iPod to the computer to which it is linked.

5. Copy the music files from the iPod onto the computer.

6. Add the files you copied to the iTunes Library on that computer. (The next time you update the iPod from this computer, the music files you added to the Library will be placed in the iPod's music collection if they meet the update's criteria.)

7. Delete the music files you copied onto the iPod from the iPod.

note

For help using iTunes to accomplish these steps, see Part II of this book, titled "iTunes."

note

By default, the music files on an iPod are hidden from view when you use the iPod as a disk. There are ways to make them visible so that you can work with them directly. This isn't hard, but it is beyond the scope of this chapter and isn't something you really need to do anyway.

Using an iPod to Capture Sound

With a recording accessory, you can use the iPod to record your voice or other sounds. This can be a handy way to capture information on the fly for use later. For example, if you use a vehicle for business use, you might want to use the iPod to keep a verbal log of that use that you can document "on paper" later.

Choosing a Voice Recorder for an iPod

In order to record sound on an iPod, you need to obtain a voice recorder accessory. By the time you read this, there should be at least two of these units available: the Belkin Voice Recorder for iPod and the Griffin Technology iTalk iPod Voice Recorder.

Only the Belkin unit was available when I wrote this, so that is the unit I focus on here (see Figure 10.5). This unit retails for about $50 and enables you to access the recording features that are already built in to the iPod's software.

> **note**
>
> There are some funky ways you can record a few seconds of sound without a voice recorder unit, but it requires more maneuvering than you are likely to want to do except as a novelty. If you are interested in this method, use Google to search the Internet for this information.

FIGURE 10.5

The Belkin iPod Voice Recorder enables you to use your iPod to record your voice and other sound.

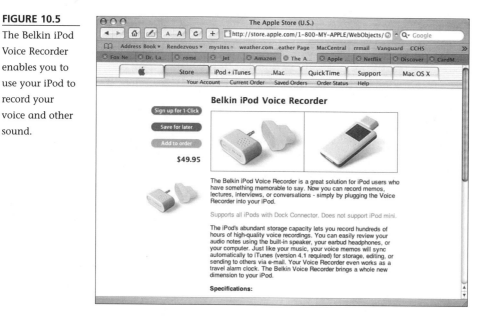

Installing the Belkin iPod Voice Recorder

Installing the Voice Recorder couldn't be easier. Simply plug the unit into the iPod's Headphones and Remote ports. When you do so, you'll see the Voice Memo screen (see Figure 10.6). That's all there is to setting up the voice recorder.

note

Unfortunately, the Belkin Voice Recorder doesn't work with an iPod mini.

FIGURE 10.6

When you connect a Voice Recorder to your iPod, you'll see this Voice Memo screen.

Recording Sound on an iPod

To record sound, use the following steps:

1. Move to the **Voice Memo** screen; if you aren't there already, choose **Main menu**, **Extras**, **Voice Memos**, **Record Now**.

2. Highlight **Record** and press the **Select button**. Your iPod will begin recording, and the counter on the Voice Memos screen will begin counting the time of the current recording. At the same time, the Pause and Stop and Save commands will appear on the screen (see Figure 10.7).

FIGURE 10.7

As you record, your iPod displays the length of the recording you are making.

tip

You aren't limited to recording your own speech; you can record any sound that is close enough to be picked up by the microphone in the voice recorder.

3. Speak into the voice recorder. Whatever sound you make will be recorded.

4. To pause the recording, highlight **Pause** and press the **Select button**. The counter and recording will pause.

5. To resume recording from where you left off, highlight **Resume** and press the **Select button**. Your iPod will start recording again.

6. When you are done recording, highlight **Stop and Save** and press the **Select button**. The recoding process will stop, and you'll move back to the Voice Memos screen on which your recording will be listed. It will be named with the date and time on which you made it (see Figure 10.8).

FIGURE 10.8

On the Voice Memos screen, you'll see the recordings you have made.

Voice Memos ▣
Record Now >
3/11 6:29 AM >
3/11 6:31 AM >
3/11 6:33 AM >

You can repeat the previous steps to continue recording sound until you have captured all that you are interested in or until you run out of disk space to store the sound you have recorded, whichever comes first.

Working with Sound You Have Recorded

There are a number of things you can do with sounds you have recorded. These include the following:

- You can play sounds you have recorded by highlighting the sound you want to hear on the Voice Memos screen and pressing the **Play button**. You'll see the Now Playing screen, and the sound will play.

- You can delete sounds you have recorded by highlighting the sound you want to delete and pressing the **Select button**. You'll see a screen with Play and Delete options. Select **Delete** and then select **Delete Memo** on the resulting screen. The sound you recorded will be deleted.

note

Because you install the voice recorder in the Headphones port, you must remove it in order to connect headphones to the iPod to be able to listen to sound you have recorded.

- The next time you connect your iPod to your computer, the sounds you recorded will be uploaded into your iTunes Library. To find them, search for the dates on which you recorded the sounds, and the sounds you recorded on those dates will be shown in the Content pane (see Figure 10.9). After a recorded sound is in your Library, you can work with it just like the songs in that Library. For example, you can play the sounds, add them to playlists, put them on CD, and so on.

FIGURE 10.9

These are sounds I recorded on an iPod.

■ You can also access the recording files you made directly by connecting the iPod to a computer and opening it as a hard drive from the desktop. Then open the Recordings folder, and you will see one WAV file for each recording stored on the iPod. You can play these WAV files or import them into an audio application for editing or other purposes.

Using an iPod to Store Digital Pictures

If you have ever been taking photos away from your computer and run out of room on your camera's memory card, you'll immediately understand why being able to store images you take on your iPod is a good thing. You can quickly upload images from your camera's memory onto your iPod and erase the card so that you can take more pictures. When you get back to your computer, you can upload the images from the iPod to your favorite photo application.

Choosing a Memory Card Reader for an iPod

To be able to store images on an iPod, you need some way to move the images from the camera's memory card onto the iPod's hard drive. At press time, there is only one device that allows you to do

note

Unfortunately, the iPod Media Reader is not supported on the iPod mini.

this: the Belkin iPod Media Reader (see Figure 10.10). This very versatile device enables you to read files from the most common types of memory cards used in digital cameras, including CompactFlash, SmartMedia, Secure Digital, Memory Stick, or MultiMediaCard.

FIGURE 10.10

The Belkin iPod Media Reader enables you to move files from a memory card onto an iPod's hard drive.

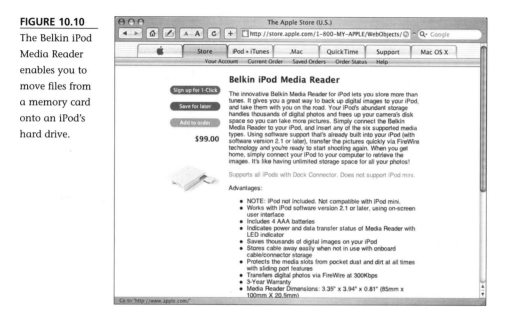

Storing Photos on an iPod

To store images on an iPod, perform the following steps:

1. Use a digital camera to capture images.

2. Remove the memory card containing the images you want to move to the iPod.

3. Open the card slots on the Media Reader by sliding its protective cover open.

4. Insert the memory card into the appropriate slot in the Media Reader. Insert the card with the label side up.

5. Fold the Dock connector out of the Media Reader to expose it.

6. Connect the Media Reader's Dock connector to the iPod's Dock Connector port. The Media Reader will start communicating with your iPod, and you'll see the Import screen (see Figure 10.11). On this screen, you'll see the number of photos on the card along with information about the amount of memory being used and the amount of memory available on the card.

note

You have to install AAA batteries into the Belkin Media Reader in order to use it.

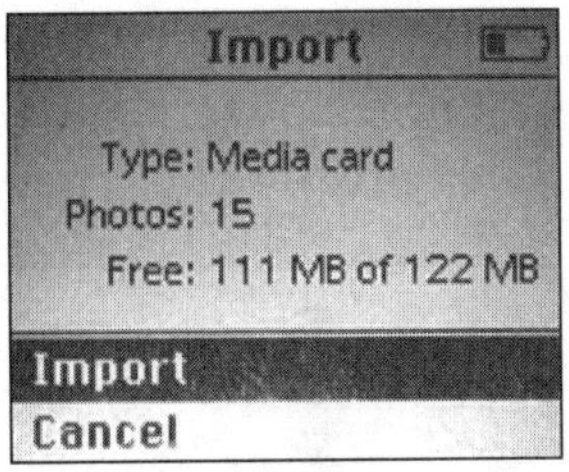

FIGURE 10.11
The Import screen shows you how many photos are on the memory card in the Media Reader.

```
         Import        
   Type: Media card
   Photos: 15
      Free: 111 MB of 122 MB
Import
Cancel
```

tip

To move to the Import screen, choose **Main menu**, **Extras**, **Photo Import**, **Import Photos**. Just like with the Voice Recorder, these commands don't appear until you have connected a Media Reader to your iPod.

7. Highlight **Import** and press the **Select button**. You'll see the Import Progress screen, which displays the progress of the import process (see Figure 10.12). When all the images have been moved from the memory card to the iPod, the Import Done screen will appear (see Figure 10.13).

FIGURE 10.12
You use this screen to monitor, and cancel if necessary, the import process.

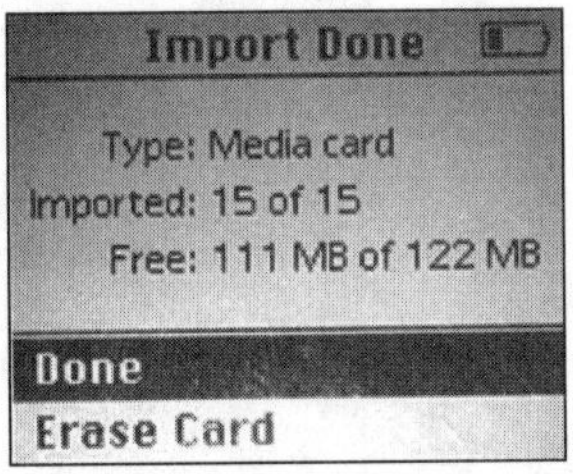

```
       Importing       
   ▬▬▬▬▬▬▬
       7 of 15
Stop and Save
Cancel
```

FIGURE 10.13
This screen informs you that the import process is complete.

```
     Import Done       
   Type: Media card
Imported: 15 of 15
      Free: 111 MB of 122 MB
Done
Erase Card
```

tip

To erase the contents of the memory card, highlight **Erase** and press the **Select button**.

8. When you are done importing, highlight **Done** and press the **Select button**. You'll move to the Photos screen on which you see the photo files you have imported onto the iPod in rolls (see Figure 10.14).

FIGURE 10.14
Photos on an iPod are organized by rolls; one import session results in one roll of photos.

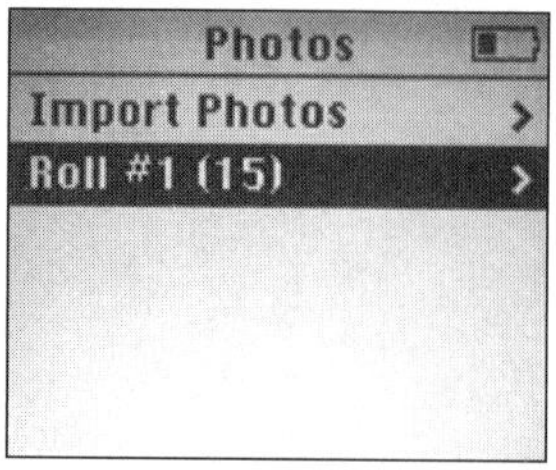

Photos
Import Photos >
Roll #1 (15) >

9. To view information about a roll of photos, select the roll in which you are interested and press the **Select button**. The Roll Information screen will appear (see Figure 10.15).

tip

To move back to the Photos screen to view roll information, choose **Main menu**, **Extras**, **Photo Import**.

FIGURE 10.15
On the Roll Information screen, you can view information about the photos imported during that session.

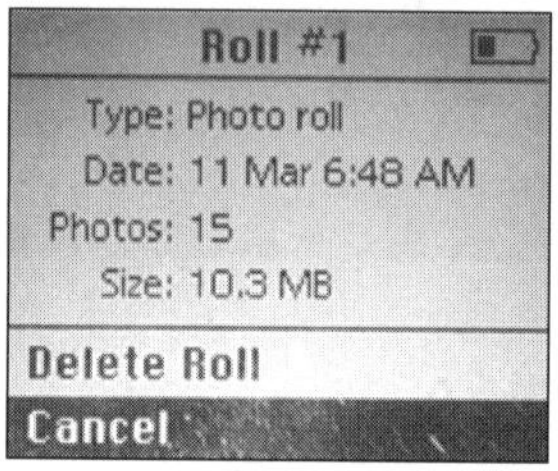

Roll #1
Type: Photo roll
Date: 11 Mar 6:48 AM
Photos: 15
Size: 10.3 MB
Delete Roll
Cancel

10. When you are done viewing information about a roll, choose **Cancel**. You'll return to the Photos screen.

Moving Images from an iPod to a Computer

To move images that you have stored on the iPod to your computer, connect the iPod to the computer on which you want to place the iPod's images. Open the **DCIM folder** and you'll see subfolders that contain the images you have downloaded. Open the folder containing photos you want to work with and you'll see those photos (see Figure 10.16). You can then open them or import them into the application you use to work with digital images.

tip

To delete a roll of photos from an iPod, open the **Roll Information** screen and choose **Delete**.

If you use a Mac and Apple's iPhoto application, you can import photos directly from the iPod. After you have connected the iPod to your computer, launch iPhoto. Click the **Import mode** button and you will see your iPod as the Import source. Click **Import** to add the photos stored on the iPod to your iPhoto Library.

FIGURE 10.16

This Finder window shows the contents of the DCIM folder that is stored on the selected iPod.

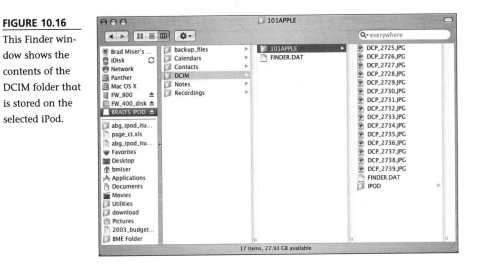

After you have moved the images from your iPod onto your computer, delete the images from the iPod to free up disk space. You can do that by using the Delete command on the iPod's Roll Information screen or by deleting the image folders from the iPod from your computer's desktop.

THE ABSOLUTE MINIMUM

As you can see, the iPod is much more than just the world's best portable music player. As you live with your iPod, you'll likely come to really appreciate its other uses, which include the following:

- Using your iPod as a portable FireWire or USB 2 hard drive just might be one of the best reasons to have an iPod. The ability to carry up to 40GB of data on a device the size of a deck of playing cards is very useful indeed.

- You can use an iPod with more than one computer; just be aware of the update option you use or you might find the contents of your iPod being replaced when you didn't intend them to be.

- Adding a Voice Recorder to an iPod is a great way to use it to record sounds, such as voice memos or reminders.

- If you use a digital camera, you can store its images on an iPod for backup purposes or to empty the camera's memory card so you can take more pictures.

IN THIS CHAPTER

- Maximize your iPod's battery life and durability.
- Update or restore your iPod's software.
- Identify and solve iPod problems.

11

MAINTAINING AN iPOD AND SOLVING PROBLEMS

The iPod is a well-designed device, and it is more likely than not that you won't ever have any trouble with it, especially if you practice good battery management and keep its software up to date. In this chapter, you'll learn how to do those two tasks, plus you'll learn how to handle any problems in the unlikely event they do occur.

Maintaining Your iPod's Power

Like any other portable electronic device, your iPod literally lives or dies by its battery. When not connected to a power source, your iPod's battery is the only thing standing between you and a musicless life. Fortunately, working with your iPod's battery isn't very difficult, but it is something you need to keep in mind.

Monitoring and Maximizing Battery Life

The Battery icon in the upper-right corner of the screen always tells you what your battery's status is at any point in time.

When your iPod is running on battery power, the amount of shading within the icon provides a relative—and I do mean relative—indication of your battery's current state (see Figure 11.1). As you use battery power, the "filled in" part of the battery will decrease until your iPod runs out of gas. When it does, you'll see an icon of a battery with an exclamation point that indicates your iPod is out of power, and the battery will have to be charged before you can use the iPod again.

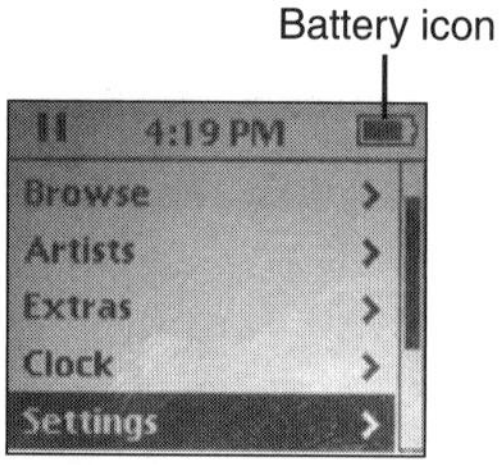

note

The iPod's and iPod mini's battery is rated for eight hours. Of course, these ratings are based on ideal conditions, which means that the iPod plays straight through for these periods with no controls being used, no backlighting, and so on. Should you expect to get that much time under actual conditions? Probably not. Later in this section, you'll learn how to test your iPod's battery to make sure it is in good condition.

Battery icon

FIGURE 11.1

Keep an eye on the battery icon to make sure you don't run out of juice while you are on the move.

To maximize your iPod's playing time per battery charge, you can do the following:

- Keep the iPod's software up to date (you'll learn how later in this chapter).
- Use the Hold switch to prevent your iPod from being unintentionally turned on when you carry it around. You'd be amazed how easy it is for the iPod to be turned on and start to play without you knowing it, especially if you carry it in your pocket, backpack, or computer bag. (It's no fun trying to listen to

tunes only to find out your iPod's battery has been accidentally drained—not that this has ever happened to me of course.)

- When you aren't listening, don't keep your iPod playing. Use the Pause button when you aren't listening to music. Playing music uses power at a greater rate than not playing music.

- Put your iPod to sleep by turning it off when you aren't using it. The Sleep, or Off, mode uses the least amount of power. (You can press and hold the Play/Pause button to turn the iPod off. You can also add the Sleep command to the Main menu if you prefer to use that instead.)

> **tip**
>
> When an iPod is turned off, it still uses some power. For example, its internal clock keeps "ticking." And, it takes some power to maintain the iPod's memory. If you don't use your iPod for 14 days or more, you should charge its battery to keep it ready to play.

- Keep backlighting at a minimum level. Backlighting is very helpful to be able to see the iPod's screen, especially in low-light conditions. However, it does use additional power, so you should use it only as needed to maximize battery life. When you don't need it, such as in daylight conditions, turn it off. When you do need it, set it such that it remains on only a few seconds when you press a control.

- Minimize track changes. Each time you change tracks, the iPod uses more power than it would just playing tracks straight through.

- Turn the Equalizer off. The Equalizer uses more power than playing music without it.

- Every 30 recharges or so, fully drain and recharge the battery.

- Keep the iPod at a comfortable temperature. Using the iPod in very cold or very hot conditions lowers its battery life.

Charging an iPod's Battery

Fortunately, there are a number of ways to charge your iPod's battery, including the following:

- Use the included FireWire power adapter.

- Connect the iPod to a six-pin FireWire port either directly with a cable or via a Dock.

- Use a power adapter designed for 12-volt sources, such as the power outlets in your vehicle.

> **note**
>
> You can't charge an iPod using a four-pin FireWire connector.

There are two different ways that the iPod lets you know it is charging.

When your iPod's battery is charging via a FireWire connection to a computer, the Battery icon will include a lightning bolt symbol and will include a filling motion from the left to the right of the icon (see Figure 11.2). When the battery is fully charged, the icon will be completely filled and the motion will stop.

Battery being charged

FIGURE 11.2

This iPod is getting its battery charged via a FireWire cable.

When you charge your iPod's battery through a separate power adapter only, the battery icon fills the iPod's screen and flashes (see Figure 11.3). When the process is complete, the battery icon remains steady.

FIGURE 11.3

This iPod is being charged with the power adapter.

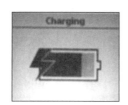

According to Apple, it takes only an hour to charge a drained battery to 80% of its capacity. It can take up to four hours to fully charge a drained battery.

Getting More Life Out of an iPod's Battery

The iPod uses a lithium-ion battery. Any battery, including the iPod's, will eventually wear out and no longer provide the power it once did. In my research, most lithium-ion batteries are rated for 300–500 charges. In this context, a charge can't be precisely defined, but it does include a full discharge and then a full recharge. A partial charge doesn't "count" as much, but the precise relationship between amount of charge and how much that charge "counts" can't be specified.

note

Unlike some other rechargeable batteries, lithium-ion batteries don't have a memory, which means that their performance is not degraded by not being fully discharged and then recharged each time.

Batteries like that in the iPod actually last longer if you don't let them fully discharge before you recharge them. Frequent "topping off" will not reduce the battery's life and in fact is better for your battery than letting it run very low on power before you recharge it.

Every 30 recharges or so, do run your iPod until it is completely out of power and then perform a full recharge. This will reset the battery's power gauge, which tends to get more inaccurate if the battery is never fully discharged.

It doesn't hurt the battery to do frequent and short recharges, such as by placing the iPod in a Dock every day after you are done using it.

However, you should make sure to run the iPod on battery power for significant periods of time. If you constantly run the iPod from the power adapter or while it is in the Dock connected to a power source, the iPod's battery's performance will degrade.

note

The fact that the iPod's battery will eventually wear out is nothing unique to the iPod. All batteries die eventually and must be replaced. However, some early iPods (the Original iPod) did have major battery problems that have left the iPod a now-undeserved reputation for having defective batteries.

Solving Battery Problems

Frankly, your iPod's battery will eventually wear out. You'll know this by the time it can play on battery power becoming shorter and shorter. And, the battery is the most likely problem you might experience.

Testing Your iPod's Battery

If your iPod doesn't seem to play for a reasonable amount of time, you should test it to get an idea of what its current battery life is. Test your iPod by performing the following steps:

1. Fully charge your iPod.
2. Remove the iPod from the charger so that it is running on battery power.
3. Make a note of the current time.
4. Use the **Settings** commands to turn off the **Equalizer** and **Backlight**.
5. Set **Repeat** to **One**.
6. Select an album or playlist and play it.

caution

Because fully discharging and then recharging an iPod's battery causes wear on it, you shouldn't do this test frequently. Only do it if you suspect that your iPod's battery is having problems.

7. Let the iPod play until it runs out of power. While the iPod is playing, don't use any of its controls. Anytime you cause the iPod to perform an action, you cause it to use additional power. In this test, you are attempting to determine what its maximum life is so you can compare it to the rated life.

8. When the iPod stops playing and the low power icon appears in the display, make a note of the time.

9. Calculate the battery life by figuring out how much time passed since you started the iPod playing (compare the time you noted in step 8 with what you noted in step 3).

If you iPod plays for four hours or longer on a full charge, Apple considers that its battery life is acceptable. If the iPod won't play for more than four hours, it likely has a problem and needs to be replaced.

Getting Help from Apple for iPod Battery Problems

If your iPod doesn't play for the expected time, the battery probably needs to be replaced. If the iPod is still under warranty (one year without the AppleCare Protection Plan or two years with it), Apple will replace the battery for free. If the iPod is not under warranty, Apple will replace the battery for you (currently this costs $99 plus $6.95 shipping). To get more information and start this process, go to www.apple.com/support/ipod/power/ and click the **iPod battery service request form** link.

If you are comfortable working with electronic devices yourself, you can replace the iPod's battery on your own. How to do this is beyond the scope of this book, but you can purchase a battery and get help on the Web at places such as www.ipodbattery.com and www.ipodresq.com.

note

Batteries are manufactured items, which means they aren't always made just right. You should test your new iPod's battery life to make sure yours is performing up to snuff prior to the warranty expiring.

Keep in mind that battery life is dependent on many factors, such as temperature, what features are being used, and so on. The guidelines are pretty loose because the conditions under which an iPod is used are so variable.

caution

According to Apple, your iPod will be replaced with an equivalent model rather than just the battery being replaced. Make sure you have all the data you need off your iPod before you send it in for service.

Replacement batteries cost from $60 to $80, including tools and instructions. Although being a bit more expensive, sending the unit back to Apple is probably a better way to go in most situations. (Who knows, if you have an old iPod, you might get a better unit back in return!)

Updating or Restoring an iPod's Software

Apple is continually improving the iPod's software to add features, make it even more stable, and so on. You should periodically check for new iPod software and, when you find it, install it on your iPod—this is called *updating* the iPod's software.

When you are having major problems with your iPod or just want to completely reformat it, you can also *restore* its software to return it to factory settings.

tip

To see the current version of iPod software installed on your iPod, choose **Main menu**, **Settings**, **About**. On the About screen, you will see the version of iPod software you are currently using next to the Version label.

You do both of these tasks in the same way, as the following steps show:

1. Open a Web browser and move to www.apple.com/support/ipod/. You'll see the iPod Support page (see Figure 11.4).

FIGURE 11.4

Apple's iPod Support page provides access to the latest iPod software.

2. Locate and click the link for the latest iPod or iPod mini software for your computer's OS, such as Mac OS X or Windows XP. You'll move to the iPod Software Update page.

3. Complete the **form**, click the **radio button** for your OS, and click **Download Update**. The update will be downloaded to your computer. Notice the name of the application you download and where you store it on your computer.

4. Launch the **iPod Update application**—in some cases, it will run automatically after you download it. On the Mac, you'll see the iPod Software Updater application (see Figure 11.5). On Windows PCs, you will have to restart your computer after running the Setup application. Then, choose **Start menu**, **iPod**, **System Software**, **Updater**. You'll then see the Updater application for Windows.

tip

If you use Mac OS X, you don't need to do this process because the Software Update feature will notify you when new iPod software is available, and then you can use the Software Update application to download and install it.

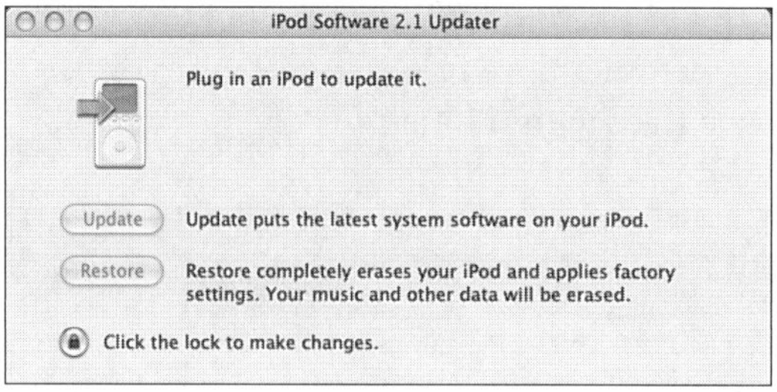

FIGURE 11.5

You use the Updater application to update your iPod's software or to restore it to original condition.

iPod Software 2.1 Updater

Plug in an iPod to update it.

Update — Update puts the latest system software on your iPod.

Restore — Restore completely erases your iPod and applies factory settings. Your music and other data will be erased.

Click the lock to make changes.

5. Connect the iPod you want to update or restore to your computer.

6. If you want to install the latest version of the iPod software on your iPod, click the **Update** button. If you want to restore your iPod, click **Restore** instead.

7. Follow the onscreen instructions to complete the update or restore process.

After you have updated your iPod, you can continue using it as you did before the update.

caution

When you restore an iPod, all of its data is erased, including its music, calendar data, contacts, and so on. If you have stored files on the iPod that aren't stored elsewhere too, make sure you copy the files you want to save from the iPod to another location before you restore it.

If you restored your iPod, you will have to perform an update from iTunes to load your music back onto it. You'll also have to replace any calendar or contact information you want to store on it.

Identifying and Solving iPod Problems

Okay, I admit it. The iPod isn't perfect. Once in a while, it might not act the way you expect it to. Hey, no one or no technology is perfect after all. In this section, you'll read some information that will help you in the event you do experience problems.

Solving iPod Problems

Troubleshooting iPod problems isn't all that different from troubleshooting other kinds of problems. First, observe exactly what is happening. Determine what you are doing and how the iPod is responding or not responding, as the case may be. Then, use the information in the following sections to see if you can solve the problem yourself.

Checking the Basics

We all do things that can be classified as dumb once in a while. And using the iPod can result in a few of these events, so use the following list to make sure you haven't done anything to shoot yourself in the foot:

- If the iPod won't respond to any controls, make sure the Hold switch isn't active. The Hold switch does just what it is supposed to—it prevents everything from working. It can be rather embarrassing to panic that your precious iPod has suffered a major failure only to realize that the Hold switch is on. (Of course you understand that this has never happened to me.)

- If the iPod won't turn on, connect it to the power adapter or to a computer using a six-pin FireWire connection. It might simply be that the battery is out of power. Remember that the iPod uses some battery power when you aren't using it, and after 14 days or so, it might not have enough battery power to wake up. Sometimes the empty battery icon will appear when you try to turn on a fully discharged iPod and sometimes it won't.

- Try connecting the iPod to a computer. If it mounts, you probably just need to do a minor reset to get it to work again.

Resetting an iPod

If you can't get an iPod to do anything (and you've checked the Hold switch) or if it is behaving badly, try resetting it. When you reset an iPod, its temporary memory is cleared, but your data won't be affected. Follow these steps:

1. Connect the iPod to the power adapter using the FireWire cable and then plug the power adapter into a wall outlet.

2. Move the **Hold switch** to the On position and then slide it to the Off position again.

3. Press and hold both the **Menu** and **Play/Pause buttons** down for about five seconds until you see the Apple logo on the iPod's screen. This indicates that the reset process is complete.

4. Try to use the iPod to do what you were trying to do when you noticed a problem.

If resetting your iPod solves your problem, you are home free. If not, you might want to try restoring it.

Restoring an iPod

As you read earlier, you can also use the iPod Software Update application to restore an iPod. When you restore an iPod, its hard drive is erased and a clean version of its software is installed. The purpose is to configure the iPod with factory settings that will likely solve many problems you are having.

For the steps to perform a restore, see "Updating or Restoring an iPod's Software" on page **155**.

Getting Help with iPod Problems

Although I could have added a lot more pages to this book with specific problems you might encounter and potential solutions to those problems, that would have been kind of wasteful

caution

Restoring an iPod also deletes any data that you have stored on its hard drive, so make sure you have any data that is unique to the iPod backed up before you restore it. You don't have to worry about its music because that will be replaced the next time you connect it to your computer to perform an update from iTunes.

for two main reasons. One, it is likely you won't ever experience the problems I would include. Two, Apple maintains an extensive iPod Web site from which you get detailed information about iPod problems. You can use this information to solve specific problems you encounter (that aren't solved with the information in the previous sections, such as a reset).

To access this help, use a Web browser to move to www.apple.com/support/ipod. On this page, you can search for help, read FAQs, and get other information that will help you solve iPod problems (see Figure 11.6).

There are a number of other Web sites that might be helpful to you as well. These include www.ipodlounge.com and www.ipodhacks.com. You can also use www.google.com to search for other iPod information; you'll find no shortage of it.

tip

Feel free to write to me with questions about your iPod or to ask for help with problems you are having with your iPod. You can reach me at

bradmacosx@mac.com.

FIGURE 11.6

Need iPod help? You got it.

THE ABSOLUTE MINIMUM

The iPod is what we hope most technology will be—it just works and works well. Here are some points to help you keep your iPod in tune:

- Understand your iPod's battery and use the practices described in this chapter to keep it maintained properly.

- Keep your iPod's software current by using the update software that Apple releases periodically.

- If you do run into problems, check the last section in this chapter for help in solving them. Fortunately, many problems are easy to solve, and you have a lot of help available.

PART

iTUNES

12

TOURING ITUNES

With not-very-sincere apologies to Mr. Edison, Apple's iTunes is the best thing to happen to music since the phonograph. This amazing application enables you to do things with your music you might have never dreamed possible. Of course, you can use iTunes to listen to audio CDs, but that is certainly nothing to write home (or a book) about. Any two-bit boom box can do that. That basic task is barely a warm-up for iTunes. If you have never used iTunes before, prepare to be impressed (and if you have used iTunes before, be impressed anyway).

What You Can Do with iTunes

I could fill a book (or at least Part II of this book) with all the great things you can do with iTunes. Following are some examples just to whet your appetite:

- Listen to audio CDs.
- Listen to Internet radio.
- Store all the music you like in a single place so you never need to fuss with individual CDs again.
- Search and organize all this music so that listening to exactly the music you want is just a matter of a few mouse clicks (and maybe a few key presses).
- Create custom albums (called *playlists*) containing the specific songs you want to hear.
- Create custom albums (called *smart playlists*) that are based on a set of criteria, such as all the Jazz music you have rated at four or five stars.
- Use the iTunes built-in Equalizer to make your music just right.
- Burn your own music CDs to play in those oh-so-limited CD players in your car, a boom box, or in your home.
- Share your music collection with other people over a wired or wireless network; you can listen to music other people share with you as well.

Audio File Formats You Might Encounter When You Use iTunes

As you work with digital music and other audio files, you'll encounter a number of different file formats that you need to understand. This is important because each of these formats offers specific benefits and limitations that impact what you do with your music. For example, some file formats offer better music quality versus file size than others. You definitely don't need to have all the specifications for each of these formats committed to memory (nor will you find them in this book); instead, all you need to be able to do is to distinguish between them and to be able to choose the format that is the most appropriate for what you are trying to do.

Most audio file formats are *encoded*. What this means is that specific compression algorithms (because this is a computer book, I am required by contract to use that word at least once) are used to reduce the size of the audio file without, hopefully anyway, lowering the quality of the resulting sound very much. The higher the compression that is used, the lower the quality of the resulting music when it is played back. Note that the words *higher* and *lower* are relative. Often, it takes a musical expert to tell the difference between encoded and unencoded music, but even if it is imperceptible to us mere mortals, it does exist.

When it comes to digital audio files, one trade-off always has to be made. And that is *file size* versus *sound quality*. When you add thousands of songs to your iTunes Library, you can easily consume gigabytes of disk space. Although you might have a humungous hard drive in your computer, you might also have other files you want to store on it, such as photos, Word docs, and so on. Even I realize that computers can be used for more than just music.

To keep the amount of disk space required to store your music to a minimum, you will encode it. When you do, you choose the settings you want to use to encode that music. The more encoding you apply, the less space the music will consume, but the lower quality the playback will be. You will quickly find a happy medium between file size and how the music sounds to you.

You'll learn about this in more detail later in the book, but for now, you should read the following sections so you can become comfortable with the various audio file formats you will encounter.

CD Audio

The CD Audio format was the world's first widely used entry in the digital audio format life cycle. The creation of this format was the start of the CD revolution. Instead of vinyl albums, which were a pain to deal with and included lots of hisses, pops, and other distractions when played, listeners began enjoying digital music. In addition to being much easier to handle than LPs, CDs provided a much better listening experience and were—and are—much more durable than records. They also sounded much better than cassettes and could be just as portable.

Eventually, CD Audio made its way to computers, which now can provide all the music-listening enjoyment of a home stereo plus much more, thanks to applications such as iTunes.

Although you can use iTunes to listen to your audio CDs, typically you will just convert those CDs into one of the newer digital formats and store that content on your computer's hard disk so you don't have to use a CD when you want to listen to music. You will also make use of this format when you put your iTunes music on your own audio CD so that you can play your iTunes music when you are away from your computer.

caution

Some audio CDs use copyright-protection schemes that prevent you from listening to them on a computer (with the idea being that you won't be able to make copies of the songs for illegal purposes). Unfortunately, not only do these CDs not work in your computer, they can actually cause damage. Before playing a CD in your computer, check the CD's label carefully to make sure it doesn't contain any warnings about playing the CD in a computer or state that the CD is copy-protected. If it does have these warnings, don't try to use the CD in your computer.

MP3

Even if this book is your first foray into the wonderful world of digital music, you have no doubt heard of MP3. This audio file format started, literally, an explosion in music technology that is still reverberating and expanding today.

MP3 is the acronym for the audio compression scheme called *Moving Picture Experts Group (MPEG) audio layer 3*. The revolutionary aspect of the MP3 encoding scheme was that music data could be stored in files that are only about one-twelfth the size of unencoded digital music without a noticeable degradation in the quality of the music. A typical music CD consumes about 650MB of storage space, but the same music encoded in the MP3 format shrinks down to about 55MB. Put another way, a single 3.5-minute song shrinks from its 35MB on audio CD down to a paltry 3MB or so in MP3 format. The small size of MP3 files opened up a world of possibilities.

> **note**
>
> Because MP3 files are relatively small, storing an entire music collection in a relatively small amount of disk space is possible, thus eliminating the need to bother with individual CDs. Using a digital music application such as iTunes, you can easily store, organize, and access an entire music collection on your desktop or laptop computer.

For example, MP3 enabled a new class of portable music devices. Because MP3 files can be stored in small amounts of memory, devices with no moving parts can store and play a fair amount of music; these were the early MP3 players, such as the Rio. Then came other devices containing small hard drives—can you say iPod?—that can store huge amounts of music, enabling you to take your entire music collection with you wherever you go. These devices are extremely small and lightweight, and their contents can be easily managed.

You will encounter many MP3 files on the Internet, and with iTunes, you can convert your audio CDs into the MP3 format so that you can store them in iTunes and put them on an iPod.

AAC

The newest digital audio format is called *Advanced Audio Coding* or *AAC*. This format is part of the larger MPEG-4 specification. Its basic purpose is the same as the MP3 format: to deliver excellent sound quality while keeping file sizes small. However, the AAC format is a newer and better format in that it can be used to produce files that have better quality than MP3 at even smaller file sizes.

Also, as with MP3, you can easily convert audio CD files into the AAC format to store them on a computer and add them to an iPod. What's more, you can convert

AAC files into the Audio CD or MP3 format when you want to put them on a CD to play on something other than your computer, such as a car stereo.

The AAC format also enables content producers to add some copy-protection schemes to their music. Typically, these schemes won't have any impact on you (unless of course, you are trying to do something you shouldn't).

One of the most important aspects of the AAC format is that all the music in the iTunes Music Store is stored in it; when you purchase music from the store, it is added to your computer in this format.

WAV

The *Windows Waveform (WAV)* audio format is a standard on Windows computers. It has been widely used for various kinds of audio, but because it does not offer the "quality versus file size" benefits of the MP3 or AAC formats, it is mostly used for sound effects or clips that people have recorded from various sources. Millions of WAV files are available on the Internet that you can play and download.

You can load WAV files into iTunes, and you can even use iTunes to convert files into the WAV format. However, because MP3 and AAC are much newer and better file formats, you aren't likely to want to do this very often. Occasionally, you might want to add WAV files to your iTunes music collection; this can be easily done, as you will learn later in this book.

AIFF

The *Audio Interchange File Format (AIFF)* provides relatively high-quality sound, but its file sizes are larger than MP3 or AAC. As you can probably guess from its name, this format was originally used to exchange audio among various platforms.

note

Frankly, you aren't likely to notice any difference between AAC music files and MP3 files, except in one area—some portable digital music players (such as MP3 players) don't support AAC-formatted music. The iPod does, so if you use one (given that you are reading this book, I assume you do), you don't have to be concerned about this difference.

tip

If you ever want to find a sound byte from your favorite movie or TV show, you can probably do so at one of the many WAV Web sites on the Internet. One example is www. wavcentral.com. Interestingly enough, even the sound clips on these sites are being largely converted into MP3.

As with the WAV format, because the MP3 and AAC formats provide better sound quality in smaller file sizes, you aren't likely to use the AIFF format very often. The most likely situation in which you might want to use it is when you want to move some music or sound from your iTunes collection into a different application that does not support the MP3 or AAC format.

The iTunes Music Library

Earlier, you read that one of the great things about iTunes is that you can use it to store all your music on your computer. This is done with the iTunes Music Library (see Figure 12.1). This is the place in which you store all the music and sound you import into iTunes, such as from audio CDs or other sources. You can then browse or search your Library to find the music you want to listen to or work with.

FIGURE 12.1

The iTunes Library is the one place to go for all the good music in your life.

As you use iTunes, you will frequently be accessing your Library; it will often be your first stop when you do things with your music.

Where Does All That Music Come From?

You have three primary sources of the music and sounds from which you will build your iTunes Library:

■ **Audio CDs**—You can add music from your audio CDs to the iTunes Library. In iTunes lingo, this process is called *importing*.

■ **The Internet**—You can download music and other audio files from the Internet and add those files to your iTunes Library.

■ **The iTunes Music Store**—Part III of this book, titled "The iTunes Music Store," is dedicated to this music source, and for good reason. Using the iTunes Music Store, you can search for, preview, and purchase music online and add that music to your Library.

Playlists: Customize Your Music Experience

I've saved one of the best features of iTunes for nearly last—*playlists*. Playlists enable you to create custom collections of music from the songs in your iTunes Library. (If you think of a playlist as a custom CD without the disc, you will be very close.)

When you create playlists, you can mix and match music to your heart's content. For example, you can build your own "greatest hits" collections that include multiple artists, music genres, and so on. You can repeat the same song multiple times in the same playlist. You can also get rid of songs you don't like by not including them in the playlists you listen to. What's more, you can create a playlist to include a specific amount of music from a single CD or endlessly repeat all the music in your Library.

Basically, you can use playlists to organize a collection of songs in any way you choose. You can then listen to your playlists, put them on a CD, or move them to an iPod.

You'll learn all you need to know about playlists in Chapter 17, "Creating, Configuring, and Using Playlists."

note

iTunes uses a more civilized term (importing) for the process of converting an audio CD into a different format and adding the resulting music to your Library. The more traditional term for converting audio CD music into the MP3 format is *ripping*. I kind of like *ripping* myself, but because *importing* is the term iTunes uses, I guess we will go with that.

The Other Members of the Band: The iPod and the iTunes Music Store

When it comes to citizenship, iTunes definitely gets an A+ because it plays so well with others.

If you have read Part I, "The iPod," you know that the iPod might just be the coolest portable electronic device ever to hit the streets. Although the iPod is indeed an awesome piece of technology, it wouldn't get very far without a tool to manage the music it contains. iTunes is that tool. iTunes and the iPod go together like a 1-2 combination punch, peanut butter and jelly, jalapenos on a pizza, Bing Crosby and Bob Hope (well, you get the idea). Using iTunes, you can determine which parts of your music library are on the iPod. iTunes manages moving the music files to the iPod and organizing them, so the process is quite simple (from your perspective anyway). In fact, iTunes will manage the process for you automatically if you prefer; when you connect your trusty iPod to your computer, iTunes will recognize it and then synchronize the music it has in your Library with that on your iPod.

When you get to Part III of this book, you will learn in detail about the last part of the digital music triumvirate: the iTunes Music Store. With the iTunes Music Store, you can shop for music to add to your Library. When you find songs you'd like to have, you can purchase and download them into your iTunes Library with just a couple mouse clicks. And you can do all this from within iTunes itself. It feels like the iTunes Music Store is just an extension of iTunes, which, in fact, it is. You access the iTunes Music Store from within iTunes, and the Store uses an interface that looks very similar to iTunes. So, once you know iTunes, you won't have any problems with the iTunes Music Store.

The Absolute Minimum

Now that you have met iTunes, I hope you are jazzed (pun intended) to get into it and start making its musical magic work for you. In the chapters following this one, you'll learn how to do everything from listening to audio CDs and Internet radio to building playlists to sharing your music over a network. Here are the major topics you learned about in this introduction to iTunes:

- You can use iTunes to do just about anything you want to with your music, from listening to CDs to putting your entire music collection on your hard drive to managing the music on an iPod.

- The primary audio file formats you can use with iTunes are AAC and MP3. However, you can also use WAV and AIFF.

- The iTunes Music Library is where you store and can work with all your iTunes music.

- You can get music for your iTunes Library from audio CDs, the Internet, and the iTunes Music Store.

- You can use playlists to create and listen to customized collections of music.

- iTunes works seamlessly with the iPod and the iTunes Music Store.

13

GETTING STARTED WITH iTUNES

It's time to put iTunes through it paces so you can see and hear for your-self what it can do. Fortunately, you will find that iTunes is not only well designed once you start using it, but it is also easy to get started with.

In the first part of this chapter, you'll learn how to install and launch iTunes. Although using iTunes on a Windows PC and on a Macintosh are nearly identical, there are slight differences in how you install the applications on each platform. So, I've included an installation section for each kind of computer. It should go without saying, but I will say it anyway just in case: You don't need to read both installation sections. Just read the section that is applicable for the type of computer you use.

After you have installed and launched iTunes, read the section called "Getting to Know iTunes," where you'll get the grand tour of the amaz-ing iTunes features you will be using throughout the rest of this part of the book.

Installing iTunes on a Windows PC

Over the years, Apple has produced a few applications designed for both Windows PCs and Macintoshes. Thank goodness for Windows users that iTunes is also in this group. (None of the others are worthy of much mention, but iTunes is definitely a crossover hit!)

In order to use iTunes on a Windows computer, you must be running Windows 2000 or Windows XP. If you are running Windows 98, Me, or 95, you are out of the iTunes game. (Of course, those older versions of Windows are really old and you should be using a newer version for more reasons than just the ability to run iTunes!)

You have two primary ways to get a copy of iTunes and install it on your computer. (The good news is that neither way will cost you any more money than you have already spent.) First, if you have purchased an iPod, which is a likely case given that you are reading a book about iPods, a copy of iTunes is provided on the CD included with every iPod. Second, if you don't have an iPod or if you don't have the CD that came with it for some reason, you can download iTunes from the Internet.

> **note**
>
> In case you are wondering, about the only other successful application that Apple has produced for Windows computers is the database program FileMaker Pro. This originally was developed by a subsidiary of Apple called Claris. Claris spun out from Apple and is now known as FileMaker, thus giving the company the same name as its most popular product.

Downloading and Installing iTunes on a Windows PC

It can be better to download a copy of iTunes from the Internet to install it on your computer even if you have a copy on the iPod CD. That's because the application is periodically updated. When you download a copy from the Web, you get the latest and greatest version. When you install a copy from the CD, you get the latest and greatest version when the CD was produced, which might not be the current latest and greatest.

If you want to download and install a copy of iTunes, perform the following steps:

1. Open your favorite Web browser, such as Internet Explorer.

2. Move to `http://www.apple.com/itunes`.

3. Click the **Download** link. You will see the Download page.

4. Scroll down the page until you see the **Download iTunes section** (see Figure 13.1).

5. Click the **Windows 2000 or XP** radio button.

6. Enter your email address if you want to subscribe to any of Apple's iTunes newsletters; if you don't, you can leave this blank.

7. Enter your first and last name if you want to (this is optional information).

8. Choose the area in which you live in the drop-down list.

9. Check the boxes for the Apple newsletters you want to receive (or uncheck the boxes for any Apple newsletters you don't want to receive). For example, the *New Music Tuesdays* newsletter lets you know about music that has been added to the iTunes Music Store.

10. Click **Download iTunes**. In most cases, you will see the **Security Warning** dialog box. If you don't have your Web browser configured to present this, you will move directly to the **Save As** dialog box, in which case you can skip the next step.

note

For information about installing iTunes from the CD included with iPods, see "Installing the iPod's Software (Including iTunes)" on page **20**. If this is the option you chose, you can skip over the rest of this section and move ahead with launching the application, as I explain in "Launching and Performing the Initial Configuration of iTunes on a Windows PC," on page **176**.

FIGURE 13.1

Downloading iTunes is easy and free; what could be better?

Apple - iTunes - Download iTunes 4.2 - Microsoft Internet Explorer

File   Edit   View   Favorites   Tools   Help

Back ▾   ·   Search   Favorites   Norton AntiVirus   SnagIt

Download iTunes
Now playing for both Mac and Windows

iTunes 4 is the best software jukebox in the world, with a great music store inside. With it, you can create your own personal digital music library to manage and listen to your music collection, all with drag-and-drop simplicity.

iTunes encodes high-quality MP3s as well as pristine AAC, all in a free application. If you don't like getting charged a subscription fee or paying for additional features like fast CD burning, your digital music experience is about to get a whole lot better.

Available for Mac OS X, Windows XP, and Windows 2000, iTunes 4.2 allows you to sign in and buy music from the iTunes Music Store with your AOL or Apple Account.

Select Download:

◉ Windows 2000 or XP

◯ Mac OS X v10.1.5 or later

Sign up

Email Address (required for newsletters)

First Name (optional)

☑ **Send me New Music Tuesdays,** a weekly e-mail showcasing new releases and highlights of music recently added to the iTunes Music Store.

Why use iTunes?

- **Easy to Buy.** Buy songs with one click for 99¢ and download music instantly.
- **Great Selection.** More than 500,000 tracks including over 100,000 from 200 independent labels.
- **Download Audiobooks.** 5,000+ audiobooks — best-sellers, classics, public radio programs, language lessons, more.
- **Allowance Accounts.** Set an allowance to let your kids download music legally without giving them your credit cards.
- **Gift Certificates.** Send presents in email.
- **Reviews, Bios and Lists.** Discover new music more ways with iTunes.
- **Celebrity Playlists.** Who's listening to what?
- **Email Music Links.** Share discoveries by dropping store links into email.

Done   Internet

11. In the **Security Warning** dialog box, click **Yes** to indicate that you want to install and run the iTunes Installer. The InstallShield Wizard will open and start the installation process. After a moment or two, you will see the **iTunes for Windows** window (see Figure 13.2).

FIGURE 13.2

Working through the iTunes Installer is mostly a matter of reading and clicking Next.

12. Read the information in the Installer window and click **Next**.

13. If you have a lot of time and patience, read the license agreement; when you are done, click **Yes** if you agree or **No** if you don't. (Of course, if you don't agree, you can skip the rest of these steps and the rest of this part of the book because you won't be able to use iTunes.)

14. In the resulting Information window, you can read information about iTunes, such as what it can do and what you need to install it. Because you have this book, you don't really need to read this information, but it can't hurt to do so! When you are done reading, click **Next**. You'll see the Setup Type window (see Figure 13.3) .

15. Check the following options to make them active or uncheck them to make them inactive:

   ■ **Install desktop shortcuts**—This option places a shortcut to iTunes on your desktop. Unless you don't like desktop shortcuts for some reason, you should usually leave this option checked.

   ■ **Use iTunes as the default player for audio files**—This option causes iTunes to be used to play most audio files that you will access on the Internet, your computer, CDs, and so on. If you prefer to use another application, such as Window Media Player, uncheck this check box. However, I recommend that you leave it checked for now. You can always change the default application to be something else after you have become comfortable with iTunes (not that you'll want to!).

■ **Use QuickTime as the default player for media files**—If you choose this option, the QuickTime Player application will be used when you view video or other multimedia content. Just like the previous option, if you prefer to use a different application, uncheck this check box.

FIGURE 13.3

As you install iTunes, you have several options, such as whether you want iTunes to be the default player for audio files.

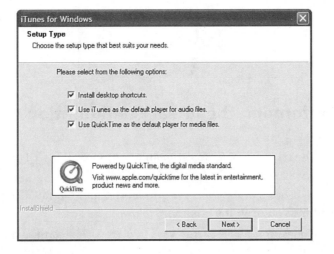

16. Click **Next**. You'll see the **Choose Destination Location** dialog box.

17. If you don't want to accept the default installation location (which is C:\Program Files\iTunes\), click the **Browse** button and choose the location you do want to use. Then click **Next**. You'll see a window advertising the iPod.

18. Click **Next**. As the Installer starts to work, you will see the Setup Status window. This window provides you with information about the installation process (see Figure 13.4).

When the process is complete, you will see the Installation Successful window.

19. Click **Finish** to restart your computer and complete the installation process. When your computer restarts, iTunes will be ready for you.

caution

If you have other open applications that contain documents with unsaved changes, make sure you save them before you restart your computer.

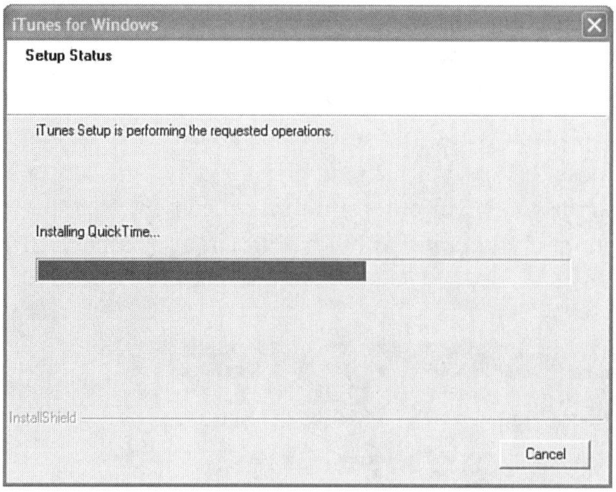

FIGURE 13.4
Here, you can
see that the
iTunes Installer
is currently
installing
QuickTime.

Launching and Performing the Initial Configuration of iTunes on a Windows PC

Whichever path you have taken to this point, I am sure all is well and you are ready to start cutting your teeth on iTunes.

To open the application and perform the initial configuration (which you need to do only the first time you open the program), follow these steps:

1. Open iTunes. You have several ways to do this. You can use the desktop icon to open it (assuming you chose to have an icon placed there). You can also choose **Start**, **All Programs**, **iTunes**, **iTunes** to launch the application from the **Start** menu. Or, you can click the shortcut that was conveniently placed in the taskbar for you.

   After you have used one of these methods, the iTunes window will open. The first time you launch the application, the iTunes Setup Assistant will appear (see Figure 13.5). The helpful assistant will guide you through the few configuration decisions you need to make before you start working with the application. As with other assistants, you will move through the iTunes Setup Assistant by reading its information, making choices, and using the **Next** button.

tip

If you find yourself to be opening iTunes every time you use your computer, and you probably will, consider adding it to the list of startup programs so it will open automatically when you turn your computer on.

FIGURE 13.5

The iTunes Setup
Assistant
appears the first
time you open
the application;
get a good look
at it because you
won't be seeing
it again.

2. Click **Next** to move to the Find Music Files
   screen. The purpose of this screen is to indicate
   whether you want iTunes to search your
   Music folder to find any existing music and
   then add that music to your iTunes Library.
   If you have music in this folder, I recommend that you let iTunes add it to your
   Library.

   If you want iTunes to search for music on
   your computer, click the **Yes** radio button
   (which isn't really necessary because it is the
   default selection) and then click **Next**.

   If you want to skip this search, click **No** and
   then click **Next**.

3. Use the Keep iTunes Music Folder Organized
   window to indicate whether you want
   iTunes to automatically rename and organize the music in your iTunes Music folder
   when you change that music's information
   (such as genre).

note

After the first time you
launch iTunes, you won't
ever need to access the Setup
Assistant again because you can
configure iTunes using its
Preferences command. (Each time
you reinstall the application, the
Setup Assistant will appear the
first time you launch the application from the new installation.)

Unless you have a very specific reason not to want this feature, click **Yes** and
then click **Next**.

If you do have some reason why you don't want iTunes to rename or move
your music files, click **No** and then click **Next**.

4. Use the iTunes Music Store window to determine whether you want to move to the iTunes Music Store immediately after the Setup Assistant is done.

Because you will learn about the iTunes Music Store in detail in Part III, "The iTunes Music Store," click the **No** radio button and click **Finish**.

The Setup Assistant will run and you will see the iTunes window (see Figure 13.6). If you indicated that you want iTunes to find any music in your Music folder and add it to the iTunes Library, you will see the music that the application found.

FIGURE 13.6

Okay, so the iTunes window doesn't look so exciting yet; soon, there will be lots of great music to listen to.

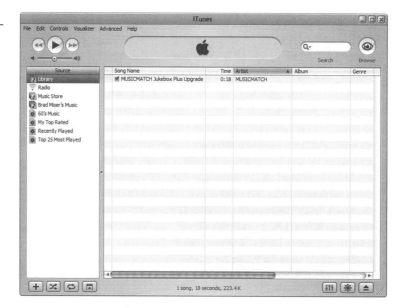

Now you are ready to learn about the major elements of the iTunes window. Unless you also have a Macintosh that you also want to install iTunes on, you can skip ahead to the section "Getting to Know iTunes" on page **181**. However, because my writing is so scintillating (don't you love that word!), I wouldn't blame you if you read the next section even if you don't have a Mac!

Installing and Configuring iTunes on a Macintosh

Because iTunes is developed by Apple, it is as integrated into the Macintosh operating system as much as any application can be. You have a number of ways to get iTunes installed on your Mac, including the following:

- **Install Mac OS X**. When you install Mac OS X, iTunes is also installed, unless you specifically tell the Installer not to install it. If you have installed OS X on your Mac, you don't need to do any installation, but you should make sure you have the current version installed (to do so, see the section "Keeping iTunes Up to Date on a Macintosh" on page **305**.

- **Buy a new Mac**. Okay, this might be the most expensive option, but, hey, you get a free Mac with your copy of iTunes!

- **Install iTunes from the iPod Software CD**. The software installation CD included with an iPod also enables you to install iTunes.

- **Buy a copy of the Apple iLife suite**. In addition to iTunes, you'll get iMovie, iPhoto, iDVD, and Garage Band.

- **Download and install iTunes from the Internet**. You can always download and install the latest version of iTunes from the Internet.

If you have installed Mac OS X on your computer, you probably don't need to do any installation because it is likely that you already have iTunes installed on your machine.

To use one of the CD options, just insert the CD, launch the installer, and follow the onscreen instructions.

If you don't already have some version of iTunes installed on your Mac, you can download and install a copy from the Internet. This is often the best option because you are sure to get the most current version of the application.

note

Not to push my other books (okay, to push my other books), but if you need help with Mac OS X in general, see *Special Edition Using Mac OS X, v10.3 Panther* (catchy title, huh?).

note

If you are still using Mac OS 9, you aren't totally out of the iTunes game because you might have an early version installed. However, because Mac OS X is the future (not to mention most of the present) of the Mac platform, I don't cover installing or using iTunes under Mac OS 9 in this book.

The process for downloading and installing iTunes on a Mac is almost identical to what you use to download and install iTunes on a Windows computer. To save a few trees, I haven't included the steps to do this on a Mac. Just refer to the section "Downloading and Installing iTunes on a Windows PC" on page **172**. The most important difference is that you should choose to download the version for Mac OS X (as if you couldn't guess that!). After that, just follow the onscreen instructions.

You have a number of ways to open iTunes on a Mac, including the following:

■ Click the **iTunes** icon on the Dock.

■ Open the **Applications** folder and double-click the **iTunes** icon.

■ Insert an audio CD into your Mac; by default, iTunes is set to launch whenever you mount an audio CD.

note

Because you are probably using Mac OS X and therefore already have iTunes, you should go ahead and make sure you are using the latest version by running the Software Update application. To do so, choose **Apple menu**, **Software Update**. If a more current version of iTunes is available than the one installed on your computer, you will be prompted to download and install it.

The first time you open iTunes, you will need to work through a basic configuration of the application. Following are the steps you need to perform:

1. Launch iTunes. You will see yet another **License Agreement** screen. (I guess Apple was kidding with the others.)

2. Click **Agree**. You will see the iTunes Setup Assistant, which will guide you through the rest of the process (see Figure 13.7) .

3. Click **Next**. You will see the Internet Audio Settings window. These settings control whether iTunes is the default application for audio content from the Internet and if iTunes should automatically connect to the Internet when it needs to.

4. Click both **Yes** radio buttons and then click **Next**. You'll see the Find Music Files window.

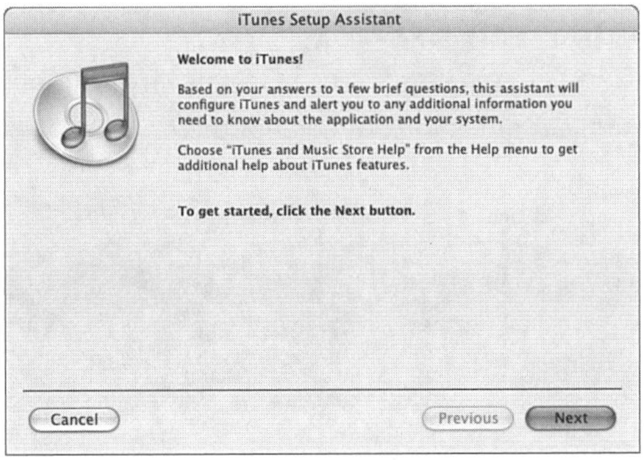

FIGURE 13.7

The iTunes Setup
Assistant lives
up to its name.

FIGURE 13.7

The iTunes Setup
Assistant lives
up to its name.

5. If you want iTunes to search for music on your Mac and then add that music to the iTunes Library, click **Yes**. If you don't want this to happen, click **No**. Click **Next**. You'll see the iTunes Music Store window.

6. Because we will explore the iTunes Music Store in detail later, click the **No** radio button and then click **Done**. The iTunes window will open (see Figure 13.8) and you will be ready to tour the application in the next section.

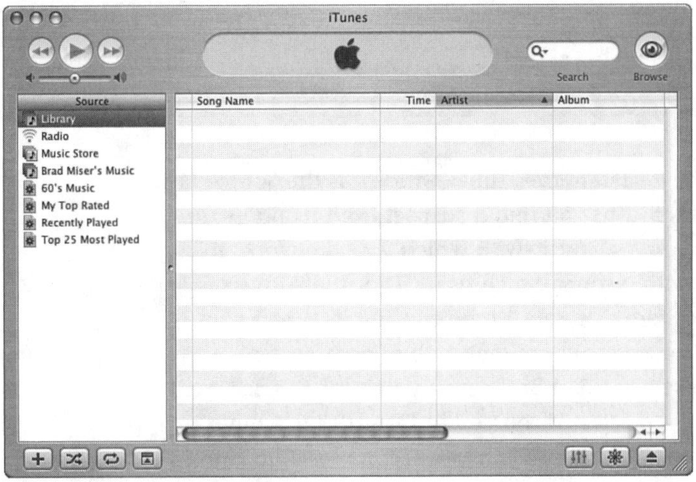

FIGURE 13.8

There aren't any
songs in the
Library yet, so
this iTunes win-
dow looks a bit
boring; we'll
soon fix that!

Getting to Know iTunes

The required but mundane work of installing iTunes on your computer is done. Now, let's take a quick tour so you get the overall feel of this excellent application. In the following chapters, you'll get down and dirty (well, because we are dealing with elec- trons here, there isn't really any dirt) with the details.

Seeing Through the iTunes Window

The iTunes window, like the windows on your house, consists of a number of panes (see Figure 13.9). Let's take a quick look at each of these.

Source List   Browser   Content Pane

FIGURE 13.9

Working with
iTunes panes
won't cause
you any (pain,
that is).

On the far left of the iTunes window is the Source List. On this list, as you might suspect from its name, are the sources of music with which you can work. To work with a source, such as a CD or the iTunes Music Store, you select it by clicking it. When you select a source, its contents will appear in the Content pane and Browser (if you have the Browser open for a selected source). In Figure 13.9, I have selected the Library as the source; its contents are shown in the Browser at the top of the window while the list of individual songs that make up the Library is at the bottom of the window.

You will use many types of sources, including the Library, the Radio, the iTunes Music Store, audio CDs, playlists, and more. As we work though the rest of this part of the book, you will get experience with all these kinds of sources.

Different sources have different icons in the Source List. For example, the Library has a yellow box containing a music note, whereas playlists have a blue box with a musical note.

The Browser presents the contents of the selected source at a summary level, by genre, artist, and album. You can view the contents of the selected source by clicking it in the appropriate column. For example, in Figure 13.9, I have selected the Blues/R&B genre. The Artist column then shows all the artists whose music I have in the selected genre. The Album column shows all the albums for the selected artists.

The Browser can be shown or hidden. For example, take a look at Figure 13.10, which shows the iTunes window with the Browser hidden.

FIGURE 13.10

Where, oh where, has my Browser gone? Where, oh where, can it be?

At the bottom of the iTunes window (or filling it if the Browser is hidden) is the Content pane. This area lists each song in the selected source. For each song, you will see a variety of information, such as Song Name, Track #, Time, Artist, and so on. You can even choose the information you see on this list. The order in which songs are listed in the Content pane is the order in which they will play when you play the selected source.

Going back to Figure 13.9, you can see that several songs by B.B. King and Dave McKenna are listed in the Content pane.

tip

We will get to working with the Browser later, but for now know that you can open and close it by clicking the **Browse** button or by choosing **Edit**, **Show Browser** or **Edit**, **Hide Browser**.

Controlling Your Music

Surrounding those panes are the controls you use to work with and get information about your music. At the top of the window, from left to right, you will see the following areas (see Figure 13.11):

FIGURE 13.11

At the top of the iTunes window, you see a number of controls you can use to play and manage your music.

- **Playback controls**—Here, you can see the familiar Play/Stop, Fast Forward, and Rewind buttons along with the Volume Control slider. These work as you probably expect them to.

- **Information window**—In the center of the iTunes window is the Information window. In this area, you will see a variety of information about what you are doing at any point in time. For example, when you are playing music, you will see information about the music currently being played. When you import music, you will see information about the import process.

- **Search tool**—You use the Search tool to search for songs.

- **Action button**—The Action button changes depending on the context you are in. For example, if you have selected the Library, it becomes the **Browse** button, which you use to open or close the Browser. If you select a playlist, it becomes the **Burn** button, which enables you to burn a CD.

When you move to the bottom of the iTunes window, you will see the following (see Figure 13.12):

- **Add Playlist button**—You can use this button to create your own playlists.

- **Shuffle and Repeat buttons**—You use the Shuffle button to shuffle the music in the selected source so that it doesn't play in the listed order. You can use the Repeat button to cause songs to repeat within a selected source.

- **Show/Hide Album Art button**—Songs can have album art associated with them. When you click this button, you will see the Art Album box at the bottom of the Source pane. In it will appear any art associated with the song that is currently selected.

- **Source information**—This information shows you the number of songs, total playing time, and disk space of the selected source. This becomes very useful at certain times, such as when you are burning a CD or building a playlist.

Because I don't see much value (not even entertainment value) in the Visualizer, I won't be mentioning it again in this book. You can play with it by using the Visualizer menu if you want to. Oh, by the way, the images you see in the Visualizer are not related to any music that might be playing anyway. Want proof? Fire up the Visualizer with no music playing; it looks just like it does when music is playing.

- **Equalizer button**—This button opens the Equalizer window, which provides you with a graphic equalizer.

- **Visualizer button**—Okay, this was one of the most promoted features of iTunes when it was initially released, but I didn't get it then, and I still don't today. When you click this, the iTunes window fills with a graphic display reminiscent of the 1960s (see Figure 13.13).

- **Eject button**—When you have selected an ejectable source, such as an audio CD, you can click this button to eject it.

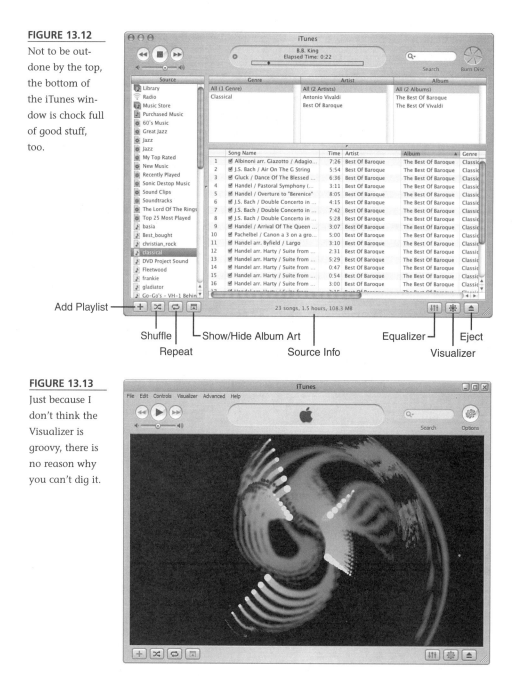

FIGURE 13.12
Not to be out-done by the top, the bottom of the iTunes win-dow is chock full of good stuff, too.

Add Playlist

Shuffle

Repeat

Show/Hide Album Art

Source Info

Equalizer

Visualizer

Eject

FIGURE 13.13
Just because I don't think the Visualizer is groovy, there is no reason why you can't dig it.

THE ABSOLUTE MINIMUM

You are well on your way to total iTunes nirvana. If you have read this chapter, you should be hip to the following iTunes jazz:

- You have a number of ways to install iTunes on your computer—whether it's a Mac or a Windows PC. The best way is to download and install it from the Internet.

- No matter how you installed iTunes, make sure you keep it up to date (you'll get to that in Chapter 21, "Maintaining iTunes and Solving Problems").

- When you first open iTunes, you work through several configuration settings using the iTunes Setup Assistant. However, you can change these settings at any time using the iTunes Preferences dialog box, which you will be working with throughout the rest of this part of the book.

- The iTunes window is an elegant mix of functionality and good interface design. As you learn more about the application, you will likely be impressed. The primary components of the iTunes window are the controls, the Information area, the Source List, the Browser, and the Content pane.

- Although iTunes is one my favorite applications and I use it constantly, it sports one of the silliest features that was ever part of an application. What is it?

IN THIS CHAPTER

- Learn the basics of listening to iTunes sources by listening to audio CDs.
- Use the iTunes Information window.
- Control your tunes like a pro.
- Make iTunes be heard, but not seen.
- Check out Internet radio.
- Change the size of the iTunes window.
- Affect your music with iTunes Effects.

14

LISTENING TO AUDIO CDS AND INTERNET AUDIO WITH ITUNES

The basic reason to have and use iTunes is to listen to music and other audio, such as audio books. Which, not coincidentally, is the basic point of this chapter. Here, you will learn how to use iTunes to listen to a couple sources: audio CDs and Internet radio. The good news is that once you know how to use iTunes to listen to these two sources, you know how to listen to other sources you will use as well, such as songs in the MP3 format, playlists, an iPod, and shared music.

After you become an iTunes-playing guru, we'll take a look at some of the ways you can configure iTunes to suit your playing preferences.

Listening to an Audio CD

What iTunes has in common with its much less sophisticated cousins the boom box and the standard CD player is the ability to play audio CDs. Although the basic function is the same, iTunes has several tricks in its bag to make listening even better. So, grab a CD and give it a try:

1. Open iTunes.

2. Insert an audio CD into your computer. In a moment, the CD will be mounted on your computer, and it will appear and be selected in the **Source List** (see Figure 14.1).

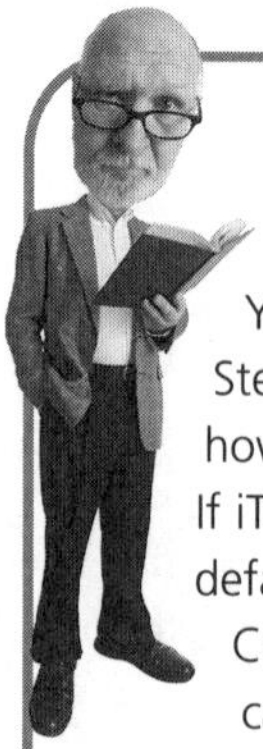

A CD is the selected source

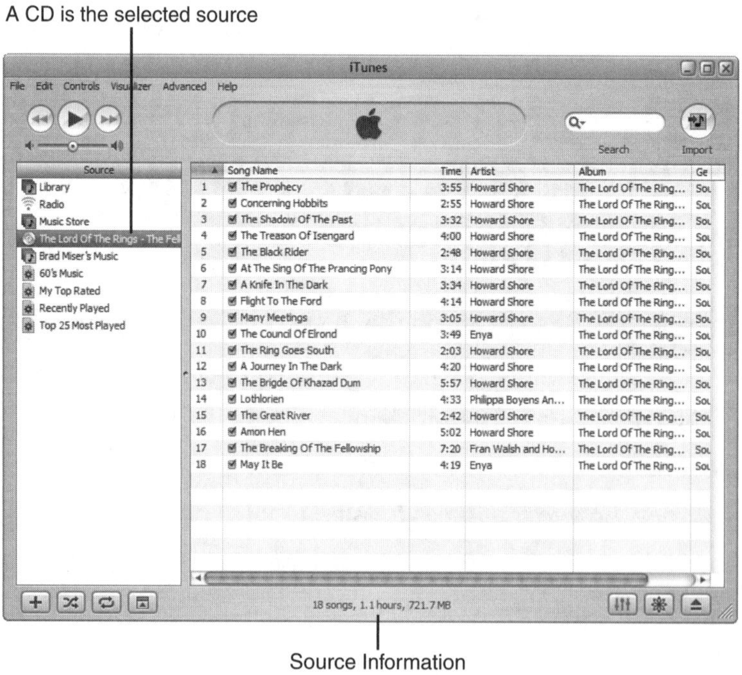

FIGURE 14.1
When a CD appears on the Source List, it awaits your listening pleasure.

Source Information

By default, iTunes will automatically connect to the Internet and attempt to identify the CD you have inserted. If it finds it, it will display the CD's information, including CD name, track names, times, artist, and genre, in the Content pane (in Figure 14.1, you can see the CD's information has been found). This is really cool because iTunes does most of the labeling work for you; this comes in very handy when you want to search or browse for music to create playlists or just to listen to specific tracks.

If iTunes finds information for a CD, it remembers that information and displays it each time you insert the CD.

At the bottom of the iTunes window is the Source Information display. This will show you the total number of songs on the CD, how long it plays, and the total disc space used.

If the CD's information isn't located, you can add it yourself (see Chapter 16, "Labeling, Categorizing, and Configuring Your Music").

If you don't want iTunes to check for a CD's information automatically, you can disable this feature as you will learn a little later in this chapter.

3. To play the CD, do any of the following: click the **Play** button in the top-left corner of the window (when a CD is playing, this becomes the **Pause** button), choose **Controls**, **Play**, or press the **spacebar**.

The CD will begin to play. As a song plays, a speaker icon appears next to it in the Content pane to indicate it is the current song, and information about that song appears in the Information window (see Figure 14.2).

Song currently playing   Information window

FIGURE 14.2

You can tell this CD is playing because of the Pause button and the speaker icon next to the song currently being played.

	Song Name	Time	Artist	Album	Ge
1	The Prophecy	3:55	Howard Shore	The Lord Of The Ring...	Sou
2	Concerning Hobbits	2:55	Howard Shore	The Lord Of The Ring...	Sou
3	The Shadow Of The Past	3:32	Howard Shore	The Lord Of The Ring...	Sou
4	The Treason Of Isengard	4:00	Howard Shore	The Lord Of The Ring...	Sou
5	The Black Rider	2:48	Howard Shore	The Lord Of The Ring...	Sou
6	At The Sing Of The Prancing Pony	3:14	Howard Shore	The Lord Of The Ring...	Sou
7	A Knife In The Dark	3:34	Howard Shore	The Lord Of The Ring...	Sou
8	Flight To The Ford	4:14	Howard Shore	The Lord Of The Ring...	Sou
9	Many Meetings	3:05	Howard Shore	The Lord Of The Ring...	Sou
10	The Council Of Elrond	3:49	Enya	The Lord Of The Ring...	Sou
11	The Ring Goes South	2:03	Howard Shore	The Lord Of The Ring...	Sou
12	A Journey In The Dark	4:20	Howard Shore	The Lord Of The Ring...	Sou
13	The Bridge Of Khazad Dum	5:57	Howard Shore	The Lord Of The Ring...	Sou
14	Lothlorien	4:33	Philippa Boyens An...	The Lord Of The Ring...	Sou
15	The Great River	2:42	Howard Shore	The Lord Of The Ring...	Sou
16	Amon Hen	5:02	Howard Shore	The Lord Of The Ring...	Sou
17	The Breaking Of The Fellowship	7:20	Fran Walsh and Ho...	The Lord Of The Ring...	Sou
18	May It Be	4:19	Enya	The Lord Of The Ring...	Sou

18 songs, 1.1 hours, 721.7 MB

4. Control the volume of the sound by dragging the Volume slider to the left to turn it down or to the right to turn it up. You can also control the volume by choosing **Controls**, **Volume Up** or **Controls**, **Volume Down**. For yet another option, use the **Ctrl+up arrow** and **Ctrl+down arrow** keys on Windows PCs or the ⌘**+up arrow** and ⌘**+down arrow** keys on Macs to set the volume from the keyboard.

To mute the sound, choose **Controls**, **Mute**. On Windows PCs you can press **Ctrl+Alt+down arrow**, whereas on Macs you can press **Option+**⌘**+down arrow** to do the same thing.

5. To pause a song, click the **Pause** button, choose **Controls**, **Pause**, or press the **spacebar**.

That's it. You now know everything you need to listen to an audio CD. However, there are lots more ways to control the tunes, some of which are in the following list:

- Double-click any song to play it. When you do that, the speaker icon will jump to the song on which you double-clicked and it will play.

- When a song is playing and you click and hold the **Rewind** or **Fast Forward** button down, the song will rewind or fast forward until you release the button.

- If a song is not playing or a song is playing but you single-click (but don't hold the button down) the **Rewind** or **Fast Forward** button, the previous or next song, respectively, will be selected. You can also choose **Controls**, **Next Song** or **Controls**, **Previous Song** to move to the next or the previous song. And for yet another method to do the same thing, use the **Ctrl+right arrow** and **Ctrl+left arrow** keys on a Windows PC or the ⌘**+right arrow** and ⌘**+left arrow** keys on a Mac to move to the next or previous song.

tip

When a song is playing, its speaker icon has waves radiating from it to show it is playing. When you pause, the speaker icon remains to show it is the current song, but the waves go away to let you know the song isn't currently playing.

note

Using the Volume slider within iTunes only changes the volume of iTunes relative to your system's volume. If you can't make the music loud or quiet enough, check your system volume level.

■ You can set a default action for iTunes to perform each time you insert a CD into your computer. You do this with the **iTunes Preferences** dialog box, which you will be using throughout this part of the book. Choose **Edit**, **Preferences** (Windows) or **iTunes**, **Preferences** (Mac). The **Preferences** dialog box will appear. The **Preferences** dialog box has several panes that you access by clicking the related tab (Windows) or icon (Mac). Click the **General** tab (Windows) or **General** icon (Mac). Use the **On CD Insert** drop-down list to choose the default action iTunes should perform when it recognizes an audio CD. **Show Songs** just displays the list of tracks on the CD. **Begin Playing** starts playing the CD as soon as it is mounted on your computer (this does the same thing as clicking the **Play** button). **Import Songs** adds the selected songs on the CD to your Library. **Import Songs** and **Eject** does the same thing as **Import Songs**, but it ejects the CD when all its tracks have been added to your Library. (You'll see the value of the last two settings in the next chapter.)

■ To remove a CD from your computer, select it in the **Source List** and choose **Controls**, **Eject Disc**, press **Ctrl+E** (Windows) or ⌘+**E** (Macintosh), or click the **Eject** button located in the lower-right corner of the iTunes window.

tip

Yet another way to eject a disc is to point to it with the cursor, open its contextual menu, and choose Eject. On Windows machines, you right-click to open this menu. On Macs, you Ctrl-click with a single-button mouse or right-click if you have a two-button mouse (which hopefully you do).

Viewing Information While Listening to Tunes

You can view different information in the Information window, such as the name, artist, and album of the currently playing song. When you first view this window, it contains a timeline bar that represents the total length of the song being played (see Figure 14.3). A black diamond indicates the relative position of the music you are hearing at any point in time compared to the total length of the song.

At the top of the Information window is a line of text. What appears here changes over time; it automatically rotates between the artist's name, album name, and name of the song currently playing. You can freeze this display on a specific attribute, such as song name, by clicking the text. Each time you

note

When you "freeze" information in the Information window, it remains frozen until the next track is played, at which point it starts rotating again.

click, the information will change from album to artist to song name. Whichever one you last clicked on will remain showing in the window.

Artist, album title, or song name

Timeline bar   Time   Current location in the playing song

FIGURE 14.3

The iTunes Information window looks basic, but there is much hidden behind its quiet demeanor.

Underneath the album, artist, and song name line is the time information. This can display elapsed time (the amount of time a song has been playing), remaining time (the amount of time a song has left), or total time (the song's total length). Unlike the name information, this display does not rotate among these values. You can set the value being displayed by clicking the text; each time you click, a different time value will be shown until you have rotated among all three values.

Finally, if you click the **Change Display** button, the display will become a graphical representation of the volume levels at various frequency groups (see Figure 14.4). You can return to the title information by clicking the button again.

note

The neat thing about the Information window is that it changes based on the context of what you are doing. You have seen how it works when you listen to music. When you add music to your Library, the information and tools in the window become those you use for the import process.

FIGURE 14.4
Why would you want to use the volume level display in the Information window? No real reason, but it does look kind of cool.

Controlling the Tunes

Playing an audio CD from start to finish and controlling the volume are useful and required tasks, but with iTunes you can take control of your music so that you hear only what you want to hear, in the order in which you want to hear it. In the following sections, you'll see how iTunes lets you take control of your tunes. For example, in the next section, you'll learn how to choose the songs you want to hear.

Choosing the Songs You Hear

Let's face it, you probably don't like every song on a CD no matter how much you like the CD on the whole. With iTunes, you can choose the songs that play when you play the CD. You can cause a song to be skipped by unchecking the **Select** check box (see Figure 14.5). When the CD plays, it will skip over every song whose check box is unchecked.

To have iTunes include and thus play the song again the next time you play the CD, simply check the **Selected** check box.

tip

Along with a CD's information, iTunes remembers the settings you make for a CD and reuses them each time you insert and play the CD. This includes skipping songs, changing the order in which they play, and so on. Cool!

Select check box

FIGURE 14.5

Here, the song "Concerning Hobbits" will be skipped because its Select check box is unchecked (of course, this is only an example; all the songs on this CD are excellent).

Choosing the Order in Which Songs Play

iTunes determines the order in which songs play by the order in which they are shown in the Content pane, starting from the top of the pane and moving to the bottom. By default, songs are listed and therefore play in the order they appear on the CD, from track 1 to the last track on the disc. However, you can make songs on a CD play in any order you choose. You have a couple ways to do this.

You can change the order in which songs are listed in the Content pane (and thus the order in which they play) by dragging the songs up or down in the pane (see Figure 14.6). When you change the order of the songs in the pane, you change the order in which they will play.

You can also change the order of tracks by sorting the Content pane by the various attributes shown, such as **Song Name**, **Time**, **Artist**, and so on. You can do this by clicking the column heading of the attribute by which you want to sort the list. When you do so, the tracks will be sorted by that column (see Figure 14.7). To change the direction of the sort (from ascending to descending or from descending to ascending), click the **Sort Order** triangle; the sort direction will be reversed, and the songs will be reordered accordingly. Just like when you manually move songs around, they will play in the order in which they are listed in the pane.

FIGURE 14.6
Order! Order!
Compare the
order of the
songs in this fig-
ure with the pre-
vious one;
listening to the
CD now will be
an entirely
different
experience.

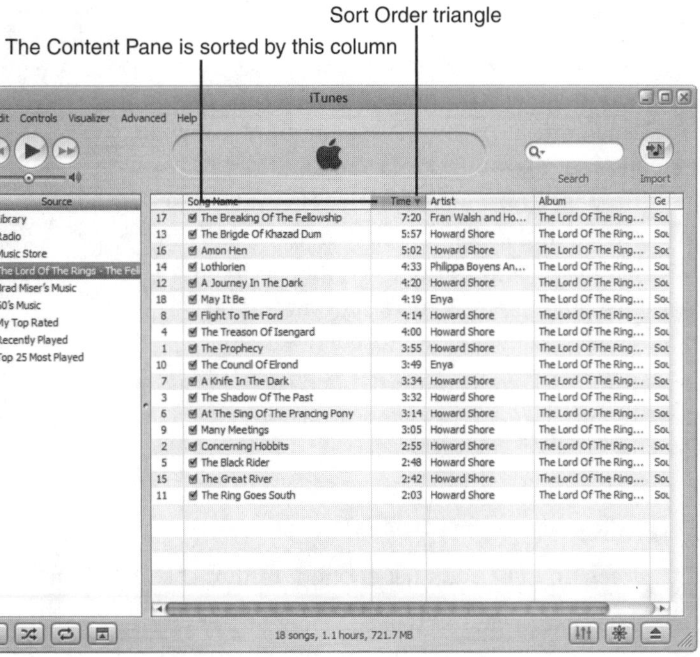

The Content Pane is sorted by this column

Sort Order triangle

FIGURE 14.7
Now the order of
the songs is
based on their
length; in this
case, the longest
song on the CD
will play first,
the next longest
second, and
so on.

The column by which the pane is sorted is indicated by the column heading being highlighted in blue—this defaults to the first column, which is the track number. (When a CD is the source, the Track Number column is always the first or leftmost column in the Content pane, and it's unlabeled.) When you select a different column, its heading becomes blue to show that it is the current sort column.

You can also tell which column is the sort column as well as the direction of the sort by the **Sort Order** triangle. It only appears in the sort column. When the triangle is pointing down, the sort is descending. When the triangle is pointing up, the sort is ascending.

Getting Random

For a little variety, you can have iTunes play songs in a random order. This feature is called Shuffle. To use this feature, click the **Shuffle** button located at the bottom of the window (second one from the left) or choose **Controls**, **Shuffle**. The songs will be reordered in the Content pane and will play in the order in which they are listed (hopefully in a random fashion). The **Shuffle** button will be highlighted to indicate that it is active.

To return the CD to its natural order, click the **Shuffle** button again or choose **Controls**, **Shuffle**.

Repeating Tracks

Sometimes, you just can't get enough. In that case, you can set iTunes to repeat an entire CD once or to repeat only a single song. To repeat your tunes, check out these pointers:

- To have iTunes repeat an entire CD, choose **Controls**, **Repeat All** or click the **Repeat** button located at the bottom of the window (third one from the left). The **Repeat** button will become highlighted to show you that it is active, and the CD will repeat when you play it.

- To repeat only the selected song, choose **Controls**, **Repeat One** or click the **Repeat** button a second time. A "1" will appear on the **Repeat** button to indicate that only the current song will be repeated.

- To turn off the repeat function, choose **Controls**, **Repeat Off** or click the **Repeat** button until it is no longer highlighted in blue.

Controlling iTunes from the Desktop

Using the controls you have seen so far is fine, but you might not want to have the iTunes window foremost all the time. You must be able to see iTunes to control it, right? Wrong!

Controlling iTunes from the Windows System Tray

When iTunes is running on a Windows machine, an iTunes icon is displayed in the System Tray. Right-click this icon and you will see an iTunes menu (see Figure 14.8). At the top of the menu, you will see information about the song that is playing (if iTunes is paused, this text will be grayed out). You can use the commands on this menu just as you can from within iTunes itself. For example, you can skip to the next song by choosing **Next Song**. After you choose a command, you can move off the menu and it will disappear. This is a handy way to control iTunes without having to make its window active or even show it.

note

If you used the menu to shuffle a disc, you will notice that the Shuffle command on the menu has a check mark next to it. This check mark shows you that the command is currently active. When it isn't, the check mark will disappear. This is true of other settings as well, such as Repeat.

tip

Using Repeat, you might hear a song you don't like all that much more than once. Remember to uncheck the Selected check box for any songs you don't want to hear. They will be skipped no matter how you play the CD.

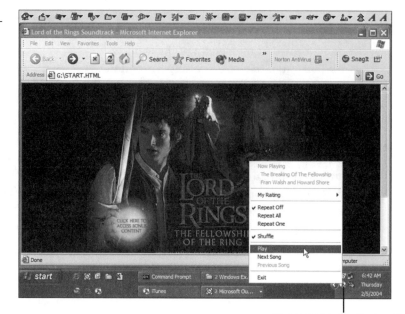

iTunes icon in the System Tray

If you don't want the iTunes icon to appear in the System Tray for some reason, you can remove it. Open the **iTunes Preferences** dialog box (**Ctrl+,**), click the **Advanced** tab, uncheck the **Show iTunes Icon in System Tray** check box, and click **OK**. The icon will no longer appear in your System Tray.

Controlling iTunes from the Mac's Dock

The iTunes icon on the Mac OS X enables you to control iTunes when it is in the background, when its window is minimized, or when the application is hidden. When you Ctrl-click the **iTunes Dock** icon (or right-click if you have a two-button mouse), the **iTunes** menu will appear (see Figure 14.9). At the top of this menu, you will see information about the song currently playing (the text

tip

To keep iTunes out of the way, open it and select a source, such as an audio CD. Then configure and play the source. Minimize (Windows) or hide (Mac) the iTunes window so it no longer appears on your desktop. Then, you can use the iTunes System Tray icon menu (Windows) or iTunes Dock icon menu (Mac) to control it—for example, to pause when you receive a phone call.

is grayed out if iTunes is paused). You control iTunes by choosing a command on this menu. For example, you can pause the music by choosing **Pause**. After you choose a command, the menu will disappear, and you can get back to what you were doing.

FIGURE 14.9
On the Mac, you use its Dock menu to control iTunes even when you can't see it.

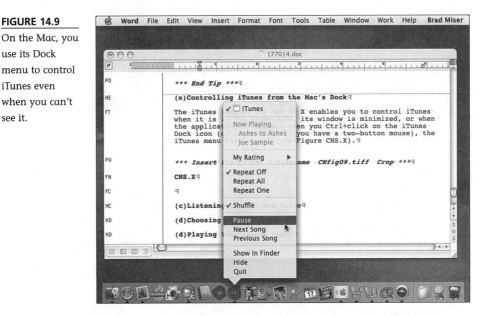

Listening to Internet Radio

iTunes supports Internet "radio" stations; you can choose one of the available stations and listen to its content similarly to how you listen to a radio station over the air. (The stations are actually Web sites that offer streaming MP3, but they are analogous to radio, so using that as a model is a good way to think about them.) iTunes offers a number of genres from which you can choose, such as Pop, Classic Rock, Jazz, and so on. Listening to one of these stations is much like listening to a CD (or any other source for that matter).

note

This is likely obvious to you from the title of this section, but your computer must be able to connect to the Internet to be able to listen to Internet radio.

Playing Your iTunes Radio

To tune in iTunes radio, perform the following steps:

1. Open iTunes and select the **Radio** source by clicking it. The Content pane will contain the list of genres available to you. The column headings will be updated to be appropriate to the content. For example, you will see **Stream**, **Bit Rate**, and **Comment**.

2. Click the **expansion triangle** for the genre in which you are interested (see Figure 14.10). iTunes will connect to the Internet to update the list of channels for the genre you selected, and the genre will expand. You will see the various channels it contains. Look at the stream name, bit rate, and comment for the channels to decide which you want to try. Usually, the comment will provide a description of the kind of music the stream contains.

> **note**
>
> When you view the Content pane with Radio source, Stream provides the names of the channels available to you. Bit Rate is a measure of the quality of a channel. The higher the bit rate, the better the quality, but the higher bandwidth connection you need to play it successfully. The Comment column contains a description of each channel.

Expansion triangle

Radio source

FIGURE 14.10

Most of these radio stations (called streams) don't include commercials.

Expanded genre

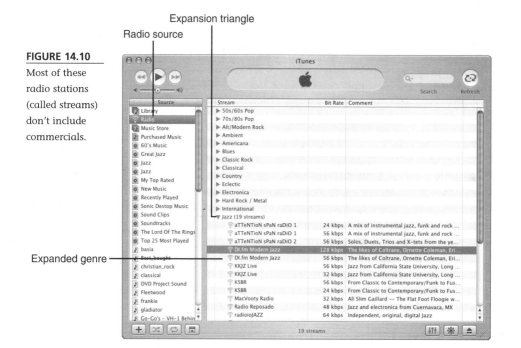

3. To play a channel, select it and click **Play** or double-click the stream you want to hear. The channel will begin to play (this will be instantaneous if you have a fast connection to the Net, or there will be a slight delay if you use a dial-up connection). Just like when you play a song on a CD, the speaker icon will appear next to the channel to which you are listening.

Also just like when you listen to a CD, information about the channel will appear in the Information window (see Figure 14.11). This includes the stream name, the song currently playing, and the Web site with which the channel is associated.

note

If you have a dial-up Internet connection, you will likely have the best results if you choose a channel with a bit rate of 56Kbps or less. If you have a broadband connection, you should choose the highest bit rate version of the available channels (some channels are offered at multiple bit-rate levels).

FIGURE 14.11
Smooth Jazz is an appropriate name for this stream.

You can use the Volume slider to change the volume level and the **Stop** button to stop playback. The **Rewind** and **Fast Forward** buttons work a little differently than you might expect. Rather than moving you in the selected stream, they instead take you to the previous or next stream, which makes sense when you think about each stream as being like a track on a CD.

Refreshing Your Radio

When you choose the **Radio** source, the **Action** button becomes the **Refresh** button. When you click this, all the genres are refreshed with the latest content. If you leave the **Radio** source selected for a long time, you might want to click the **Refresh** button once in a while to see if new channels become available. (Each time you select the **Radio** source, it is refreshed, so you don't need to click the **Refresh** button if you have recently selected the **Radio** source.)

Configuring iTunes for a Slow Internet Connection

If you use a slow Internet connection, such as a dial-up account, traffic on the Internet can cause the stream of music to slow or even stop, resulting in pauses in the music, even if you choose a lower bit-rate channel, such as 32Kbps. If this is a problem for you, perform the following steps:

1. Choose **Edit**, **Preferences** (Windows) or **iTunes**, **Preferences** (Mac). The **Preferences** dialog box will appear.

2. Click the **Advanced** tab (Windows) or the **Advanced** icon (Mac). The **Advanced** pane will appear (see Figure 14.12).

3. On the **Streaming Buffer Size** drop-down list, choose **Large**. This increases the amount of buffer space used to store a stream before it actually starts to play.

4. Click **OK**. The dialog box will close.

tip

The name of the song currently playing is especially useful when you hear a song you like that you might want to add to your collection. Make a note of the song's name and artist. Then, you can look for CDs containing that song or, even better, buy it from the iTunes Music Store.

note

There are more than just tunes on the iTunes Radio. You can also hear talk, news, and other audio content.

tip

A faster way to open the Preferences dialog box is to press **Ctrl+,** (Windows) or ⌘**+,** (Mac).

FIGURE 14.12

The iTunes Preferences dialog box is very useful, and you will be coming back here again and again.

Hopefully, this will eliminate any pauses in the streams to which you like to listen. If not, choose a different stream or one with a lower bit rate.

Playing Around with Internet Audio

You can do a couple other things with Internet audio using iTunes.

If you want iTunes to be used to play Internet audio by default, open the **Preferences** dialog box (**Ctrl+,** on Windows computers or ⌘**+,** on Macs). Open the General pane. Then check the **Use iTunes as the Default Player for Audio Files** check box (Windows) or click the **Set** button (Mac). When your browser hits an audio file that iTunes supports, iTunes should play it.

You can also play audio streams for which you have a URL within iTunes. To do this, use the following steps:

1. Find the URL pointing to the stream to which you want to listen. Hopefully, you can copy the URL from the Address bar of the Web browser because that is a lot easier than trying to remember the URL or writing it down and then typing it in.

tip

If you want to play the content to which the URL points more than once, download it to your computer and add it to the Library. You'll learn how to do this in the next chapter. You can also add a stream to a playlist by selecting it and choosing **File, New Playlist from Selection**.

2. Choose **Advanced**, **Open Stream**. The **Open Stream** dialog box will appear.

3. Paste in or type the URL in the **URL** field (see Figure 14.13).

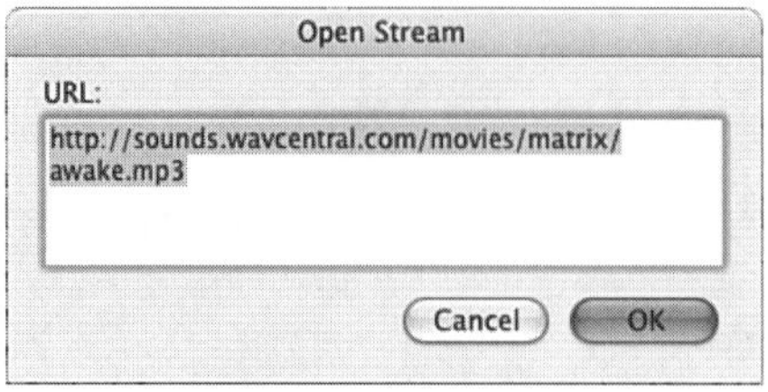

FIGURE 14.13

Here, I've
pasted in a URL
to an MP3 file
that contains a
line from the
movie *The
Matrix*.

4. Click **OK**. The stream will play.

Customizing the iTunes Window

You can configure iTunes in various ways to suit your preferences. You can also change the size of the iTunes window in different ways.

Setting General iTunes Preferences

On the General pane of the **Preferences** dialog box are several settings you might want to use (see Figure 14.14):

FIGURE 14.14

The General
pane of the
iTunes
Preferences dia-
log box pro-
vides..., well,
general
preferences.

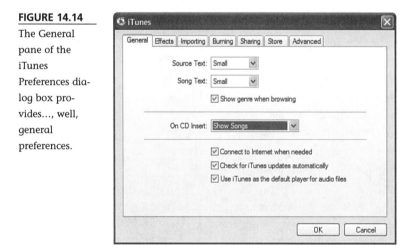

- ■ **Source Text**—Use this drop-down list to change the size of the font of the sources shown in the **Source List**. The options are **Small** (default) and **Large**.

- ■ **Song Text**—This setting changes the size of the text used in the Content pane. Again, your options are **Small** and **Large**.

■ **Show Genre When Browsing**—Earlier, you learned about the Browser. This check box controls whether the **Genre** column appears in the Browser (the check box is checked) or not (the check box is not checked). I like the **Genre** column, so I leave this checked, but if you don't, you can uncheck the check box.

■ **Connect to Internet When Needed**—If you don't want iTunes to try to connect to the Internet automatically, such as when you are using it on a laptop, uncheck this check box. Because iTunes uses the Internet to get CD information, provide Internet radio, and access the iTunes Music Store, you should leave this check box checked whenever you are using iTunes on a computer that can connect to the Internet.

Changing the Size of the iTunes Window

Like the windows of other applications, you can change the size of the iTunes window. For example, you might want to make the window smaller so that it doesn't consume so much desktop space (remember that you can minimize or hide the window and use its System Tray or Dock controls to control it).

Changing the Size of the iTunes Window on a Windows PC

As you use iTunes, keep in the mind the following tips for keeping the window out of your way:

■ **You can minimize/maximize the window**. Use the standard Minimize and Maximize controls in the iTunes window to hide it or make it full-screen size.

■ **You can make the window smaller**. If the iTunes window is in the resize mode (click the Maximize button so the window's size is maximized, then click it again), you can drag its **resize handle** to make the window smaller until it reaches the smallest possible size (see Figure 14.15). Then, you can slide the window out of the way.

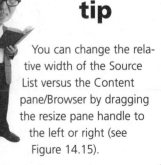

note

You have many ways to customize how contents are displayed in the Content pane. You will learn about these later in the book.

tip

You can change the relative width of the Source List versus the Content pane/Browser by dragging the resize pane handle to the left or right (see Figure 14.15).

Resize pane handle   Resize window handle

FIGURE 14.15

Smaller is sometimes better, when it comes to window size that is.

Changing the Size of the iTunes Window on a Mac

When you use iTunes on a Mac, you can change the window's size in the following ways:

- **You can hide the application**. Press ⌘+**H** to hide the application. Its window will be hidden from the desktop. You can control iTunes by using its Dock menu. Click the **iTunes Dock** icon to show the window again.

- **You can toggle the size of the window**. If you click the Toggle Size button (the green "light") on the window's title bar, the iTunes window will collapse so that only the playback controls and the Information window are shown (see Figure 14.16). Click the button again to open the window to its full size.

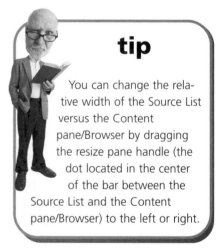

tip

You can change the relative width of the Source List versus the Content pane/Browser by dragging the resize pane handle (the dot located in the center of the bar between the Source List and the Content pane/Browser) to the left or right.

- **You can change the size of the window**. In either the full or collapsed state, you can change the size of the window by dragging its resize handle located in the bottom-right corner of the window.

FIGURE 14.16

On the Mac, you can quickly collapse the iTunes window to this handy size.

Setting iTunes Effects Preferences

You can use iTunes Effects to control how your music plays. For example, you can get rid of the gap of silence between songs or make songs play back at a consistent volume level. You can take advantage of these features by using the Effects pane of the **iTunes Preferences** dialog box. On this pane, you can configure the following effects for your music (see Figure 14.17):

- **Crossfade playback**—This effect causes one song to fade out and the next one to fade in smoothly, eliminating the gaps of silence between songs. To activate it, check the **Crossfade Playback** check box and use the slider to see the amount of fade time. If you move the slider to the left, songs will fade out more quickly. If you set it to 0, there is no fading, and as soon as one song ends, the next one starts. If you move the slider to the right, the fades will last longer. Click **OK** and the effect will take effect.

- **Sound Enhancer**—This effect is iTunes' attempt to "add depth and enliven" the quality of your music. The actual result of this effect is a bit difficult to describe, so the best thing to do is try it for yourself. Check the **Sound Enhance** check box and use the slider to set the relative amount of enhancement. Click **OK** and then listen to some

tip

If you toggle the window to its reduced size and then make it even smaller with the resize handle, the window will contain only the playback controls.

note

This Crossfade setting does not impact audio CDs. Because there is a physical gap between tracks on the CD, iTunes can't do anything about it. This setting applies to other sources, such as your Library and playlists. (So why cover it in the CD chapter you ask? Because this seemed like the place to cover the other effects, so I added this one here, too.)

music. It if sounds better to you, increase the amount of the effect. If not, decrease it or turn it off.

■ **Sound Check**—This effect sets the relative volume level of all songs the same. It is useful if you have changed the relative volume level of songs (perhaps you cranked up your favorite classical tunes) and want to have all your music play at the same volume level. To implement this effect, check its check box and click **OK**.

note

You'll learn how to change the relative volume level of songs later in this part of the book.

FIGURE 14.17

Are these effective effects? You be the judge.

Effects

General Effects Importing Burning Sharing Store Advanced

☑ Crossfade playback

0   seconds   12

☑ Sound Enhancer

low   high

☐ Sound Check
Automatically adjusts song playback volume to the same level.

Cancel   OK

THE ABSOLUTE MINIMUM

By learning how to use iTunes to play audio CDs and Internet radio, you've picked up a lot more knowledge than you might realize. That's because you use the same steps and controls to listen to other music sources, such as your Library, playlists, and so on. In the next couple chapters, you'll learn about these other sources; once you do, you'll be able to use the techniques you picked up in this chapter to work with them.

For now, keep the following tidbits in mind:

- Many of the controls in the iTunes window work just like similar controls on a CD player.

- The iTunes Information window doesn't look like a lot, but you'll learn to really love it when you are building your Library in the next chapter.

- If a song's Selected check box is checked, it will play. If it's not checked, the song won't play.

- You determine the songs you want to hear and the order in which you want to hear them for all your sources by the order in which they appear in the Content pane (except for the Radio source, which you have to take as it comes). Each time you insert a CD, iTunes remembers the settings you used last time and uses those settings again. Just wait until you get to playlists— you can take this concept to the extreme!

- You can repeat or randomize the music in any source, such as a CD or playlist.

- Don't forget about the iTunes System Tray (Windows) or Dock (Mac) menu. This is a great way to keep iTunes music going while not consuming any of your valuable desktop real estate.

- You can change the width of columns within the iTunes window, and you can also resize the iTunes window to make it the size you want. As you work through later chapters, you'll also learn how to customize the information you see inside the window as well.

- Listening to the Radio source provides access to lots of music available on the Internet.

- You can use iTunes Effects to control the gap between songs, to equalize the relative volume of songs, and to enhance the sound you hear.

- Both CDs I used as examples in the screenshots in this chapter are sound-tracks from a couple of my favorite movies. You get bonus points if you can name them.

IN THIS CHAPTER

15

BUILDING, BROWSING, SEARCHING, AND PLAYING YOUR ITUNES MUSIC LIBRARY

Are you ready for some real iTunes? If the material in the previous chapters covered good features of iTunes, which it did, then this chapter starts the coverage of the amazing, awesome [insert your own superlative here] features that make iTunes something to write a book about. Here is where we start taking your iTunes game to the next level, hitting some home runs, scoring touchdowns, and some other sports clichés that all good books use. It's time to start working with that mysterious Library I have mentioned a number of times but into which you have only had glimpses.

The iTunes Library is where you can store all your music, such as that from your audio CDs and the Internet, and where any music you purchase from the iTunes Music Store is stored. After you have added music to your Library, you never have to bother with individual CDs again because you can access all your music from the Library. And, you can use the music in your Library in many ways, such as to create playlists, burn CDs, and so on.

Right now, your iTunes Library is probably sort of sad. Like a book library with no books in it, your iTunes Library is just sitting there gathering dust on its digital shelves. You will change that shortly. The first step is to add music to the Library. Then, you'll learn how to browse, search, and listen to the tunes you have added there.

Gathering Your Music from All the Right Places

If you are going to add music to your Library, you have to get it from somewhere, right? The following are the three main sources of tunes for your Library:

- **Audio CDs**—Who wants to bother with audio CDs? Wouldn't it be nice if you could store all of the content of your CD collection in one place so you can listen to any music you want to at any time just by browsing or doing a quick search? Obviously, that is a loaded question because you already know you can use iTunes to do just that. In this chapter, you'll learn how to copy the music from audio CDs into your Library (as you'll remember from Chapter 12, "Touring iTunes," this is called *importing*) so that you never have to use the original CDs again.

- **MP3 and other audio files**—You can add audio files in just about any format to your Library. For example, there are lots of free and legal MP3 files on the Web that you can add to your own Library. In this chapter, you will learn how to add music to your Library in this way too.

- **iTunes Music Store**—With the iTunes Music Store, you can browse and search among hundreds of thousands of songs. When you find music you like, you can purchase an entire CD's worth of songs or you can buy individual songs (can you say one-hit wonders!). When you buy a song, it is downloaded and added to your iTunes Library. Instead of ordering a CD or, even worse, buying one in a real store, your music is available to you instantly, and you don't even have to import it. Because the iTunes Music Store is so cool, I have devoted an entire part of this book to it (Part III, "The iTunes Music Store"). In that part, you will see how to build your Library by purchasing music online.

Determining Where and How the Music Library Music Is Stored

It is much easier to organize an empty room, so it is good practice to set up the organization of your iTunes Library before you fill it with music. In this section, you'll learn how iTunes organizes the music in your Library. If its standard practices aren't good enough for you, you can change its ways to suit your own organizational preferences.

Working with the iTunes Music Folder

As you import music into the Library, files are created for each song you add (whether it's from a CD, downloaded from the iTunes Music Store, or imported from an existing file). When you first started the application, iTunes created a folder in which it stores all the music it manages for you.

The default location of this folder depends on the kind of computer you are using. On Windows computers, the folder will be stored in a folder called iTunes Music, located within your My Music folder. On Macs, this folder is also called iTunes Music, but it is located in the Music folder within your Home folder.

To see the current location of the iTunes folder on your computer, open the **iTunes Preferences** dialog box and then open the **Advanced** pane (see Figure 15.1). At the top of this dialog box, you will see the iTunes Music Folder Location box. Within this box, you will see the path to your iTunes Music folder.

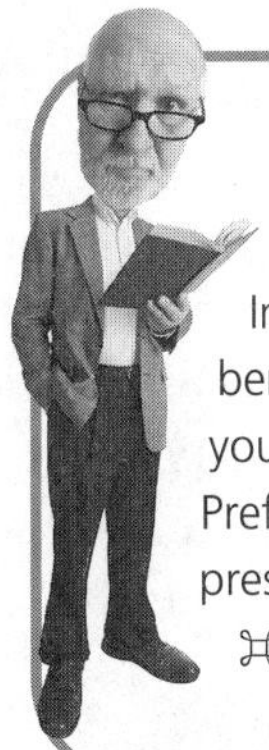

tip

In case you don't remember from the last chapter, you access the iTunes Preferences dialog box by pressing **Ctrl+** (Windows) or ⌘**+** (Macs) .

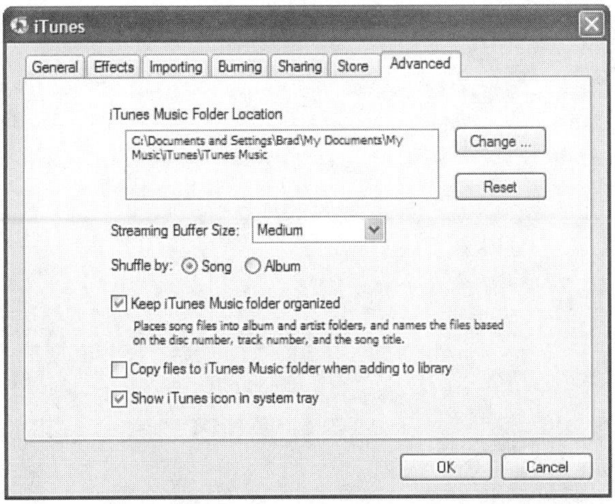

FIGURE 15.1

The current location of your iTunes folder is shown on the Advanced pane of the iTunes Preferences dialog box.

Just for fun, go ahead and open your iTunes Music folder so you can see it for yourself. Use the path you see on the Advanced pane to find it. If you haven't added any music to your Library yet, it might be pretty dull. To see what a full folder looks like, check out Figure 15.2.

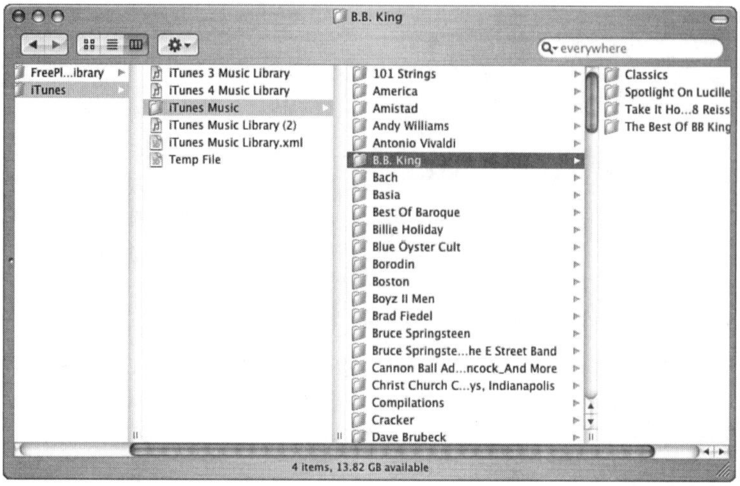

FIGURE 15.2
Don't be envious—soon your iTunes Library will soon be as full of good tunes as mine is.

As you can see, within the iTunes Music folder is a folder for each artist (in the figure, my B.B. King folder is highlighted). Within the artists' folders, each album from which you have added music is shown. Within each of those folders, the tracks you have added are individual files (see Figure 15.3). If you take a close look at Figure 15.3, you can see that the files have the extension .mp3, which means these files were imported in the MP3 format.

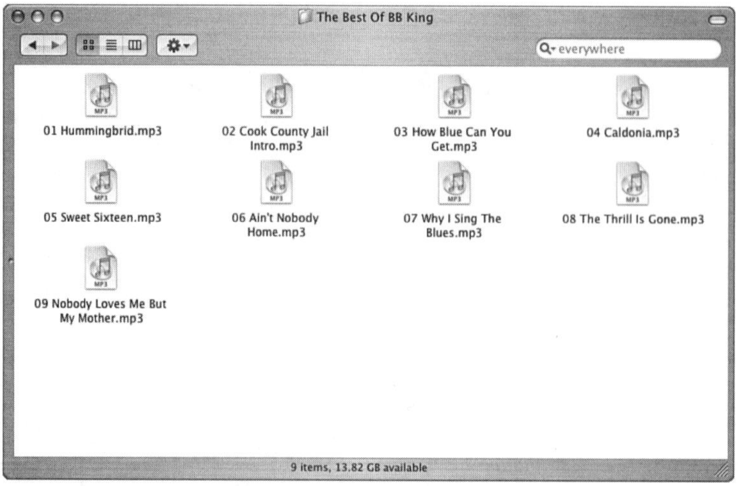

FIGURE 15.3
In this folder, you can see all the songs contained on the album *The Best of BB King* (which is an excellent album by the way, not that I am qualified to be a music critic).

Configuring the Location of the Music Folder

In most cases, the default location of your iTunes Music folder will be fine, and you don't have to do anything about it. However, there are some cases in which you will want to change the location of this folder. For example, suppose you have several hard drives in your computer and the one on which the folder is currently stored doesn't have a lot of room. Even though individual song files are relatively small, you are likely to end up with thousands or tens of thousands of them in your Library. That can add up to a lot of disk space. You might want to change the location of your iTunes Music folder so that it is on a drive with more room.

If you already have music in your Library, changing the location of the iTunes Music folder won't hurt you. When you select a new folder, iTunes will remember the location of any previous music you have added to the Library and will update its database so that music will still be part of your Library.

To change the location of this folder, do the following:

1. Open the **Advanced** pane of the iTunes Preferences dialog box.

2. Click the **Change** button. On a Windows PC, you will see the Browse For Folder dialog box (see Figure 15.4). On a Mac, you will see the Change Music Folder Location dialog box (see Figure 15.5).

FIGURE 15.4

You use the Browse For Folder dialog box to move to or choose a new home for your iTunes Music folder.

> **Browse For Folder**
>
> Change Music Folder Location
>
> - ⊞ 🗀 Adobe
> - ⊞ 🗀 Combat Flight Simulator 3.0
> - ⊞ 🗀 downloads
> - ⊞ 🗀 fce
> - 🗀 Max Payne Savegames
> - 🗀 My eBooks
> - ⊟ 🗀 My Music
>   - ⊟ 🗀 iTunes
>   - ⊞ 🗀 iTunes Music
>
> [Make New Folder]   [OK]   [Cancel]

3. Use the dialog box to move to and select the folder in which you want your iTunes Music folder to be located.

4. Click **OK** (Windows) or **Open** (Mac). You'll return to the Advanced pane, and the folder you selected will be shown in the iTunes Music Folder Location area.

5. Click **OK** to close the iTunes Preferences dialog box.

FIGURE 15.5

The Change Music Folder Location dialog box looks a bit different from its Windows counterpart, but the purpose is exactly the same.

Change Music Folder Location

Setting Other Organization Preferences

The location of the folder in which your music will be stored is likely the most important part of the organization preferences. However, you'll need to understand a couple more preferences. These are also located on the Advanced pane of the iTunes Preferences dialog box:

- **Keep iTunes Music Folder Organized**—This preference causes iTunes to organize your music as described earlier—that is, by artist, album, and song. Because this is a logical way to organize your music files, I recommend that you leave this option active by making sure this check box is checked.

- **Copy Files to iTunes Music Folder when Adding to Library**—This preference causes iTunes to make a copy of audio files that already exist on your computer (such as MP3 files you have downloaded from the Internet), and it places those copies in your iTunes Music folder, just like files you create by importing them from a CD. If this preference is inactive, iTunes uses a pointer to song files you are adding instead of making a copy of the files; it doesn't actually place the files in your iTunes Music folder. I recommend that you make this preference active by checking its check box. This way, all your music files will be in the same place, no matter where they came from originally. If you don't have iTunes make copies when you add songs to your Library and then you delete or move the song files you added, iTunes will lose track of the song and you will experience the "missing song file" problem. To learn how to solve that problem, see "Solving the Missing Song File Problem" on page **307**.

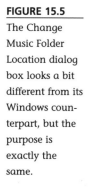

caution

If you have iTunes copy files to your iTunes Music folder when you add them to your Library, be aware that it does actually make a copy of the file you are adding. This means you will have two files for each song you add to the Library. After you have successfully added songs to your Library, you should delete the song files from their original location so that you aren't wasting disk space.

Understanding Encoding and Other Important Format Options

Back in Chapter 12, you learned about the major music file formats that you need to be aware of as you use iTunes. As you will recall, the two primary formats you use when dealing with music are AAC and MP3. When you add music to your Library, you choose the format and then you choose the specific configuration of that format. Just in case you don't remember, AAC is a new and better file format than MP3 because it produces higher quality files with smaller file sizes.

Choosing a Format Option

Although I am sure that going into the specifications for each kind of format would make for fascinating reading, there isn't really any need to get into that detail. Frankly, the benefit of using an application such as iTunes is that it manages all this complexity for you so that you don't have to be concerned with it. If you are like me, you just want to work with the music, not diddle around with complicated settings.

Generally, when you add music to your Library, you should use either the AAC or MP3 format. Because the AAC format is better (with *better* meaning that it provides higher quality music in smaller file sizes), it is usually the best choice.

note

About the only case I can envision where MP3 would be a better option is if you use a portable music player that can only play MP3 music. But because you are reading this book, you are probably using an iPod, and iPods are designed to work with the AAC format as well as the MP3 format.

Picking Quality Levels

After you select a format, you decide the quality with which the music will be encoded. Higher quality levels mean better-sounding music, but larger file sizes. If file size is not a problem, then choosing a higher quality setting is the way to go. If you have relatively little disk space, you might want to experiment to see which is the lowest quality setting you can choose that results in music that still sounds good to you.

Note that when it comes to music, quality is in the ear of the beholder. Also, it heavily depends on the type of music you listen to as well as how you listen to it. For example, if you listen to heavy metal rock using a low-quality pair of speakers (in other words, cheap speakers), quality will be less of an issue for you because you likely won't hear any difference anyway. However, if you listen to classical music on high-quality speakers, the differences in quality levels will likely be more noticeable.

The trade-off for quality is always file size. The higher the quality setting you choose, the larger the resulting files will be. If you don't have disk space limitations and have a discriminating ear, you might want to stick with the highest possible quality setting. If disk space is at a premium for you, then consider using a lower quality setting if you can't detect the difference or if that difference doesn't bother you.

Configuring iTunes to Import Music

When you add music to your Library, you start by choosing the import options (mainly format and quality levels) that you want to use. Here are the steps to follow:

1. Open the **Importing** pane of the iTunes Preferences dialog box (see Figure 15.6).

> **note**
>
> Nothing against heavy metal rock, of course (I like some of it myself). It's just that it usually includes lots of distortion and constant noise, which means that minor flaws in the encoded music won't be as noticeable.

FIGURE 15.6

Here, you can see that the AAC format (the AAC encoder) is selected.

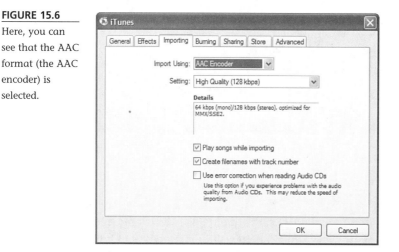

2. Select the format in which you want to add music to your Library on the Import Using menu. For example, to use the AAC format, choose **AAC Encoder**. To use the MP3 format, choose **MP3 Encoder**. The other encoder options are WAV and AIFF. For music, you should use AAC or MP3.

3. Choose the quality level of the encoder you want to use on the Setting menu. The options you see in this list depend on the format you selected in step 1. If you chose AAC Encoder, you have two quality options: High Quality and Custom. If you chose MP3 Encoder, you have four options: Good Quality, High Quality, Higher Quality, and Custom. The Custom option enables you to configure specific settings that the encoder will use. Because you don't typically need to do this, we won't explore doing so in this chapter. If you want to check it out, choose **Custom** on the Setting menu and explore the options you see.

   In the Details box, you will see a summary of the settings you have selected. For example, you will see the data rate of the encoder, such as 128Kbps, and the processor for which the encoder has been optimized. (Do you need to worry about these details? Not really.)

   If you use the AAC encoder, the High Quality setting will likely be all you ever need.

   If you use the MP3 encoder, try the High Quality setting. If music at this quality sounds good to you, try the Good Quality setting to see whether you can detect any difference. If not, use that setting. If the High Quality setting doesn't sound good enough, increase the quality to the Higher Quality setting.

4. If you want music you add to your Library to play while it is being added, check the **Play songs while importing** check box. This is a personal preference, and it doesn't impact the encoding process significantly.

5. If you want the files that iTunes creates when you import music to include the track number in their filenames, check the **Create filenames with track number** check box. Because this helps you more easily find files for specific songs, I recommend that you keep this preference active.

6. The **Use error correction when reading Audio CDs** check box causes iTunes to more closely control the encoding process. You should use this option only if you notice problems with the music you add to your Library, such as cracking or popping sounds. If that happens, check this check box and try the import process again.

7. Click **OK** to close the dialog box.

Adding Music from Audio CDs to Your iTunes Music Library

Now that you know all you need to about configuring iTunes to build your Library, you are ready to start adding your own audio CDs to your Library.

Adding Audio CDs to Your Library

Use these steps to add a CD to your Library:

1. Configure the encoder you want to use for the import session (see the section "Configuring iTunes to Import Music" on page **220**).

2. Insert the CD you want to add to your Library. iTunes will attempt to identify it. When it does, the CD will appear in the Source List and will be selected (see Figure 15.7). Notice that the Action button in the upper-right corner of the screen is now the Import button.

3. If there are songs that you don't want to add to the Library, uncheck their **Selected** check box. Only songs with their check boxes checked will be imported. Unless you really hate a song or disk space is at a premium for you, it is generally better to import all the songs. You can use the Selected check box in another source, such as in your Library, to cause those songs to be skipped when you play that source.

4. Click the **Import** button. It will become highlighted, and the import process will start (see Figure 15.8).

> **tip**
>
> You can also choose **File**, **Import** or press **Shift+Ctrl+O** (Windows) or **Shift+⌘+O** (Mac) to start the import process. You will see a dialog box that enables you to move to and select the CD you want to import.

If you left the Play songs while importing preference active, the music will begin to play as it is imported.

The Information window will show information related to the import process, such as the name of the song currently being imported and the rate at which the import process is happening. The rate of the import process depends on the hardware you are using and the import settings. In most cases, the import process will occur at a much greater rate than the playing process. For example, with moderate hardware, you can usually achieve import rates of 10×, meaning 10 minutes of music will be imported in 1 minute of time.

FIGURE 15.7

iTunes is ready
to add this CD to
the Library.

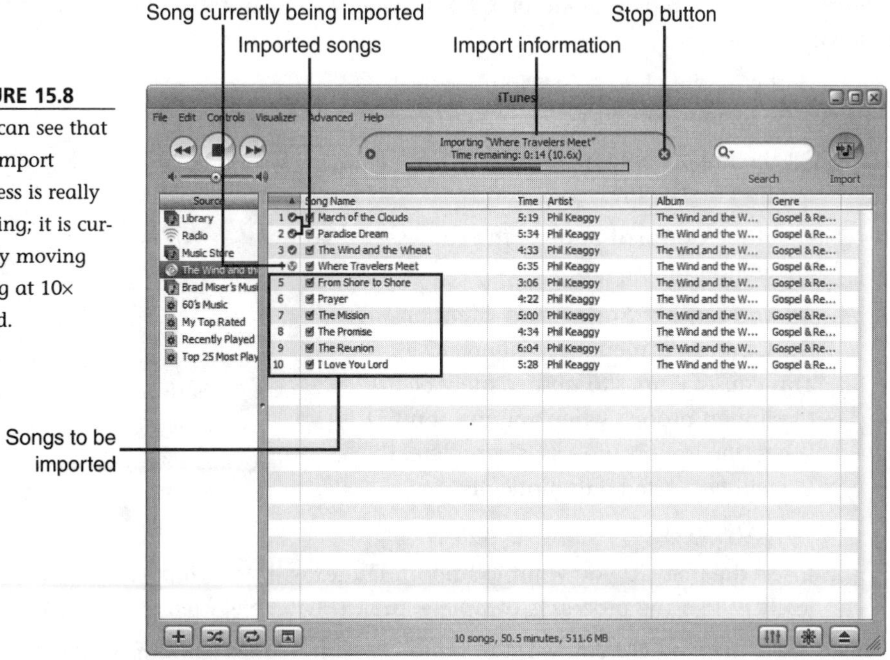

FIGURE 15.8

You can see that
the import
process is really
moving; it is cur-
rently moving
along at 10×
speed.

Song currently being imported

Imported songs

Import information

Stop button

Songs to be
imported

An orange circle with a "squiggly" line inside it marks the song currently
being imported. When a song has been imported, it is marked with a green
circle containing a check mark.

If you want to stop the import process for some reason, click the **Stop** button (the small "x" within a circle) in the Information window.

When the process is complete, you will hear a tone, and all of the songs will be marked with the "import complete" icon.

If you have the Play songs while importing preference active, the music will keep playing long after the import process is complete (because importing is much faster than playing is). Listen for the complete tone or keep an eye on the screen to determine when all the music on the CD has been imported.

5. Eject the CD.

> **tip**
>
> During the import process, you don't have to listen to what you are importing. You can select a different source, such as a playlist, and play it while the CD is being imported.

Building Your iTunes Music Library in a Hurry

The import process moves along pretty quickly, but you can make it even faster by following these steps:

1. Gather a pile of your CDs in a location close to your computer.

2. Set the import preferences (encoder and quality) for the import session.

3. Open the **General** pane of the iTunes Preferences dialog box.

4. Choose **Import Songs and Eject** on the **On CD Insert** menu (see Figure 15.9). This causes iTunes to immediately begin the import process when you insert a CD. When the import process is complete, the CD will be ejected automatically.

5. Click **OK** to close the dialog box.

> **tip**
>
> Consider turning off the Play songs while importing preference on the Importing pane so that the import process doesn't impact the music to which you are listening.

6. Insert the first CD you want to import. iTunes will start importing it automatically. When the process is complete, the CD will be ejected automatically.

7. Insert the next CD you want to import. Again, iTunes will import the music and eject the disc when it is done.

8. Repeat step 7 until all the CDs have been imported. You'll be amazed at how quickly you can build a Library, even if you have a large number of CDs. When you are done batch importing your CDs, you might want to reset the On CD insert menu to **Show Songs** to prevent unintentionally importing a CD.

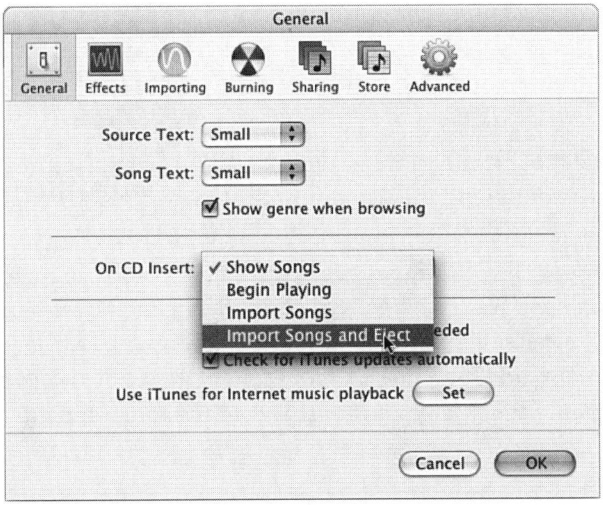

FIGURE 15.9

Choosing the Import Songs and Eject option makes adding lots of CDs to your Library as fast as possible.

Importing Audio Files into Your Library

Another potential source of music for your Library is the Internet. There are millions of audio files there, and you can download these files and add them to your Library.

Or, you might have lots of MP3 files on your computer already. You can add all these to your iTunes Library so that you can use that music from within iTunes as well.

You can add music that is stored on your hard drive to your iTunes Library by following these steps:

1. Locate the files you want to add to your Library. For example, find the MP3 files on your hard drive or go to a Web site that has audio files, such as MP3 files, and download them to your computer.

caution

Make sure that you don't download and add illegal files to your Library. In addition to this being the wrong thing to do, you can get prosecuted for downloading files illegally. Make sure any Web sites from which you get files have those files legally with permission of the files' creators.

2. In iTunes on a Windows computer, choose **File**, **Add File to Library** to add individual music files or **File**, **Add Folder to Library** to add a folder full of music files. On a Mac, choose **File, Add to Library**. If you used the Add Folder to Library command, you'll see the Browse For Folder dialog box. If you used the Add File to Library command, you'll see the Add to Library dialog box.

> **tip**
>
> On a Mac, you can choose a folder containing files you want to import using the Add to Library dialog box.

3. Use the dialog box to move to and select the folder containing the files you want to add or to select the files you want to add to the Library.

4. Click **Open**, **OK** or **Choose** (the name of the button you see depends on the command you use). The files you selected will be imported into your Library. If you selected a folder, all the songs it contains will be added to your Library. You can also add song files to your iTunes Library by dragging them from the desktop onto the Content pane. This does the same thing as using one of the Add to Library commands.

Browsing and Searching Your Music Library

It won't be long until you have a large Library with many kinds of music in it. In fact, you are likely to have so much music in the Library that you won't be able to find songs you are interested in just by scrolling up and down the screen. In this section, you'll learn how to find music in your Library, first by browsing and then by searching.

Browsing in the Library

You've already seen the Browser a couple of times. Now it is time to put it to work:

1. Select the **Library** on the Source List.

2. If the Browser isn't showing, click the **Action** button, which is now labeled Browse (it looks like an eye). The Browser will appear (see Figure 15.10). The Browser has three columns: Genre, Artist, and Album. The columns start on the left with the most general category, Genre, and end on the right with the most specific category, which is Album. If you don't see the Genre column in the Browser, open the **General** pane of the iTunes Preferences dialog box and check the **Show Genre when Browsing** check box.

FIGURE 15.10

The Browser offers a good way to find songs in your Library.

	iTunes

Source	Genre	Artist	Album
Library	All (24 Genres)	All (174 Artists)	All (155 Albums)
Radio	Alternative	101 Strings	1
Music Store	Blues	Al Green	16 Biggest Hits
Purchased Music	Blues/R&B	The Alan Parsons Project	20th Century Masters – The Miller
60's Music	Business & Finance	America	20th Century Masters – The Miller
Great Jazz	Classical	Amistad	A Fresh Aire Christmas
Jazz	Country	Amy Grand/Sandi Patti	A Legendary Performer
Jazz	Dance	Andy Williams	Acoustic Sketches
My Top Rated	Easy Listening	Antonio Vivaldi	America

Song Name	Track #	Time	Artist	Album
☑ Love Me Do	1 of 27	2:20	The Beatles	1
☑ From Me To You	2 of 27	1:56	The Beatles	1
☑ She Loves You	3 of 27	2:21	The Beatles	1
☑ I Want To Hold Your Hand	4 of 27	2:25	The Beatles	1
☑ Can't Buy Me Love	5 of 27	2:11	The Beatles	1
☑ A Hard Day's Night	6 of 27	2:33	The Beatles	1
☑ I Feel Fine	7 of 27	2:18	The Beatles	1
☑ Eight Days A Week	8 of 27	2:44	The Beatles	1
☑ Ticket To Ride	9 of 27	3:10	The Beatles	1
☑ Help!	10 of 27	2:18	The Beatles	1
☑ Yesterday	11 of 27	2:05	The Beatles	1
☑ Day Tripper	12 of 27	2:48	The Beatles	1
☑ We Can Work It Out	13 of 27	2:15	The Beatles	1
☑ Paperback Writer	14 of 27	2:18	The Beatles	1

1831 songs, 4.9 days, 9.10 GB

The contents of the "path" selected in the Browser are shown in the Content pane that now occupies the bottom part of the right side of the window. At the top of each column is the All option, which shows all the contents of that category. For example, when All is selected in the Genre column, you will see the contents of all the genres for which you have music in the Library. In Figure 15.10, you can see that I have selected All in each category, so the Contents pane shows the entire contents of my Library.

tip

You can also open and close the Browser by choosing **Edit**, **Show Browser** or **Edit**, **Hide Browser**. Pressing **Ctrl+B** (Windows) or ⌘+**B** (Mac) also works.

At the bottom of the screen, you will see Source Information for the selected source. Again, in Figure 15.10, you can see that my Library had 1,831 songs in it when I captured the screenshot and that I could play music for 4.9 days without hearing the same song twice.

3. To start browsing your Library, select the genre in which you are interested by clicking it. When you do so, the categories in the other two columns are scoped down to include only the artists and albums that are part of that genre (see Figure 15.11). Similarly, the Content pane now includes only jazz music. Notice in Figure 15.11 that the Source Information has been scoped, too. It now shows that I can listen to only 21.5 hours of jazz before I run out of music.

FIGURE 15.11

Because Jazz is selected in the Genre column, the Artist and Album columns contain only the jazz that is in my Library.

4. To further limit the browse, click an artist in which you are interested in the Artist column. The Album column will be scoped down to show only those albums for the artist selected in the Artist column (see Figure 15.12). Also, the Content pane will show the songs on the albums listed in the Album column.

FIGURE 15.12

Now I am browsing all my music in the Jazz genre that is performed by Dave McKenna.

5. To get down to the most narrow browse possible, select the album in which you are interested in the Album column. The Content pane will now show the songs on the selected album.

6. When you have selected the genre, artist, and album categories in which you are interested, you can scroll in the Content pane to see all the songs included in the group of songs you are browsing.

To make the browse results less narrow again, choose **All** in one of the Browser's columns. For example, to browse all your music again, click **All** in the Genre column.

Hopefully, you can see that you can use the Browser to quickly scan your Library to locate music that you want to hear or work with. As you use the Browser more, you will come to rely on it to get you to a group of songs quickly and easily.

tip

You can change the size of the Browser relative to the Content pane by dragging the resize handle (the small circle located in the center of the bar between the two panes) up or down to make the Browser larger or smaller. Of course, making the Browser larger makes the Content pane smaller, and vice versa. Remember that you can also make the Source List narrower or wider by dragging its resize handle to the left or right.

Searching Your Music Library

You can use iTunes Search tool to search for specific songs. You can search for songs by any of the following criteria:

- All (searches all possible data)
- Artists
- Albums
- Composers
- Songs

tip

If you want to search by all data at the same time, you don't need to perform step 2 because All is the default selection.

To search for music in your Library, perform the following steps:

1. Select the source you want to search (in this case, click the **Library** source). As you might surmise, you can search any source in the Source List, such as a CD, playlist, and so on, by selecting it and then performing a search.

2. Click the **magnifying glass** icon in the **Search** tool (see Figure 15.13). You will see a menu containing the list of data by which you can search.

FIGURE 15.13

By selecting
Artists on the
menu, you can
search the Artist
field for all the
songs in your
Library.

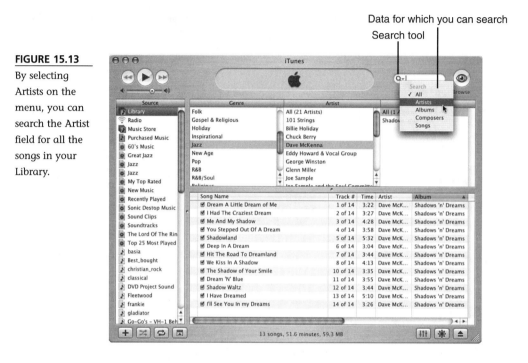

Data for which you can search

Search tool

3. Select the data for which you want to search in the menu. When you release
   the mouse button, the data you selected will appear in gray inside the search
   box and in regular text underneath it so you can see which data you are
   searching for. For example, choose **Artists** to search by the Artist field.

4. Type the data for which you want to search in the field. As you type, iTunes
   searches the selected source and presents the songs that meet your criterion in
   the Content pane. It does this on the fly so that the search narrows with each
   keystroke. As you type more text or numbers, the search becomes more
   specific (see Figure 15.14).

5. Keep typing until the search becomes as narrow as you need it to be to find
   the songs in which you are interested.

After you have found songs, you can play them, use them in playlists, and so on.

To clear your search, click the **Clear Search** button that appears in the Search tool
after you have typed in it. The songs shown in the Content pane will again be
determined by your selections in the Browser.

FIGURE 15.14

Because I selected Artist and typed "lyn" in the Search tool, the Content pane shows all songs whose artist includes the text "lyn," as in The Lyndhurst Orchestra, Lynyrd Skynyrd, and so on.

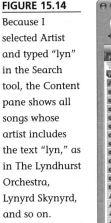

Clear search

Playing Music in Your Music Library

Remember earlier when I said that you use the same listening techniques to listen to music in your Library as you do when listening to a CD? Now it's time to prove my words.

When you listen to music in your Library, you start by choosing the scope of the music you want to hear. You do this by browsing or searching for music (if you don't know how to do this, here's a hint: Read the previous two sections).

After you have the group of songs to which you want to listen showing in the Content pane, use the listening tools you learned about in the previous chapter to listen to your music. For example, you can click **Play** to play the songs, use the Repeat button to repeat them, sort the Content pane by one of the column headings to change the order in which the songs play, and so on.

note

When you are listening to your Library, I don't recommend that you uncheck a song's Selected check box in the Library or move songs up and down in the list to control how they are played. Use playlists for that kind of customized listening instead (playlists are explained in Chapter 17, "Creating, Configuring, and Using Playlists"). Changes you make to songs in the Library can result in unexpected things happening if you forget to undo a change before making a playlist, burning a CD, and so on.

Removing Tunes from the Music Library

Not all that glitters is gold, nor are all tunes that are digital good. Sometimes, a song is so bad that it just isn't worth the hard disk space it consumes.

To remove songs from your Library, ditch them with the following steps:

1. Find the songs you want to delete by browsing or searching.

2. Select the songs you want to trash. They will become highlighted to show you they are selected (see Figure 15.15).

> **tip**
>
> Remember that you can stop a song from playing by unchecking its check box in the Content pane. If you aren't sure you want to dump a song permanently, use that method instead so that you can always use the song again should you change your mind.

FIGURE 15.15

If I hit the Delete key now, "La Paloma" will be removed from my Library.

3. Press the **Delete** key. You will be prompted to confirm that you really want to delete the song you have selected.

4. Click **Yes** to confirm the deletion. You will see another prompt asking if you want the selected files to be moved to your Recycle Bin (Windows) or Trash (Mac).

5. Click **Yes**. The selected songs will be deleted from your Library, and their song files will be moved to the appropriate trash receptacle on your computer. The next time you empty that receptacle, they will be gone forever.

Of course, songs you delete probably aren't really gone forever. You can always add them back to the Library again by repeating the same steps you used to place them in there the first time. This assumes that you have a copy somewhere, such as on a CD or stored in some other location. If you imported the music from your hard disk and had iTunes move the songs files to your iTunes Music folder, your only copy will reside in your iTunes Library, so make sure you have such music backed up before you delete it if you might ever want it again.

> **tip**
>
> In many of the prompts iTunes presents to you, you have the option of telling the application not to present those prompts to you again. Just look for the appropriate **Don't Tell Me Again** check boxes in such prompts and check them to hide those prompts.

THE ABSOLUTE MINIMUM

Although it might not smell like a book library, your iTunes Library is at least as useful and is a heck of a lot easier to get to. In this chapter, you learned how to build and use your iTunes Library. Before we move on to the next great thing about iTunes, check out some related points of interest (well, my interest anyway; hopefully, they will be yours, too):

- Through the Audible.com service (accessible via the iTunes Music Store), you can also add audio books to your iTunes Library to listen to them on your computer and you can add them to an iPod. Working with audio book content is very similar to working with music. Unfortunately, covering the details of doing so is outside the scope of this book.

- You learned that you can choose the import encoder and quality settings when you import music from audio CDs to your Library. You can import the same songs at different quality levels to experiment with various settings or to create different versions of the same song. For example, you might want a high-quality version to play from your computer and a lower-quality version with a smaller file size for a portable device. To create another version of a song, you can change the import settings and import it from a CD again. You

continues

can also reimport a song already in the Library by setting the encoding settings and adding its file (which will be located in the iTunes Music folder) to the Library, just like other music files stored on your computer.

■ Although we focused on the AAC and MP3 formats in this chapter, in some cases you might want to use the WAV or AIFF format. For example, suppose you want to use part of a song as a sound byte in an application that doesn't support either of the primary formats, but does support WAV files. You could choose the WAV format and then import the song you want to use in that format. The WAV file, which would be located in your iTunes Music folder, could then be added to the other application you are working with.

■ If you are listening to music while doing something else, such as browsing your Library, you might move away from the song that is currently playing. If you want to move back to it again, choose **File**, **Show Current Song** or press **Ctrl+L** (Windows) or ⌘+**L** (Mac).

■ If you like to shuffle while you listen, you can determine whether iTunes shuffles by song or by album. It can be interesting when listening to the Library if you shuffle by album because iTunes will pick an album and play a song from it, then pick another album, play a song, and so on, rather than just randomly picking songs on the same album. To set this behavior, open the **Advanced** pane of the iTunes Preferences dialog box and click the **Album** radio button next to the Shuffle by text. (The default option is **Song**.)

■ You can use the Browser with any source, although it defaults to being closed with CDs and some playlists because it usually isn't that useful in those contexts (especially when the source is a single CD). Just select the source you want to browse and open the Browser.

IN THIS CHAPTER

- Get to know and love tags.
- Get the details for your music.
- Label your music so that you can do cool things with it, such as creating playlists based on a music's information.
- Rate your songs, set the relative volume level, and hear only the parts you want to hear.
- Don't miss out on album artwork just because you have gone digital.
- Work the Content pane like a pro.

16

LABELING, CATEGORIZING, AND CONFIGURING YOUR MUSIC

It's confession time. I admit it. This topic might not seem too exciting at first glance. Who wants to spend their time labeling and categorizing music? That is a fair question; I hope by the time you read through this chapter, you answer that question with an enthusiastic "I do, that's who!" Of course, I would be almost as happy even if your response is, "It might not be as fun as building my Library, but it will make my iTunes world a lot better." Think of this chapter as learning the nuts and bolts of how iTunes works so that you can become an iTunes wizard later on.

After you have worked through the labeling content in this chapter, I think you will find the ability to configure the songs in your Library to be pretty exciting because that is where you start really bending iTunes to your will (which isn't as dramatic as it sounds because iTunes is really pretty easy to command).

Understanding Song Tags and Knowing Why You Should Care About Them

In the previous chapter, you saw how you can browse your iTunes music collected by genre, artist, and album. This makes finding music fast and easy, even if you have thousands of songs in your Library. This functionality is enabled because each song in your Library has information—also called *tags*—that categorizes and identifies those songs for you. Genre, artist, and album are just three of the possible tags for each song in iTunes. There are many more items of information that iTunes manages.

These types of data fall into two groups: data that iTunes assigns for you and that you can't change, and data that you or iTunes assigns and that you can change.

Not all songs have all the data fields listed. You will only see data that is applicable to a specific song. For example, only music purchased from the iTunes Music Store has information about the purchase.

Data that iTunes assigns and that you can view but can't change include the following:

- **Kind**—The type of file the song is, such as AAC, MP3, and so on.
- **Size**—The amount of disk space required to store the song.
- **Bit Rate**—The quality level at which the song was encoded. Larger numbers, such as 128Kbps, are better.
- **Sample Rate**—The rate at which the music was sampled when it was captured.
- **Date Modified**—The date on which the song file was last changed.
- **Play Count**—The number of times the song has been played.
- **Last Played**—The last time the song was played.
- **Profile**—A categorization of the song's complexity.
- **Format**—The format in which the song was encoded, such as MPEG-1, Layer 3, and so on.
- **Channels**—Whether the track is stereo or mono.
- **Encoded With**—The tools used to encode the song, such as iTunes, QuickTime, and so on.
- **ID3 Tag**—Data formatted according to a set of specifications. If a song's data has been formatted with this specification, the ID3 version number will be shown.

■ **Purchase By** and **Account Name**—Information that identifies who purchased the music from the iTunes Music Store and what account was used.

■ **Where**—A path to the song's file on your computer along with the file's name.

Data collected for songs that you can change includes the following:

■ **Name**—The name of the song.

■ **Artist**—The person who performs the song.

■ **Album**—The name of the album from which the song comes.

■ **Grouping**—A label you can assign to group songs together in some fashion.

■ **Composer**—The person who is credited with writing the song.

■ **Comments**—A free-form text field in which you can make comments about a song.

■ **Genre**—A song's musical genre, such as jazz or classical.

■ **Year**—The year the song was created.

■ **Track Number**—The song's position on the CD from which it came, such as "2 of 12."

■ **Disc number**—The number of the CD. This is meaningful only for multiple CD sets.

■ **BPM**—The song's beats per minute.

■ **Compilation**—An indicator of whether the song is part of a compilation in the Library, such as coming from a CD that is stored in the Library.

When you add a song to your Library, iTunes will add as much of this data as it can find for each song. However, you can add or change the data in the previous list.

So, why should you care about all this data? There are a couple of reasons.

The first is that, as you already know because you learned how to browse and search your Library in the previous chapter, this data can be used to find music in which you are interested. That reason alone should be enough to convince you that these types of data are important to you.

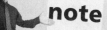

note

When you insert a CD, iTunes attempts to get that CD's information from the CDDB (the online CD database), which is why it connects to the Internet. If iTunes finds the CD in this database, the information for that CD is applied to the CD and carried into the Library if you import the songs from that CD into iTunes. If you purchase music from the iTunes Music Store, it also contains many of these tags.

The second reason is, when it comes time to create playlists (which you will learn about in Chapter 17, "Creating, Configuring, and Using Playlists"), you can use song tags to determine which songs are included in your playlists. For example, you can configure a playlist to include the last 25 songs you have played from the Jazz genre. This is just a basic example—you can get much more sophisticated than that. In fact, you can include lots of different combinations of these types of data as criteria in playlists to create very interesting sets of music to listen to.

Viewing Song Information

Now that you understand the types of data that can be associated with songs in your Library, it's time to learn how to view that information. You have three basic areas in which to view song information: the Browser, the Content pane, and the Info window.

Viewing Tags in the Browser

If you read through the previous chapter, you have already used this technique. When you view the Browser, you see the genre, artist, and album tags associated with the songs you are browsing (see Figure 16.1).

FIGURE 16.1

Each column in the Browser is a tag associated with songs in your Library.

Viewing Tags in the Content Pane

Even if you don't realize it, you have also seen tags in the Content pane. The column headings you see in the Content pane are actually the tags associated with the songs you are viewing (see Figure 16.2).

FIGURE 16.2

Each column heading in the Content pane is a tag.

You can customize the columns (tags) shown in the Content pane, as you will learn later in this chapter.

Viewing Tags in the Info Window

The Info window is probably the only area in which you haven't seen tags yet. To view the Info window, select a song in your Library and choose **File**, **Get Info** or press **Ctrl+I** (Windows) or ⌘**+I** (Mac). The Info window will appear (see Figure 16.3). This window has four panes that you will be using throughout the rest of this chapter. The Summary pane provides a summary view of the song's information, starting at the top with any album art associated with the song and including its name, artist, and album. In the center part of the pane, you see the data iTunes manages (you can view this data, but you can't change it). At the bottom of the pane, you can see the path to the song's file on your computer.

When you click the Info tab, you will see the tags that you can change (see Figure 16.4). You'll learn how to change this data in the next section.

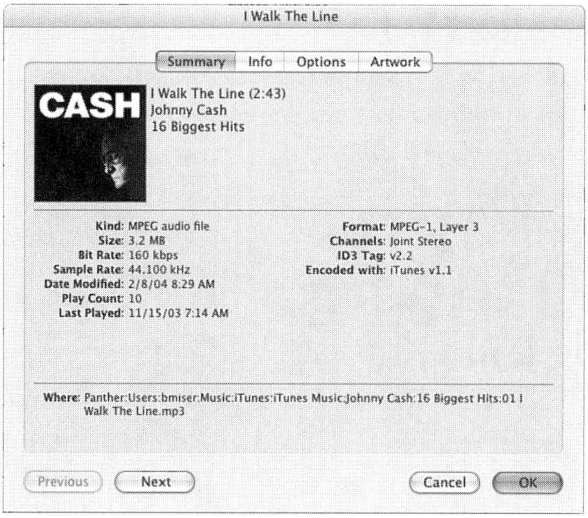

FIGURE 16.3

The Info window enables you to view the tags associated with a song, and you can change many of them.

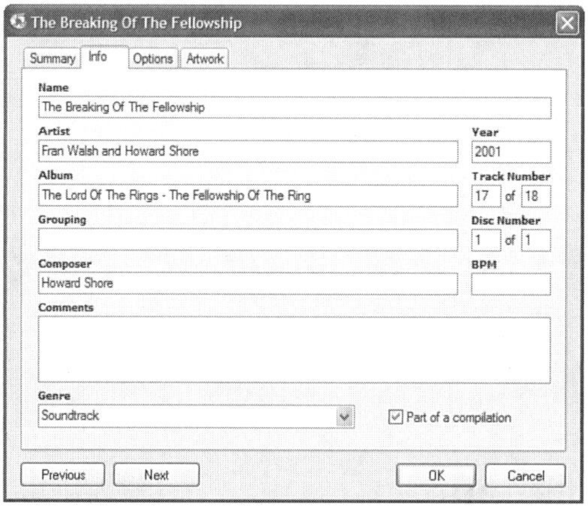

FIGURE 16.4

Although you can't change the tags shown on the Summary pane, you can change the ones on the Info pane.

The other two panes of the window, Options and Artwork, are used to configure specific aspects of a song (again, we'll get to these topics in a few pages).

You can view information for other songs without closing the window. Click **Next** to move to the next song in the source you are viewing (such as your Library) or **Previous** to move to the previous song. When you do, that song's information will be displayed in the Info window.

To close the window, click **OK**.

Labeling Your Music

Typically, if you have imported a CD or purchased music from the iTunes Music Store, you shouldn't change most of the data that came from the source, such as name, artist, album, track number, and so on. Occasionally, a CD's information will come in incorrect (such as a misspelling in the artist's name); you'll probably want to fix such mistakes. Also, you can certainly add data in those fields that are empty. There are a couple of places in which you can change a song's tags.

Labeling a Song in the Info Window

You can use the Info window to change a song's tags, as you can see in the following steps:

1. Open the **Info** window for the song whose information you want to change.

2. Click the **Info** tag. The Info pane will appear.

3. Enter or change the information shown in the various fields. For example, you can change the song's name or artist. Or you might want to add comments about the song in the Comments box.

   One of the more useful tags is Genre. This can be used for browsing and also in playlists.

4. To change a song's genre, select the new genre on the Genre menu.

5. When you are done entering or changing tags, click **OK**. The Info window will close, and any changes you made will be saved.

Labeling Multiple Songs at the Same Time

You can change some tags, such as Genre, for a group of songs at the same time. This can be a faster way to enter data because you can change multiple songs at the same time. Here are the steps to follow:

1. Select the songs whose data you want to change.

2. Open the **Info** window. You'll be prompted to confirm that you want to change the information for a group of songs.

tip

If a genre isn't listed on the menu, you can add it to the menu by choosing Custom on the menu and then typing the genre you want to add. That genre will be added to the menu and associated with the current song. You can use the genres you add just like the default genres.

3. Click **Yes** to clear the prompt. The Multiple Song Information window will appear (see Figure 16.5). The information and tools in this window work in the same way as they do for individual songs. The difference is that the information and settings apply to all the songs you have selected.

4. Enter data in the fields, make changes to existing data, or use the other tools to configure the songs you have selected. As you change information, the check box next to the tag will become checked to show that you are changing that data for all the selected songs.

> **tip**
>
> To select multiple songs that are next to each other, hold the **Shift** key down while you click songs. To select multiple songs that aren't next to each other, hold the **Ctrl** (Windows) or ⌘ (Mac) key down while you click songs.

5. When you are done making changes, click **OK**. The window will close and the changes you made will be saved.

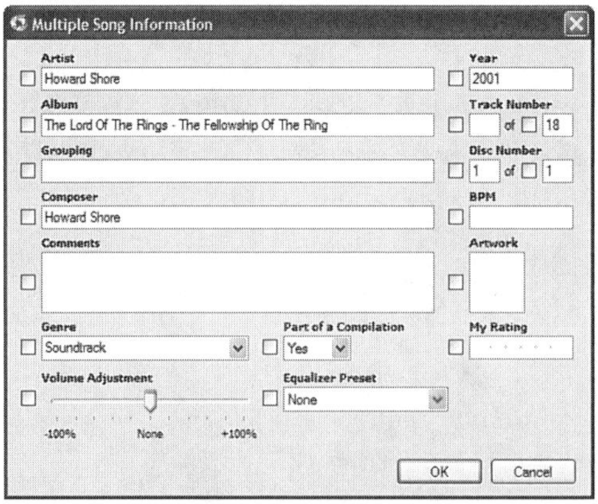

FIGURE 16.5

You can use this window to change the data for multiple songs at the same time.

Labeling a Song in the Content Pane

You can also edit tags within the Content pane:

1. Click once on a song to select it.

2. Click once on the tag you want to edit. The tag will become highlighted to show that it is ready to be edited (see Figure 16.6).

3. Type the new information.

4. Press **Enter** (Windows) or **Return** (Mac). The changes you made will be saved.

FIGURE 16.6

You can also change tags from the Content pane.

Configuring a Song's Options

You can configure a number of options for the songs in your Library, including the following:

- **Relative Volume**—You can change a song's relative volume so that it is either louder or quieter than "normal." This is useful if you like to listen to songs that are recorded at a variety of volume levels so that the volume remains somewhat similar as you move from song to song.

- **Equalizer Preset**—You can use the iTunes Equalizer to configure the relative volume of sound frequencies. You'll learn about the Equalizer in Chapter 18, "Equalizing Your Music."

- **My Rating**—You can give tunes a rating from one to five stars. You can use ratings in various ways, such as to create criteria for playlists (such as include only my five-star songs) or to sort the Content pane.

- **Start and Stop Time**—You can set songs to start or stop at certain points in the track. This can be useful if you don't want to hear all of a track, such as when a song has an introduction that you don't want to hear each time the song plays.

Configuring Song Options in the Info Window

You can configure a song's options in the Info window by performing the following steps:

1. Select the song whose options you want to set.

2. Open the **Info** window.

3. Click the **Options** tab (see Figure 16.7).

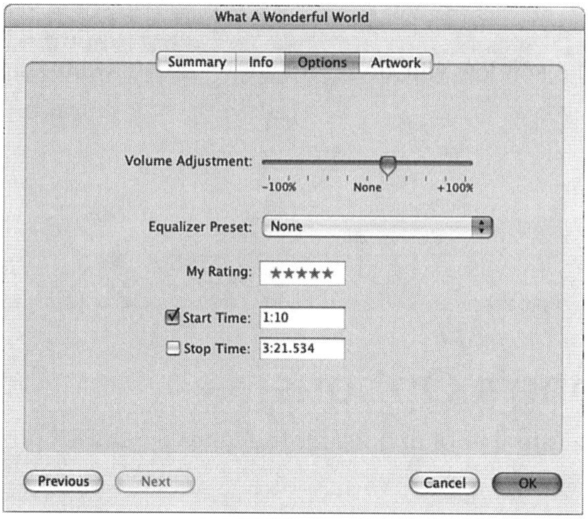

FIGURE 16.7

Using the Options tab, you can configure a number of settings for a song.

4. To change the song's relative volume, drag the **Volume Adjustment** slider to the left to make the song quieter or to the right to make it louder.

5. To rate the song, click the dot representing the number of stars you want to give the song in the My Rating field. For example, to give the song three stars, click the center (third) dot. Stars will appear up to the point at which you click. In other words, before you click you'll see a dot. After you click a dot, it becomes a star.

tip

If you want to configure options for a group of songs at the same time, select those songs and open the Info window. Use the resulting Multiple Song Information window to make changes to all the songs you have selected at the same time.

6. To set a start time, check the **Start Time** check box and enter a time in the format *minutes:seconds*. When you play the song, it will start playing at the time you enter.

   When you set a start or stop time, you don't change the song file in any way. You can play the whole song again by unchecking the Start Time or Stop Time check box.

7. To set a stop time, check the **Stop Time** check box and enter a time in the format *minutes:seconds*. When you play the song, it will stop playing at the time you enter.

8. Click **OK**. The window will close and your changes will be saved.

Ratings Songs in the Content Pane

You can also rate songs in the Content pane. To do so, follow these steps:

1. Scroll in the Content pane until you see the **My Rating** column (see Figure 16.8).

2. Select the song you want to rate. Dots will appear in the My Rating column for that song.

3. Click the dot representing the number of stars you want to give the song. The dots up to and including the one on which you clicked will become stars.

FIGURE 16.8

You can also rate songs from the Content pane.

Adding and Viewing Album Artwork

Many CD and album covers are works of art (though many aren't!), and it would be a shame never to see them just because your music has gone digital. With iTunes, you don't need to miss out because you can associate artwork with songs and display that artwork in the iTunes window.

Most of the music you purchase from the iTunes Music Store will include artwork that you can view. You can also add artwork to songs and view that in the same way.

Viewing Album Artwork

To view a song's artwork, do one of the following:

- Click the **Artwork** button located under the Source list. The Artwork pane will appear and display the artwork associated with either the currently playing song or the currently selected song (see Figure 16.9). At the top of the artwork, you will see **Selected Song**, which indicates you are viewing the artwork associated with the selected song, or **Now Playing**, which indicates you are viewing artwork associated with the song currently playing.

- Double-click the artwork to see a larger version in a separate window (see Figure 16.10). The title of the window will be the name of the song the artwork is associated with.

FIGURE 16.9

You can view the artwork associated with a song in the Artwork pane.

Artwork button

FIGURE 16.10

You can view a large version of a song's artwork in a separate window.

- To choose between viewing artwork associated with the selected song or the song currently playing, click the text at the top of the Artwork pane. The artwork will change to the other option (for example, if you click Now Playing, it will become Selected Song), and you will see the artwork for that song.

- If you choose the Now Playing option, the artwork will change in the Artwork pane as the next song begins playing (unless, of course, the songs use the same artwork).

- If the song has more than one piece of artwork associated with it, click the arrows that appear at the top of the pane to see each piece of art.

note

If you view the artwork in a separate window, it does not change with the music. When you open the artwork in a new window, it is static, meaning you can only view the image you double-clicked.

Adding Artwork for Songs

You might want to associate artwork with a song. For example, if a song doesn't have album art associated with it, you can add the art yourself. Or, you might want to add the artist's picture or some other meaningful graphic to the song. You can add one or more pieces of art to songs by using the following steps:

1. Prepare the artwork you are going to associate with a song. You can use graphics in the usual formats, such as JPG, TIFF, GIF, and so on.

2. Select the song with which you want to associate the artwork.

3. Open the **Info** window and then click the **Artwork** tab (see Figure 16.11). If the selected song has artwork with it, you will see it in the Artwork pane. You can add multiple images for the same song.

FIGURE 16.11

You use the Artwork pane to add artwork to a song.

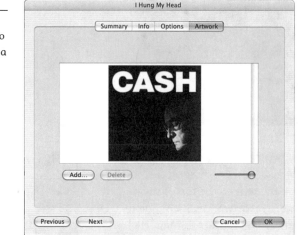

You can use the slider under the image box to change the size of the previews you see in the window. Drag the slider to the right to make the image larger or to the left to make it smaller. This doesn't change the image; instead, it only impacts the size of the image as you currently see it in the Info window. This is especially useful when you associate lots of images with a song because you can see them all at the same time.

4. Click **Add**. A dialog box that enables you to choose an image will appear.

5. Move to and select the image you want to associate with the song.

6. Click **Open** (Windows) or **Choose** (Mac). The image will be added to the window (see Figure 16.12).

> **tip**
>
> You can also add artwork to a song by dragging the image file from your desktop onto the Artwork pane of the Info window.

7. Continue adding images to the Artwork pane until you have added all the images for a song.

   The default image for a song is the one on the left of the image box.

8. To change the order of the images, drag them in the image box.

9. Click **OK**. The window will close and the images will be saved with the song (see Figure 16.13).

FIGURE 16.12

This song now has two images associated with it.

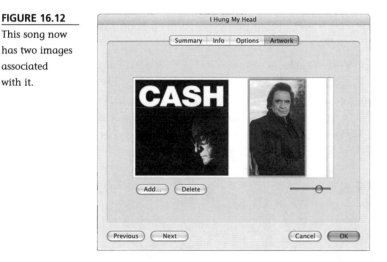

FIGURE 16.13

You can tell this song has multiple images associated with it by the arrows at the top of the Artwork pane. Click an arrow to see the other images.

Customizing the Content Pane

You have a number of ways to customize the columns (tags) that appear in the Content pane. What's more, you can customize the Content pane for each source. The customization you have done for a source (such as a CD or playlist) is remembered and used each time you view that source.

You can choose the tags (columns) that are shown for a source by using the following steps:

1. Select the source whose Content pane you want to customize. Its contents will appear in the Content pane.

2. Choose **Edit**, **View Options** or press **Ctrl+J** (Windows) or ⌘**+J** (Mac). You will see the View Options dialog box (see Figure 16.14). At the top of the dialog box, you see the source for which you are configuring the Content pane. (In Figure 16.14, it is a playlist called Johnny Cash.) You also see all the available columns that can be displayed. If a column's check box is checked, that column will be displayed; otherwise, it won't be shown.

FIGURE 16.14

You can set the columns shown in the Content pane with the View Options dialog box.

View Options

🎵 Johnny Cash

Show Columns

☑ Album   ☐ Grouping
☑ Artist   ☐ Kind
☐ Beats Per Minute   ☑ Last Played
☐ Bit Rate   ☑ My Rating
☐ Comment   ☑ Play Count
☐ Composer   ☐ Sample Rate
☐ Date Added   ☐ Size
☐ Date Modified   ☑ Time
☐ Disc Number   ☑ Track Number
☐ Equalizer   ☐ Year
☑ Genre

Cancel   OK

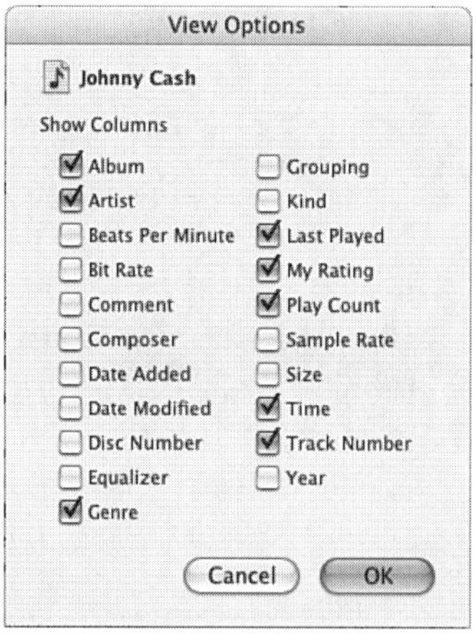

3. Check the check boxes next to the columns you want to see.

4. Uncheck the check boxes next to the columns you don't want to see.

5. Click **OK**. When you return to the Content pane, only the columns you selected will be shown (see Figure 16.15).

If you can't see all the columns being displayed, use the horizontal scrollbar to scroll in the Content pane. You can also use the vertical scroll bar to move up and down in the Content pane.

FIGURE 16.15

If you could view
all the columns
in this Content
pane, you would
see that they cor-
respond to the
check boxes
checked in the
previous figure.

Following are some other ways to customize the
Content pane:

- You can change the width of columns by
  pointing to the line that marks the bound-
  ary of the column in the column heading
  section. When you do, the cursor will
  become a vertical line with arrows pointing
  to the left and right. Drag this to the left to
  make a column narrower or to the right to
  make it wider. The rest of the columns will
  move around to accommodate the change.

- You can change the order in which columns
  appear by dragging a column heading to
  the left or to the right. When you release the
  mouse button, the column will assume its
  new position and the other columns will move to accommodate it.

note

The only column you
can't change (width or location) is the first one (which usually
displays the track if you are viewing
a CD or playlist and is empty when
you are viewing your Library).

- As you learned when playing a CD, you can sort the Content pane using any
  of the columns by clicking the column heading by which you want the pane
  to be sorted. The songs will be sorted according to that criterion, and the column heading will be highlighted to show it is the current sort column. To
  change the direction of the sort, click the **sort order triangle**, which
  appears only in the Sort column. When you play a source, the songs will play
  according to the order in which they are sorted in the Content pane, starting
  from the top of the pane and playing toward the bottom.

THE ABSOLUTE MINIMUM

Hopefully this chapter turned out to be more exciting than you might have expected based on its title. Although labeling your music might not be fun in itself, it does enable you to do fun things. Setting options for your music enables you to enhance your listening experience, and adding and viewing artwork is fun. Finally, you saw that the Content pane can be customized to your preferences. As we leave this chapter, here are some nuggets for you to chew on:

- If iTunes can't find information about a CD, you can enter that information yourself by using the Info window that you learned about in this chapter.

- If you want to check for information about a CD on command, choose **Advanced**, **Get CD Track Names**. (You can also use this command if you turned off the preference that allows iTunes to perform this task automatically.) iTunes will connect to the Internet and attempt to get the CD's information.

- Occasionally, iTunes will find more than one CD that seems to be the one it looked for. When this happens, you will see a dialog box that lists each candidate that iTunes found. Select the information you want to apply to the CD by clicking one of the candidates.

- You can submit track names for a CD. Label the CD and select it. Then choose **Advanced**, **Submit CD Track Information**. The CD's information will be uploaded into the CDDB and will be provided to other people who use the same CD.

- When adding artwork to songs, you aren't limited to just the related album cover. You can associate any kind of graphics with your songs. For example, you can use pictures of the artists, scenes that relate to the music, pictures you have taken that remind you of the music, and so on.

- If you have looked at the figures in this chapter, you should be able to guess who one of my favorite artists is. Can you remember that far back?

17

CREATING, CONFIGURING, AND USING PLAYLISTS

Of all the cool features that iTunes offers (and as you have seen, there are lots of cool features), this chapter's topic—playlists—just might be the coolest of them all. Playlists enable you to listen to exactly the music you want to hear, when and how you want to hear it. Do you love a CD but hate a song or two on it? Fine, just set up a playlist without the offensive song. Wish that you could hear different songs from a variety of albums? No problem. Ever thought that it would be neat if you could pick a style of music and hear your favorites tunes in that style? What about if the tunes you hear are selected for you automatically based on your preferences? With iTunes playlists, you can do all that and more.

Understanding Playlists

Simply put, playlists are custom collections of songs that you create or that iTunes creates for you based on criteria you define. After a playlist has been created, you can listen to it, put it on a CD, move it to your iPod, share it over a network, and more.

There are two kinds of playlists: standard playlists and smart playlists.

The Standard-But-Very-Useful Playlist

A standard playlist (which I'll call just *playlist* from here on) is a set of songs you define manually. You put the specific songs you want in a playlist and do what you will with them. You can include the same song multiple times, mix and match songs from many CDs, put songs in any order you choose, and, basically, control every aspect of that music collection (see Figure 17.1).

In the Source List, the playlist icon is a blue box with a musical note in its center (see Figure 17.1). A smart playlist has a purple box with a gear inside it (see Figure 17.2).

FIGURE 17.1

Here is a standard playlist that contains a wide variety of tunes from an assortment of artists.

Playlists are very useful for creating CDs or making specific music to which you might want to listen available at the click of the mouse. With a playlist, you can determine exactly what songs are included and the order in which those songs play. Playlists are also very easy to create and they never change over time—unless you purposefully change them of course.

The Extra-Special Smart Playlist

A smart playlist is smart because you don't put songs in it manually. Instead, you tell iTunes what kind of songs you want included in it by the attributes of that music, such as genre or artist, and iTunes picks those songs for you (see Figure 17.2). For example, you can create a playlist based on a specific genre, such as Jazz, that you have listened to in the past few days. You can also tell iTunes how many songs to include.

caution

Creating smart playlists depends on your music being properly tagged with information, such as genre, artist, song names, and so on. Sometimes music you add to your Library, such as by adding MP3 files that are stored on your hard drive to it, won't have all this information. Before you get going with smart playlists, make sure you have your music properly labeled and categorized. Chapter 16, "Labeling, Categorizing, and Configuring Your Music," explains how you do this.

FIGURE 17.2

On the surface, a smart playlist doesn't look all that different from a playlist, but when you take a closer look, you will see that a smart playlist lives up to its name.

The really cool thing is that smart playlists can be dynamic, meaning that the songs they contain are updated live, based on your criteria. As you add, listen to, or change your music, the contents of a smart playlist can change to match those changes; this happens in real time so that the songs included in a smart playlist can change too. Imagine that you have a smart playlist that tells iTunes to include all the music you have in the Jazz genre that is performed by Kenny G, the Pat Metheny Group, Joe Sample, and Larry Carlton. If you make this a "live" smart playlist, iTunes will automatically add any new music from any of the artists to it as you add that music to your Library. The content of a live smart playlist changes over time, depending on the criteria it contains.

note

Whether it's a standard playlist or a smart playlist, the playlist is the staring point for some iTunes activities such as burning a CD. And much of the time, a playlist makes listening to specific music easy and fast.

Building and Listening to Standard Playlists

Although they aren't as smart as their younger siblings, standard playlists are definitely very useful because you can choose the exact songs included in them and the order in which those songs will play. In this section, you will learn how to create, manage, and use playlists.

Creating a Standard Playlist

You have two ways to create a playlist. One is to create a playlist that is empty (meaning that it doesn't include any songs). The other is to choose songs and then create a playlist that includes those songs.

The place you start depends on what you have in mind. If you want to create a collection of songs, but aren't sure which specific songs you want to start with, create an empty playlist. If you know of some songs that you are going to included, choose them and create the playlist. Either way, creating a playlist is simple and you end up in the same place.

Creating an Empty Standard Playlist

You can create an empty playlist from within iTunes by using any of the following techniques:

■ Choosing **File**, **New Playlist**.

■ Pressing **Ctrl+N** (Windows) or ⌘**+N** (Mac).

■ Clicking the **Create Playlist** button (see Figure 17.3).

FIGURE 17.3

This playlist has been created and is ready to be renamed.

New playlist

Create playlist

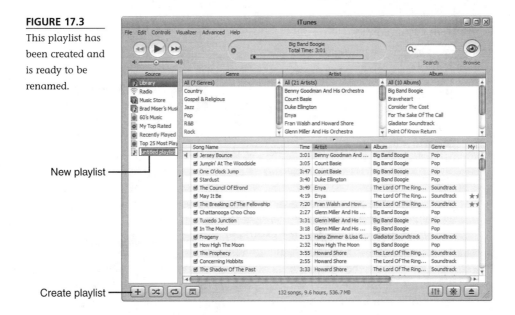

Whichever method you use will result in an empty playlist whose name will be highlighted to show you that it is ready for you to edit. Type a name for the playlist and press **Enter** (Windows) or **Return** (Mac). The playlist will be renamed and selected. The Content pane will be empty because you haven't added any songs to the playlist yet. You will learn how to do that in the section called "Adding Songs to a Playlist" on page **259**.

Creating a Standard Playlist with Songs in It

If you know some songs you want to place in a playlist, you can create the playlist so that it includes those songs as soon as you create it. Here are the steps to follow:

tip

Remember that you can choose a group of songs that are next to one another by holding down the Shift key while you click them. You can choose multiple songs that aren't next to one another by holding down the **Ctrl** key (Windows) or the ⌘ key (Mac) while you click them.

1. Browse or search the Library to find the songs you want to be included in the playlist. For example, you can browse for all the songs in a specific genre or search for music by a specific artist.

2. In the Content pane, select the songs you want to place in the playlist.

3. Choose **File**, **New Playlist from Selection**. A new playlist will appear on the Source List and will be selected. Its name will be highlighted to indicate that you can edit it, and you will see the songs you selected in the Content pane (see Figure 17.4).

    iTunes will attempt to name the playlist by looking for a common denominator in the group of songs you selected. For example, if all the songs are from the same artist, that artist's name will be the playlist's name. Similarly, if the songs are all from the same album, the playlist's name will be the artist's and album's name. Sometimes iTunes picks an appropriate name, and sometimes it doesn't.

> **tip**
>
> You can also create a new playlist containing one or more songs by selecting the songs and pressing **Ctrl+Shift+N** (Windows) or **⌘+Shift+N** (Mac). Alternatively, you can select songs and then hold down the **Shift** key (Windows) or **Option** key (Mac) and click the **Create Playlist** button (which becomes the **Create Smart Playlist** button when you press the listed key).

FIGURE 17.4

Because I created a playlist from selected songs, the new playlist contains the songs I selected when I created it.

4. While the playlist name is highlighted, edit the name as needed and then press **Enter** (Windows) or **Return** (Mac). The playlist will be ready for more songs.

Adding Songs to a Playlist

The whole point of creating a playlist is to add songs to it. Whether you created an empty playlist or one that already has some songs in it, the steps to add songs are the same:

1. Select the Library as the source.

2. Browse or search the Library so that songs you want to add to the playlist are shown in the Content pane.

3. Select the songs you want to add to the playlist by clicking them (remember the techniques to select multiple songs at the same time). To select all the songs currently shown in the Content pane, press **Ctrl+A** (Windows) or ⌘**+A** (Mac).

4. Drag the selected songs from the Content pane onto the playlist to which you want to add them. When the playlist becomes highlighted and the cursor includes a plus sign (+), release the mouse button (see Figure 17.5). The songs will be added to the playlist.

5. Repeat steps 2 through 4 until you have added all the songs you want to include in the playlist.

6. Select the playlist on the Source List. Its songs will appear in the Content pane (see Figure 17.6). Information about the playlist, such as its playing time, will appear in the Source Information area at the bottom of the iTunes window.

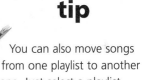

tip

For still another way to create a playlist, try this: Select a group of songs and drag them onto the Source List. When you do so, iTunes will do the same thing as it does when you create a playlist using the steps in this section.

tip

You can also move songs from one playlist to another one. Just select a playlist instead of the Library in step 1.

You can select the same song to a playlist as many times as you'd like to hear it.

note

The Source Information area becomes very important when you are creating a CD because you can use this to make sure a playlist will fit onto a CD.

You add songs to a playlist by dragging them onto the playlist in the Source pane.

This playlist, called (in a burst of creativity) "Soundtracks," contains music from some of my favorite soundtrack CDs.

Removing Songs from a Playlist

If you decide that you don't want one or more songs included in a playlist, select the songs you want to remove in the playlist's Content pane and press the **Delete** key. A warning prompt will appear. Click **Yes** and the songs will be deleted from the playlist. (If this dialog box annoys you like it does me, check the **Do not ask me again** check box and you won't ever have to see it again.)

Setting the Order in Which a Playlist's Songs Play

Just like an audio CD, the order in which a playlist's songs play is determined by the order in which they appear in the Content pane (the first song will be the one at the top of the window, the second will be the next one down, and so on). You can drag songs up on the list to make them play earlier or down in the list to make them play later.

Listening to a Standard Playlist

After you have created a playlist, you can listen to it by selecting it on the Source List and using the same controls you use to listen to a CD or music in the Library. You can even search in and browse playlists just as you can the Library or CDs. (That's the real beauty of iTunes; it works the same way no matter what the music source is!)

Deleting a Standard Playlist

If you decide you no longer want a playlist, you can delete it by selecting the playlist on the Source List and pressing the **Delete** key. A prompt will appear; click **Yes** and the playlist will be removed from the Source List. (Make sure to check the **Do not ask me again** check box if

note

When you delete a song from a playlist, it *isn't* deleted from the Library. It remains there so you can add it to a different playlist or listen to it from the Library.

tip

You can also change the order in which songs will play by sorting the playlist by its columns. You do this by clicking the column title in the column by which you want the Content pane sorted. You can set the columns that appear for a playlist by using the **Edit**, **View Options** command, as you learned to do in the previous chapter.

You can use the iTunes Shuffle and Repeat features with playlists just like you can use them with other sources. For example, to hear the songs in a playlist in a random order, select the playlist you want to hear and click the Shuffle button. The songs will playback in random order.

you don't want to be prompted in the future.) Even though you've deleted the playlist, the songs in the playlist remain in the Library for your listening pleasure.

Becoming a Musical Genius with Smart Playlists

The basic purpose of a smart playlist is the same as a standard playlist—that is, to contain a collection of songs to which you can listen, put on a CD, and so on. However, the path that smart playlists take to this end is different from standard playlists. Rather than choosing specific songs as you do in a standard playlist, you tell iTunes the kind of songs you want in your smart playlist, and it picks out the songs for you and places them in the playlist. For example, suppose you want to create a playlist that contains all of your Classical music. Rather than picking out all the songs in your Library that have the Classical genre (as you would do to create a standard playlist), you can use a smart playlist to tell iTunes to choose all the Classical music for you. The application then gathers all the music with the genre Classical and places that music in a smart playlist.

Understanding Why Smart Playlists Are Called Smart

You create a smart playlist by defining a set of criteria based on any number of different attributes. After you have created these criteria, iTunes chooses songs that meet those criteria and places them in the playlist. An example should help clarify this. Suppose you are a big-time Elvis fan and regularly add Elvis music to your Library. You could create a playlist and manually drag your new Elvis tunes to that playlist. But by using a smart playlist instead, you could define the playlist to include all your Elvis music. Anytime you add more Elvis music to your Library, that music would be added to the playlist automatically.

You can also base a smart playlist on more than one attribute at the same time. Going back to the Elvis example, you could add the condition that you want only those songs you have rated four stars or higher so that the smart playlist contains only your favorite Elvis songs.

note

iTunes includes several smart playlists by default. These include 60's Music (music based on the Year attribute being 1960 to 1969), My Top Rated (all the music you have rated three stars or above), Recently Played (songs you have played within the past two weeks), and Top 25 Most Played (the 25 songs you have played most often). To see the songs that meet these conditions, select a smart playlist and you will see its songs in the Content pane.

As the previous example shows, smart playlists can be dynamic; iTunes calls this *live updating*. When a smart playlist is set to be live, iTunes changes its contents over time to match the criteria. If this feature isn't set for a smart playlist, that playlist will contain only those songs that meet the criteria at the time the playlist was created.

Finally, you can also link a smart playlist's conditions by the logical expression All or Any. If you use an All logical expression, all the conditions must be true for a song to be included in the smart playlist. If you use the Any option, only one of the conditions has to be met for a song to be included in the smart playlist.

Creating a Smart Playlist

You can create a smart playlist by performing the following steps:

1. Choose **File**, **New Smart Playlist** or hold down the **Shift** (Windows) or **Option** (Mac) key and click the **New Playlist** button, which becomes the **New Smart Playlist** button when the **Shift** or **Option** key is pressed down. You will see the Smart Playlist dialog box (see Figure 17.7).

> **tip**
>
> You can also create a new smart playlist by pressing **Ctrl+Alt+N** (Windows) or **Option+⌘+N** (Mac).

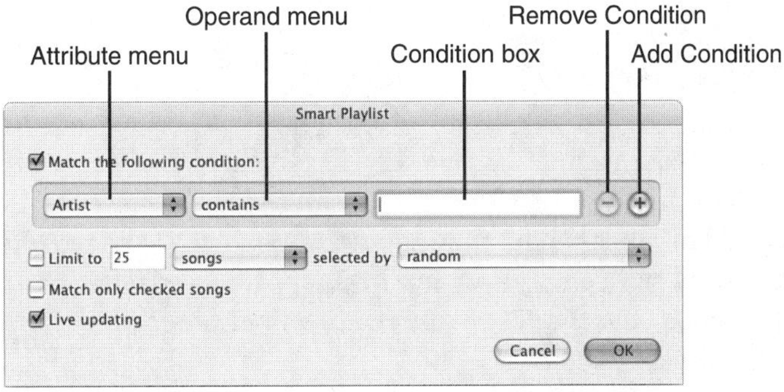

FIGURE 17.7

The Smart Playlist dialog box enables you to create playlists based on a single attribute or many of them.

2. Choose the first attribute on which you want the smart playlist to be based in the Attribute menu. For example, you can choose Artist, Genre, My Rating, Year, and so on. The Operand menu will be updated so that it is applicable to the attribute you selected. For example, if you choose Artist, the Operand menu will include Contains, Does Not Contain, Is, Is Not, Starts With, and Ends With.

3. Choose the operand you want to use in the **Operand** menu. For example, if you want to match data exactly, choose Is. If you want the condition to be more loose, choose Contains.

4. Type the condition you want to match in the **Condition** box. The more you type, the more specific the condition will be. As an example, if you choose Artist in step 1, Contains in step 2, and type **Elvis** in this step, the condition would look like the one shown in Figure 17.8 and would find all songs that include Elvis, Elvis Presley, Elvis Costello, Elvisiocity, and so on. If you typed **Elvis Presley** in the Condition box and left the Contains operand, iTunes would only include songs whose artist includes Elvis Presley, such as Elvis Presley, Elvis Presley and His Back-up Band, and so on.

> **note**
>
> As you make selections on the Attribute menu and type conditions in the Condition box, iTunes will attempt to automatically match what you type to data from the songs in your Library. If your Library includes Elvis music and you use Artist as an attribute, iTunes will enter Elvis Presley in the Condition box for you.

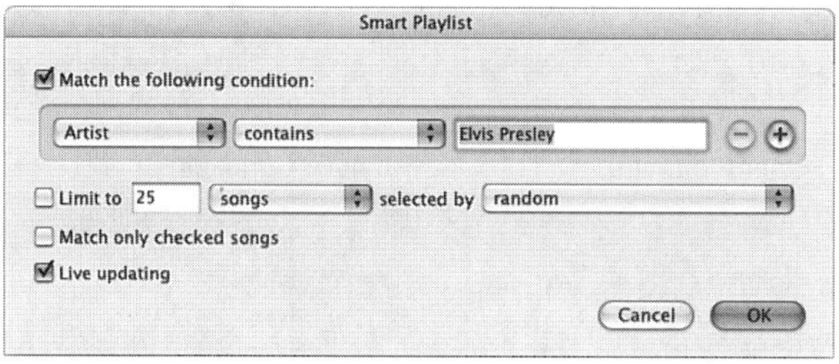

FIGURE 17.8

This smart playlist is getting smarter.

5. To add another condition to the smart playlist, click the **Add Condition** button. A new, empty condition will appear (see Figure 17.9). At the top of the dialog box, the All or Any menu will also appear.

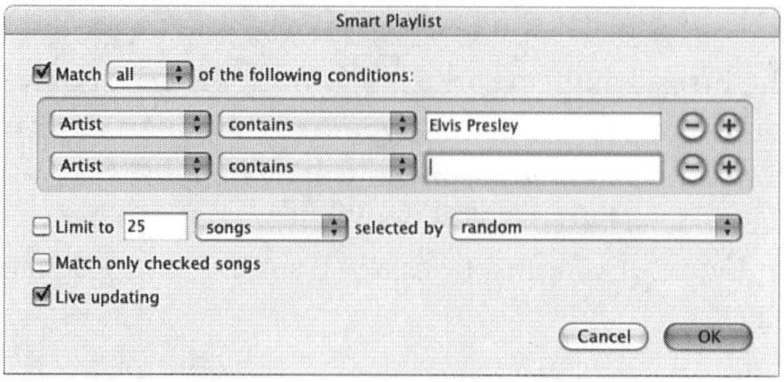

FIGURE 17.9

This smart playlist now contains two conditions; both are currently based on Artist.

6. Choose the second attribute on which you want the smart playlist to be based in the second condition's **Attribute** menu. For example, if you want to include songs from a specific genre, choose **Genre** on the menu.

7. Choose the operand you want to use in the **Operand** menu, such as Contains, Is, and so on.

8. Type the condition you want to match in the **Condition** box. If you selected Genre in step 6, type the genre that the music in the playlist should come from. As you type, iTunes will try to match the genre you type with those in your Library.

9. Repeat steps 6 through 8 to add more conditions to the playlist, until you have all the conditions you want to include (see Figure 17.10).

tip

If you want to remove a condition from a smart playlist, click the Remove button for the condition you want to remove.

FIGURE 17.10

This smart playlist is approaching the genius level; it now includes four conditions.

10. Choose **All** on the menu at the top of the dialog box if all the conditions must be met for a song to be included in the smart playlist, or choose **Any** if only one of them must be met. For example, you could create a smart playlist based on multiple Artist conditions, and the playlist would feature music by those artists. In this case, you would choose Any so that if a song is associated with *any* of the artists for which you created the condition, it would be included in the playlist. As a contrasting example, if you want the playlist to include songs you have rated as three stars or better by a specific artist, you would include both of these conditions and then choose All in the menu so that both conditions would have to be met for a song to be included.

You can limit the length of a smart playlist based on a maximum number of songs, the time it plays, or the size of the files it includes. You set these limits using the Limit to check box and menus.

11. If you want to limit the playlist, check the **Limit to** check box. If you don't want to set a limit on the playlist, leave the check box unchecked and skip to step 15.

12. Choose the attribute by which you want to limit the playlist in the first menu; by default, this menu has Songs selected (see Figure 17.11). Your choices include the number of songs (just the songs on the menu), the time the playlist will play (in minutes or hours), and the size of the files the playlist contains (in GB or MB).

note

If you include more than one condition based on the same attribute, you usually don't want to use the All option because the conditions will likely be mutually exclusive, and using the All option will result in no songs being included in the playlist, because no song will be able to meet all the conditions at the same time.

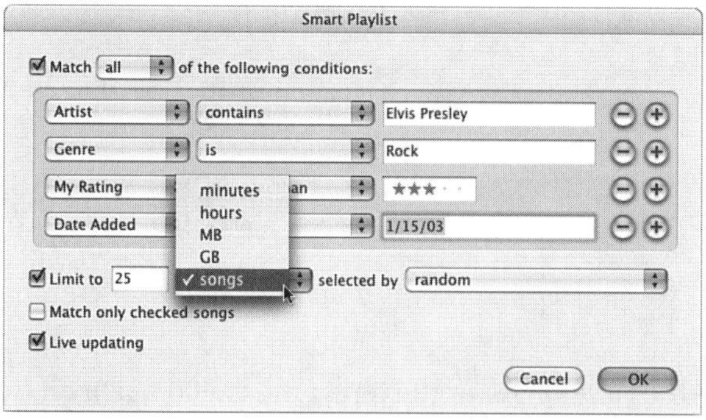

FIGURE 17.11

You can choose to limit a smart playlist to a number of songs, a length of time, or by disk space.

13. Type the data appropriate for the limit you selected in the **Limit to** box. For example, if you selected Minutes in the menu, type the maximum length of the playlist in minutes in the box. If you selected Songs, enter the maximum number of songs that can be included in the playlist.

14. Choose how you want iTunes to choose the songs it includes based on the limit you selected by using the **selected by** menu. This menu has many options, including to choose songs randomly, based on your rating, how often the songs are played, and so on (see Figure 17.12).

15. If you want the playlist to include only songs
    whose Selected box in the Content pane is
    checked, check the **Match only checked
    songs** check box. If you leave this check
    box unchecked, iTunes will include all songs
    that meet the playlist's conditions, even if
    you have unchecked their Selected check
    box in the Content pane.

16. If you want the playlist to be dynamic,
    meaning that iTunes will update its con-
    tents over time, check the **Live updating**
    check box. If you uncheck this check box,
    the playlist will include only those songs
    that meet the playlist's conditions when you
    create it.

17. Review the playlist to see whether it con-
    tains the conditions and settings you want
    (see Figure 17.13).

note

The smart playlist I
built as an example in
these steps can be interpreted as
follows: Include songs by Elvis
Presley in the Rock genre that I
have rated at three stars or more
and that I added to my Library
after 1/15/03. Limit the playlist to
90 minutes, and if I have more
songs that meet the conditions
than this time limit allows, randomly choose the songs to
include. Include only songs I
haven't skipped and keep adding
songs that meet the conditions as
I add them to my Library.

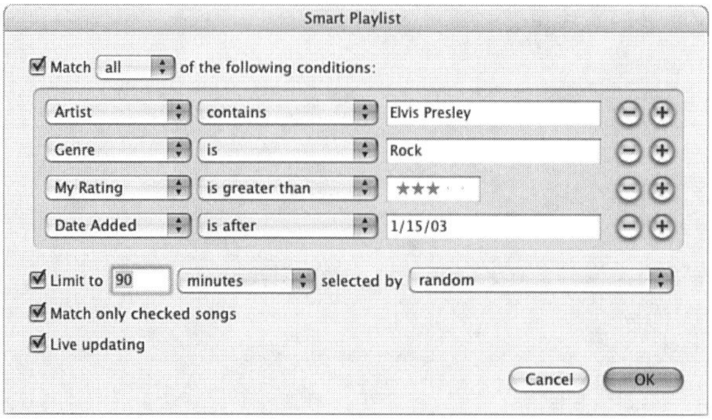

FIGURE 17.13

This playlist will include up to 90 minutes of the best of my Elvis music from the Rock genre; as I add music to my Library, it will also be added to this playlist if it meets these conditions.

18. Click **OK** to create the playlist. You will move to the Source List, the smart playlist will be added and selected, and its name will be ready for you to edit. Also, the current contents of the playlist will be shown in the Content pane.

19. Type the playlist's name and press **Enter** (Windows) or **Return** (Mac). The smart playlist is complete (see Figure 17.14).

Listening to a Smart Playlist

Listening to a smart playlist is just like listening to other sources: You select it on the Source List and use the playback controls to listen to it. The one difference is that if a smart playlist is set to be live, its contents can change over time.

note

Just like other sources, when you select a smart playlist, its information will be shown in the Source Information section at the bottom of the window. This can be useful if you want to create a CD or just to see how big the playlist is (by number of songs, time, or file size).

FIGURE 17.14

FIGURE 17.14

If you compare the songs in this smart playlist to the criteria shown in the previous figure, you will see they match.

Changing a Smart Playlist

To change the contents of a smart playlist, you change the smart playlist's criteria (remember that iTunes actually places songs in a smart playlist). Use the following steps to do this:

1. Select the smart playlist you want to change.

2. Choose **File**, **Edit Smart Playlist**. The Smart Playlist dialog box will appear. The playlist's current criteria will be shown.

3. Use the techniques you learned when you created a playlist to change its criteria. For example, you can remove conditions by clicking their Remove button. You can also add more conditions or change the other settings for the playlist.

4. Click **OK**. Your changes will be saved and the contents of the playlist will be updated to match the current criteria (see Figure 17.15).

> **tip**
>
> You can also edit a smart playlist by selecting it and opening the Info window (which also opens the Smart Playlist dialog box). You can also open the playlist's contextual menu by right-clicking (Windows or Mac) or Ctrl-clicking it (Mac) and choosing Edit Smart Playlist.

FIGURE 17.15

I changed the conditions on this smart playlist so that only five-star songs are included.

You can also change a smart playlist using the same techniques you use on other sources, such as sorting it, choosing the columns you see when you view it, and so on.

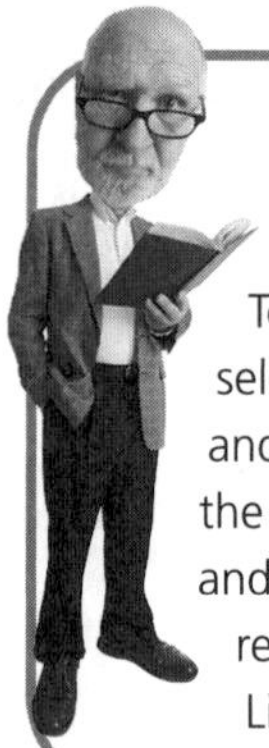

tip

To delete a smart playlist, select it on the Source List and press **Delete**. Confirm the deletion at the prompt, and the playlist will be removed from the Source List.

THE ABSOLUTE MINIMUM

Playlists are a great way to customize the music in your Library for listening purposes, to create a CD, or to manage the music on an iPod. As you learned in this chapter, playlists include a specific collection of songs that you choose, whereas iTunes chooses the songs in a smart playlist based on the conditions you specify.

Playlists are a great way to select specific music to which you want to listen. You can make them as long or as short as you like, and you can mix and match songs to your heart's content.

Smart playlists can really enhance your listening experience. Following are some ideas you might find interesting for smart playlists:

- Be diligent about rating your songs. Then create a smart playlist for one of your favorite genres that also includes a rating condition. Enable this playlist to be updated live. Such a playlist would always contain your favorites songs in this genre, even as you add more songs to your Library.

- Create a smart playlist based only on genre and allow it to be updated live. This playlist would make it easy to listen to that genre, and it would always contain all your music in that genre.

- Create a smart playlist that includes several of your favorite artists (remember to choose **Any** in the top menu) and limit the number of songs to 20 or so. Have iTunes choose the songs in random order. Playing this playlist might provide an interesting mix of music. If you include a My Rating condition, you can cause only your favorite music to be included in this group. Make a dynamic list, and it will change over time as you add music to your Library.

- If you like to collect multiple versions of the same song, create a playlist based on song name. Allow it to be updated live, and this playlist will contain all the versions of this song you have in your Library.

18

EQUALIZING YOUR MUSIC

In addition to the great tools iTunes provides to enable you to choose which music you want to listen to, the application also enables you to control *how* that music sounds. You do this with the Equalizer. Using this feature, you can customize how music sounds to suit your system, hearing, and listening preferences.

Touring the iTunes Equalizer

Like a hardware graphic equalizer, the iTunes Equalizer enables you to change the relative volume levels of various frequencies of the sounds of which music is made (see Figure 18.1).

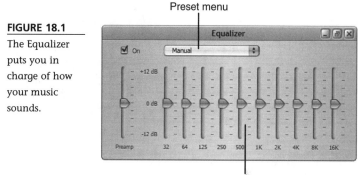

Preset menu

FIGURE 18.1

The Equalizer puts you in charge of how your music sounds.

Frequency sliders

To open the Equalizer, click the **Equalizer** button on the right side of the bottom of the iTunes window (it contains three blue sliders). On Macintoshes, you can also open the Equalizer by choosing **Window**, **Equalizer** or by pressing ⌘+2. The Equalizer window will appear.

At the top of the window, you will see the On check box. When this is checked, the Equalizer is active and will affect how your music sounds. If the check box is not checked, the Equalizer settings don't impact the way your music sounds. When you see the values in the Equalizer window, remember that they are all relative and only change the volume of frequencies relative to one another, not the volume of your system.

Along the left side of the window is the Preamp slider. The Preamp setting changes the relative volumes of all the frequencies at the same time. For example, if a song is recorded at a low volume level, you can drag the Preamp slider up to make its relative volume louder. Similarly, you can drag the slider down to make a song's relative volume level lower.

> **note**
>
> The abbreviation dB stands for *decibels*, which is a measure of the power of sound. Sounds with higher decibels are louder. The decibel measurements are on a logarithmic scale, which means they do not follow a linear progression. In other words, 100 dB is not 10 times louder than 10 dB. To give you an example of this, normal human conversation is about 60 dB, whereas a jet engine at close range is about 150 dB.

The bulk of the window consists of a set of sliders that control the relative volume of a number of sound frequencies that are listed underneath the sliders, from 32Hz to 16KHz (kilohertz). The left end of the range represents lower or bass sound, whereas the middle is the mid-range and the right end is the higher or treble sound. The sliders all have a range of –12 to +12 decibels (dB). Again, this is relative to 0, which means the volume level is not affected.

Above the frequency sliders and to the right of the On check box is the Presets menu. Presets are collections of slider settings, and you can choose to apply them without having to adjust each slider individually. iTunes includes a number of presets, and you can create and save your own presets in the menu.

You can use the Equalizer in a couple of ways: You can set it for all the music you are listening to at a specific time, or you can associate a specific preset with a song so those settings will be used each time that song plays. As you play with the Equalizer, realize that there are no right or wrong settings. It is entirely up to your listening pleasure. If some adjustment makes the music sound "worse" to you, go onto something else. You might find that some of the default presets don't help the way the music sounds at all. It is all relative to your speakers, the music to which you are listening, and your musical ear.

Configuring the Equalizer Manually

To configure the Equalizer manually, perform the following steps:

1. Select some **music**, such as a playlist, and play it.
2. Open the Equalizer.
3. Check the **On** check box, if it isn't checked already. This makes the Equalizer active.
4. Choose **Manual** on the Presets slider. This puts the Equalizer in the Manual mode. If you make an adjustment to any of the sliders, the Equalizer will switch to the Manual mode automatically.
5. If you want to change the relative volume of all the songs you are playing, drag the Preamp slider up to make the music louder or down to make the music quieter.
6. Set each of the frequency sliders to change the relative volume of that frequency. Drag a slider up to make its frequency louder or down to make it quieter. For example, to make music more bassy, drag the sliders for the lower end of the frequency scale up. This will increase the volume of lower sounds and make the bass components of music more prominent. Adjust the other sliders to change the relative volumes of their frequencies until the music sounds "better" to you (see Figure 18.2).

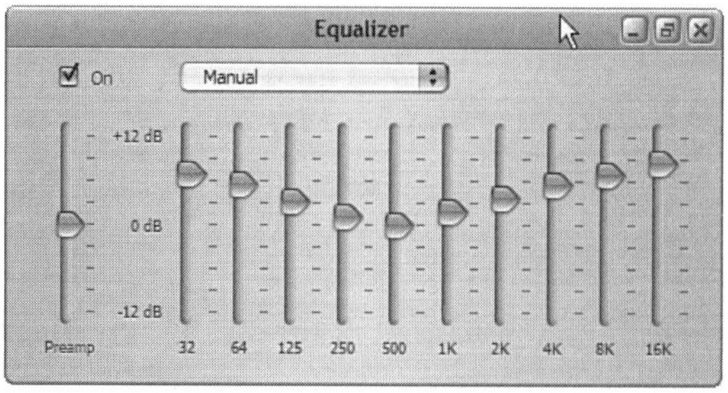

FIGURE 18.2

It's all relative; this classic equalizer pattern enhances both the bass and treble components of music.

7. When you are done making changes, you can click in the iTunes window to make it active or close the Equalizer to get it out of the way (it continues to work even if you can't see it).

Working with Presets

Dragging all the sliders up and down is lots of fun and all, but it isn't something you are likely to want to do a lot. Presets are collections of slider settings that you can apply just by choosing one on the Presets menu. You can use iTunes' default presets or you can create your own.

Selecting a Default Preset

Working with iTunes' default presets is a snap, as you can see from the following steps:

1. Play some music.

2. Open the Equalizer and turn it on.

3. Open the Presets menu (see Figure 18.3). At the bottom of the menu, you will see the set of default presets available to you.

4. Choose the preset you want to apply. When you return to the Equalizer window, the sliders will be set according to the preset you selected (see Figure 18.4).

5. Continue choosing presets until the music sounds just right. The specific slider settings you should use depend on many factors, including your sound system, the music to which you are listening, and last, but certainly not least, your personal preferences. For example, if you use speakers that have poor bass performance, you might want to consistently use higher bass settings (assuming you like to hear lots of bass of course). If you have a system with a powerful subwoofer, you might not need any bass enhancement.

FIGURE 18.3

Are there enough presets for you?

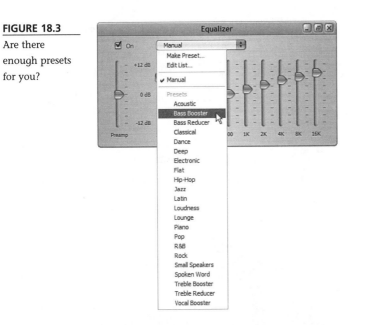

FIGURE 18.4

The Bass Booster preset does just what it sounds like it will.

Creating Your Own Presets

If none of the default presets are quite right, you can create your own presets so that you can return to a specific Equalizer configuration easily and quickly. This is useful when a preset of your own making is just what you like and you want to be able to go back to it easily. A good way to create custom presets is to choose one of the default presets and make changes to it. Then, you can save the preset with your changes as a new preset. To create a preset, follow these steps:

1. Open the Equalizer, turn it on, and set its sliders to the settings you want to reuse.

2. Open the Presets menu and choose **Make Preset**. You'll see the Make Preset dialog box (see Figure 18.5).

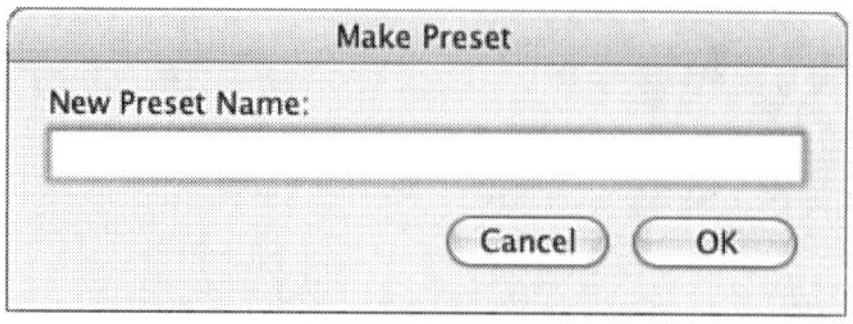

FIGURE 18.5

To save your custom Equalizer settings, you can create your own presets.

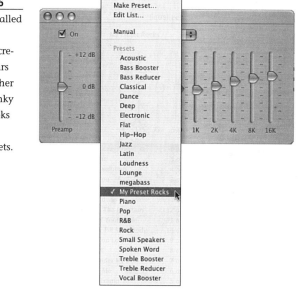

FIGURE 18.6

The preset called "My Preset Rocks" is a creation of yours truly, but other than the funky name, it looks just like the default presets.

3. In the New Preset Name box, type a name for your preset.

4. Click **OK**. The preset will be added to the Presets menu, and you can choose it just like one of the defaults (see Figure 18.6).

Configuring the Preset Menu

As you saw in the previous section, you can add presets to the Presets menu. You can also remove presets from it to create a custom Presets menu. For example, you might want to get rid of presets you will never use so that the menu offers fewer choices. Or, you might want to rename a preset. To do these tasks, use the following steps:

1. Open the Presets menu and choose **Edit List**. The Edit Presets dialog box will appear (see Figure 18.7).

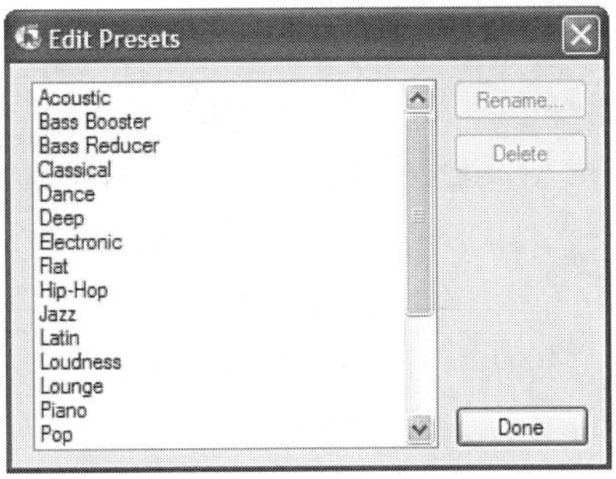

FIGURE 18.7

You can customize the Presets menu so it contains only those presets that are useful to you.

2. To remove a preset from the menu, select it, click **Delete**, and confirm your decision at the prompt by clicking **Yes**. You will see a prompt asking you if you want to remove the preset from the songs that are set to use it as well (you'll learn about this in the next section); click **Yes** if you want to remove the preset from the songs or **No** if you want to retain the settings even though the preset will be removed from the menu. The preset will be removed from the menu.

3. To rename a preset, select it and click **Rename**. The Rename dialog box will appear. Type a new name for the preset and click **OK**. It will be renamed on the menu.

Setting the Equalizer for Specific Songs

You can apply specific Equalizer presets to individual songs so that those songs will always play with the settings you associate with them. You can do this from the Info window or from the Content pane.

There are several situations in which you might want to set the Equalizer for specific songs. One case might be for songs whose recording level is so low that you have a hard time hearing it—you can use a preset so that its volume level is adjusted automatically each time you play it. Or, you might like to use different presets with different types of music. By applying a preset to the songs of a specific type, that preset will be used whenever those songs are played. Suppose you like to listen to both Classical and Rock and have a preset for each. By associating a preset with the Classical music and another with the Rock music, the appropriate preset will be used when you play that music.

Setting the Equalizer in the Info Window

To configure the Equalizer for a specific song, perform the following steps:

1. Select the song to which you want to apply Equalizer settings and open the Info window.

2. Click the **Options tab**.

3. Choose the preset you want to apply to the song in the Equalizer Preset menu (see Figure 18.8).

FIGURE 18.8

Remember the preset "My Preset Rocks" from earlier in the chapter? It's back....

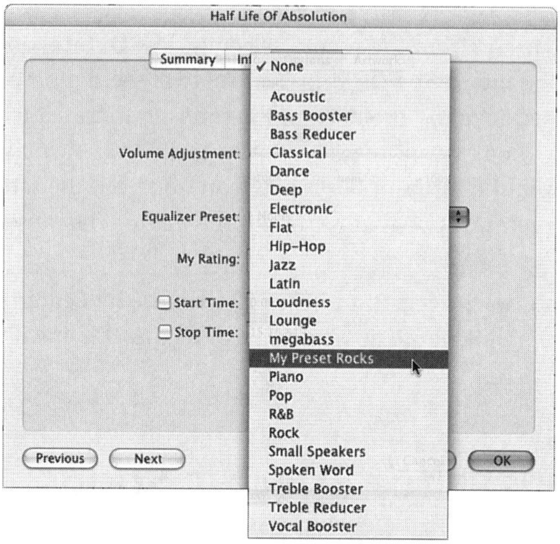

4. Click **OK**. The Info window will close and the preset will be associated with the song.

Assuming that the Equalizer is turned on, the preset you associate with a song will be used each time that song plays.

Using the Equalizer from the Content Pane

You can also configure the preset for a song from the Content pane. First, show the Equalizer in the Content pane. Then, you can choose a preset for the song.

Showing the Equalizer in the Content Pane

To show the Equalizer in the Content pane, you use the View Options dialog box to show its column. In case you don't remember how, the following steps will lead the way:

1. Select the source for which you want the Equalizer column to be displayed, such as the Library or a playlist.

2. Open the View Options dialog box by selecting **Edit, View Options**.

3. Check the Equalizer check box and close the dialog box. The Equalizer column will be added to the Content pane for the selected source.

tip

If you can't see the Equalizer column, scroll in the Content pane until you do. Or, drag the Equalizer column to the left in the Content pane so that you can see it more easily.

Setting the Equalizer in the Content Pane

After you have added the Equalizer column to the Content pane, you can easily associate a preset with a song. For the song with which you want to associate a preset, click the button that appears on the left side of the Equalizer column. The Presets menu will appear (see Figure 18.9). Choose the preset you want to apply to the song. It will be used each time the song is played. To change the preset, select a different one or choose **None** to remove the preset from the song.

FIGURE 18.9

Does this menu look familiar to you?

THE ABSOLUTE MINIMUM

You can use the iTunes Equalizer to fine-tune your music to suit your system, your listening tastes, and the kind of music you listen to. Before we leave this topic, here are a few Equalizer tidbits for you:

- You can reduce the Equalizer window so that you see only the On check box and the Presets menu. This makes it easier to keep the window out of your way, but you can still change its settings by choosing presets to apply. To do this on Windows computers, click the **Resize** button on the window's title bar. On Macs, click the **Zoom** button.

- You can apply the same preset to multiple songs at the same time by selecting the songs to which you want to apply the preset and opening the Info window (which becomes the Multiple Song Information window). Choose the preset you want to apply to the selected songs on the Equalizer Preset menu and click **OK**. The preset will be applied to all the songs you selected.

- Which is more decibels, a jet plane engine up close or a typical rock concert in front of the speakers? In general, the noise levels in these environments are roughly the same. Noises at this level can be damaging to your hearing. So if you are hanging out next to jet engines or are planning on going to a rock concert, consider wearing hearing protection. After all, you want to protect your hearing so you can take advantage of iTunes, right?

IN THIS CHAPTER

- Know the three disc formats that you can burn.
- Prepare your computer to burn.
- Burn, baby, burn.

19

BURNING YOUR OWN CDs OR DVDs

When you are at your computer, you'll likely use iTunes to listen to your music because you can easily get to the specific music to which you want to listen, such as by using your Library, creating playlists and smart playlists, and so on. When you are on the move, you'll probably use your iPod to listen to your tunes. At other times, you might want to put music on a CD to take with you, such as when you are traveling in a car with a standard CD player. Or, you might want to back up your music on a DVD to keep your collection safe. Using iTunes, you can quickly and easily burn CDs or DVDs so that they contain any collections of music you want them to.

Understanding the Types of Discs You Can Burn

You can burn several different types of disc formats with iTunes. Each of these formats is useful for specific purposes. With iTunes, you can burn the following types of discs:

- **Audio CD**—When you burn a CD in this format, you can play it in any CD player, such as the one in your car, a boom box, or a home theater. And that is the primary benefit of this format; CD players are ubiquitous, so you can play audio CDs just about anywhere.

- **MP3 CD**—You can place your tunes on a CD in the MP3 format and then play those discs using any player than can handle MP3 music. Many newer CD players for cars and home theater systems can play MP3 CDs, so this is a good thing. The benefit of using the MP3 format is just what you might think it is—you can put about three times as much music on a single disc as you can with a disc that uses the Audio CD format.

- **Data CD or DVD**—This format is the same that's used to store music files on your computer's hard drive. In fact, when you choose this format, you simply replicate songs as they are on your computer on a disc. The primary purpose of this format is to back up your music in order to protect it from loss should something go horribly wrong with your computer.

Getting Your Computer Ready to Burn

In order to burn CDs or DVDs, your computer must have a drive that is capable of writing to CD or DVD. Fortunately, most computers include a CD-RW (CD-Rewritable) drive that you can use to burn CDs. Many also include a DVD-R (DVD Recordable) or DVD-RW (DVD Rewritable) drive that you can use to create DVDs.

To determine if your computer is ready to burn, open the **iTunes Preferences** dialog box and click the **Burning** tab (see Figures 19.1 and 19.2). At the top of this pane, you'll see the text "CD Burner." If iTunes can find one or more drives capable of burning CDs or DVDs, they will be shown here. If iTunes does recognize a drive, you are good to go and can proceed to the next section.

note

In Figure 19.2, you might notice that a menu appears next to the CD Burner text. That's because the machine used for this screenshot includes two drives capable of burning CDs. In this case, you can select from the menu the drive you want iTunes to use to create a disc.

FIGURE 19.1

This Windows
computer has a
CD burner that
is ready to go.

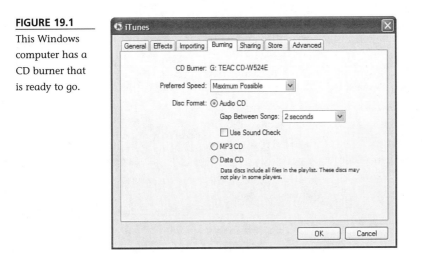

FIGURE 19.2

This Macintosh
includes a DVD-
RW drive that
can be used to
burn CDs or
DVDs.

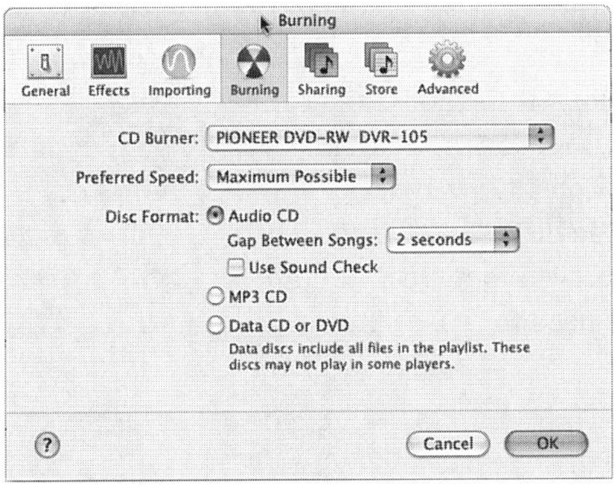

If a drive is not shown on this pane, there are two possibilities. One is that a capable
drive is installed but is not functioning correctly, so it's not recognized by iTunes. The
other is that your computer doesn't have a capable drive at all.

If your computer does have a drive that is capable of writing to a disc, but it is not
recognized by iTunes, it is likely that your drive is not working at all. You'll have to
use troubleshooting techniques to repair and configure the drive to get it working
again. I don't have room in this book to cover this topic because it can be complicated. If you don't know how to do this or you don't know someone who does, you
can consult one of the many books available on this topic to help you get the drive
working properly.

Selecting and installing a CD-RW or DVD-RW drive in your computer is beyond the scope of this book. If your computer doesn't have at least a CD-RW drive, it is likely a fairly old machine because these drives have been standard on most computers for a couple years. If you don't want to purchase a new computer that includes a writable drive, you can purchase an external or internal CD-RW drive and install it in your computer fairly easily.

Burning Discs

Burning a disc from iTunes is quite straightforward, as you will see from the information in this section.

Preparing Content to Burn

The first phase in the process is to choose the content you want to place onto a disc. You do this by creating a playlist. In Chapter 17, "Creating, Configuring, and Using Playlists," you learned everything you need to know about creating and using playlists, so I don't need to repeat that information here.

One thing you need to keep in mind as you create a playlist for CD or DVD is the size of the playlist. Obviously, you can't put more music on a CD or DVD than there is room to store files on the disc. How large a playlist can be to be put on a disc depends on the format you will be using. If you are burning an Audio CD, you can get about 70 minutes of music on the disc. If you are creating an MP3 disc, you can store about 210 minutes on a disc. If you are creating a data DVD, you can store at least 5.2GB of files on a disc.

When you are creating an Audio CD, use the play time to judge the size of the playlist; keep it to 70 minutes plus or minus a couple minutes. For the other formats, use file size (for example, a CD can typically hold 750MB).

note

In many cases, a drive that doesn't work properly can be fixed by updating the driver software for that drive. If you use a Windows computer, you might need to download and install the proper driver from your drive's manufacturer; some drivers will be updated automatically when you run Windows Update. If you use a Mac that includes such a drive, the drivers will be updated when you use the Software Update application.

note

If you choose to burn a playlist that contains more music than will fit on the type of disc you are trying to burn, iTunes will warn you about the situation. Then, you can choose to cancel the burn or you can choose to have iTunes burn the playlist across multiple discs.

In any case, use the Source Information area to check the playlist to make sure it will fit on the type of disc you are going to create (see Figure 19.3).

FIGURE 19.3

This playlist contains 1.2 hours of music, which will be just right for a CD in the Audio CD format.

The name of the playlist will become the name of the CD or DVD, so if you don't want the current playlist name to be used, change it to be what you do want the CD to be called. (To do this, click the playlist name once. It will be highlighted to show you can change it. Type the new name and press **Return** or **Enter**.)

Preparing for a Burn Session

Next, configure the burn session during which you will create a disc by opening the **Burning** pane of the iTunes Preferences dialog box. Choose the format you want to use for the burning session by clicking the appropriate radio button (see Figure 19.4).

If you choose **Audio CD**, there are two options you can configure. One is the gap between songs, which you choose by making a selection on the **Gap Between Songs** menu. Your options are **None**, which causes one song to begin immediately after the previous one ends; **1 second**, which

> The exact amount of music you can fit on a disc depends on your drive and the discs you use. The best way to figure out a maximum limit is to experiment until you find the upper limit for your system and the discs you use.

places 1 second of silence between tracks; **2 seconds**, which places 2 seconds of silence between songs; and so on, up to **5 seconds**. The other option is the **Use Sound Check** box. If you check this box, iTunes applies its Sound Check feature to the music that it places on a disc. (If you don't remember from earlier in the book, this feature causes iTunes to attempt to set the relative volume of the songs you play to the same level.)

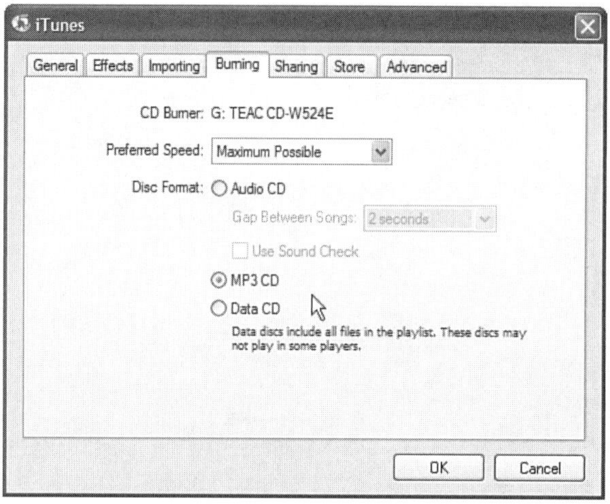

FIGURE 19.4

Because the MP3 CD radio button is selected, the next CD will be burned in that format.

To choose either the MP3 CD or the Data CD or DVD format, simply click the appropriate radio button.

Click **OK** to close the iTunes Preferences dialog box and prepare the burn session.

Burning a Disc

After you have selected the content and prepared the burning session, actually burning the disc is rather anticlimactic. You burn a disc with the following steps:

1. Make sure the playlist you want to burn is selected.

2. Click the **Burn Disc** button. The drive that is configured on the Burning pane of the iTunes Preferences dialog box will open, you will see a prompt in the Information window, and the Burn button will go radioactive (see Figure 19.5).

tip

If you are putting live music on a disc, make sure you choose None on the Gap Between Songs menu. Otherwise, the roar of the crowd will be interrupted by the silent gaps, which causes the live feeling of the tracks to be lost.

FIGURE 19.5

iTunes is ready to burn.

3. Insert the appropriate disc into the drive. If you selected the Audio CD or MP3 CD format, use a CD. If you selected the Data format, use a CD or DVD. iTunes will check the disc you inserted. If everything is ready to go, you will see the "Click Burn Disc to start" prompt in the Information area.

4. Click the **Burn Disc** button again. iTunes will start the burn process and will display information about the process in the Information area (see Figure 19.6).

   When the process is complete, iTunes will play a tone to let you know. The CD will appear on the Source List and will be selected (see Figure 19.7).

5. To eject the disc, click the **Eject** button. You can then use the CD in any player or drive that is compatible with its format.

caution

You may ruin the disc if you click stop before the burn process is finished.

FIGURE 19.6

The playlist
Soundtracks is
being put on
CD.

FIGURE 19.7

The Soundtracks
playlist has
become the
Soundtracks CD.

THE ABSOLUTE MINIMUM

Burning a CD or DVD is useful when you want to listen to music apart from iTunes or from your iPod. It is a relatively simple and very useful process. As you burn, keep the following points in mind:

- There are three types of discs you can burn with iTunes: Audio CD, MP3, and data discs.

- To prepare your computer to burn discs, you use the Burning tab of the iTunes Preferences dialog box to check to see that you have a compatible drive.

- To burn a disc, create a playlist containing the content you want to put on disc, configure the settings for the burn session, and then burn the disc.

- If you can't get discs to burn properly, open the **Burning** pane of the iTunes Preferences dialog box and choose a lower burn speed on the **Preferred Speed** menu. Then try to burn the disc again. Sometimes, using a lower burn speed will correct problems in the burn process.

- The format for a burn session must be compatible with the format of the music you are using. The most likely case that might cause you problems is when you attempt to burn a CD in the MP3 format but the music you are attempting to place on a disc is in the AAC format (such as what you purchase from the iTunes Music Store). In this case, iTunes can't burn the disc because you are trying to place music that is in the AAC format on an MP3 disc. These are different and incompatible formats. If this happens, use the Audio CD or Data CD format instead. Or, if you simply must put AAC music on an MP3 disc, you can do it with the following steps. Set the **Import** preference to the MP3 format (use the Importing pane of the iTunes Preferences dialog box). Then, select the AAC tunes you want to put on an MP3 CD and choose **Advanced, Convert Selection to MP3**. This will create MP3 versions of the selected songs and place them in the Library. Find the MP3 versions (use the **Info** window) and place them in a playlist. Then burn that playlist onto an MP3 CD.

20

SHARING ITUNES MUSIC OVER A NETWORK

If two or more computers are connected via a network—and with the broad use of high-speed Internet connections, networks are becoming common even in homes these days—you can share the music in your iTunes Library with other people on the network. They can listen to that music as if it was stored in their own Libraries. Of course, assuming other folks on your network are also generous, you can listen to music they share with you as well.

Understanding How iTunes Music Sharing Works

When iTunes computers can communicate with each other over a network, they can access the Library stored on each computer. This means that you can see music in other iTunes Libraries, and other computers can see the music stored in your Library (both cases assume that sharing is enabled on your computer).

When music is shared with you, it appears as a network source on your Source List—if more than one source is available, the Shared Music source will appear. When you share your music with others, your music appears as a network source on their Source List. In either case, the person using the computer can select the shared source and listen to it using the same tools used to listen to other sources, such as CDs and playlists.

Even better, Windows and Macintosh users can share music with each other on networks that include both kinds of computers.

To share music with others on your network, you configure iTunes to share its music, which is covered in the next section. To access shared music, you configure iTunes to look for music being shared with you; that is the topic of the "Listening to Music Being Shared with You" section, later in this chapter.

note

In case you are wondering, you can't share iTunes music over the Internet. You can only share on a local network, such as the one in your home or business.

note

This chapter assumes that you have a network set up and that the iTunes computers on that network can communicate with each other. Installing and configuring a network is beyond the scope of this book. If you need help, lots of good networking books are available to you.

Sharing Your iTunes Music with Others

Setting up an iTunes computer to share its music is a two-step process. The first step is to connect your computer to a network. The second step is to configure iTunes to share your music.

You can also use iTunes to see who is accessing the music you have shared.

Connecting an iTunes Computer to a Network

As I wrote in an earlier note, this is not a book on networking, so I can't provide the information you need to connect computers together on a network. However, to enable sharing over a network, you must be connected to a network, which makes sense because the computers have to have some way to communicate with one another.

The network over which you share iTunes music can be wired, wireless, or both, and it can include Windows and Macintosh computers. If you have such a network and your iTunes computers are connected to it, you are ready to share your music. Otherwise, you will need to build the network before you can share your iTunes tunes.

Setting Up Your Computer to Share Music

To allow other people to listen to the music in your Library, perform the following steps:

1. Open the **iTunes Preferences** dialog box and then open the **Sharing pane** (see Figure 20.1).

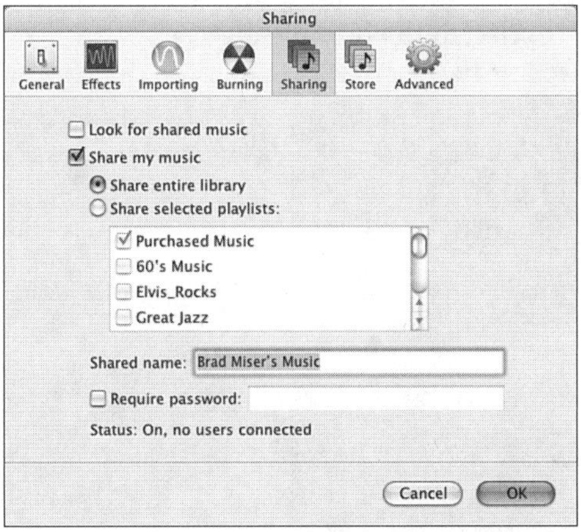

FIGURE 20.1

Using the Sharing pane of the iTunes Preferences dialog box, you can allow other people on your network to listen to your iTunes music.

2. To enable music sharing on your computer, check the **Share my music** check box. When you do so, you will see a prompt reminding you that sharing is for personal use only; click **OK** to clear the prompt.

   When you share music, you have two options for the music you share. You can share your entire Library or you can share only selected playlists.

3. To share your entire Library, click the **Share entire library** radio button.

   To share only specific playlists, click the **Share selected playlists** radio button and then check the box next to each playlist you want to share. You can scroll through the list of available playlists using the scrollbar located on the right side of the playlist list.

4. Enter the name of your shared music collection in the **Shared name** field. By default, this will be the name of your user account on the computer with *'s Music* added to it. However, you can enter any name you'd like. This name will be how others identify your music on their **Source List**.

5. If you want to require that people enter a password before they can listen to the music you share, check the **Require password** check box and enter the password they will have to use in the box.

6. Click **OK**. The music you selected to share will become available to others on your network.

7. If you require a password to let others access your music, provide them with the password.

Knowing Who Is Using Your Music

You can monitor how many people are using the music you are sharing by opening the Sharing pane of the iTunes Preferences dialog box (see Figure 20.2). At the bottom of the pane, you will see the current status of sharing (On or Off) and how many users are currently connected to your music.

FIGURE 20.2

At the moment, the Status information at the bottom of the pane shows that two users are sharing the iTunes music on this computer.

Listening to Music Being Shared with You

Two steps are required to listen to music being shared with you. The first one, which must be done only once, is to tell iTunes to look for any music being shared with you. The second one is to access and listen to that music.

Accessing iTunes Music Being Shared with You

To have iTunes look across the network and identify music that is available to you, open the **Sharing** pane of the iTunes Preferences dialog box (see Figure 20.3). Then, check the **Look for shared music** check box. Click **OK**. When you return to the iTunes window, you will see music that is being shared with you. If only one source is available, you will see the name of that source with a set of dark blue boxes and a musical note as its icon (see Figure 20.4).

FIGURE 20.3

When the Look for shared music check box is checked, iTunes will look for any music being shared with you.

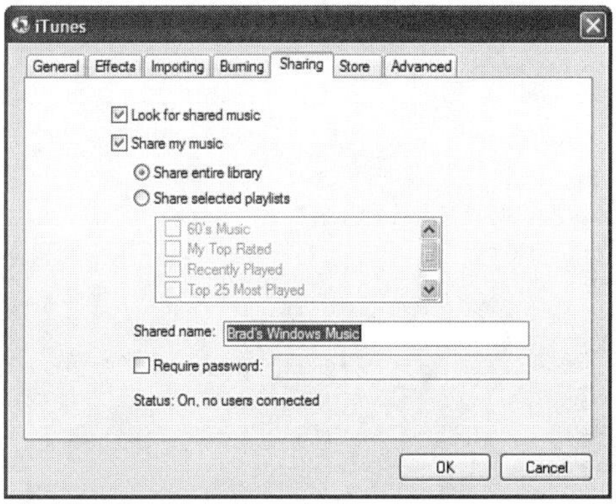

FIGURE 20.4

The source called iMac Music is being shared on the network.

If more than one source is available to you, you will see a source called **Shared Music** with an expansion triangle next to it. Click this triangle to expand the Shared Music source to see each of the music sources being shared with you (see Figure 20.5).

FIGURE 20.5

Under the expanded Shared Music source, you can see that three computers are currently sharing music with this machine.

iTunes

Source	Genre	Artist	Album
Library	All (7 Genres)	All (22 Artists)	All (11 Albums)
Radio	Country	Benny Goodman And His Orchestra	Big Band Boogie
Music Store	Gospel & Religious	Count Basie	Braveheart
Shared Music	Jazz	Duke Ellington	Consider The Cost
Brad's PowerBook Music	Pop	Enya	For The Sake Of The Call
Brad Miser's Music	R&B	Fran Walsh and Howard Shore	Gladiator Soundtrack
iMac Music	Rock	Glenn Miller And His Orchestra	Live Rust
60's Music			
My Top Rated			
Recently Played			
Top 25 Most Played			
Soundtracks			

Song Name	Time	Artist	Album	Genre
Sugar Mountain	5:02	Neil Young	Live Rust	Rock
I Am A Child	3:00	Neil Young	Live Rust	Rock
Comes A Time	3:15	Neil Young	Live Rust	Rock
After The Gold Rush	3:48	Neil Young	Live Rust	Rock
My My, Hey Hey (Out Of The Blue)	4:11	Neil Young	Live Rust	Rock
When You Dance I Can Really Love	3:42	Neil Young	Live Rust	Rock
The Loner	4:52	Neil Young	Live Rust	Rock
The Needle And The Damage Done	3:06	Neil Young	Live Rust	Rock
Lotta Love	2:52	Neil Young	Live Rust	Rock
Sedan Delivery	4:50	Neil Young	Live Rust	Rock
Powderfinger	5:43	Neil Young	Live Rust	Rock
Cortez The Killer	6:19	Neil Young	Live Rust	Rock
Cinnamon Girl	3:21	Neil Young	Live Rust	Rock
Like A Hurricane	8:20	Neil Young	Live Rust	Rock
Hey Hey, My My (Into The Black)	4:37	Neil Young	Live Rust	Rock

166 songs, 12 hours, 690.1 MB

Listening to Shared iTunes Music

To listen to shared music, do the following steps:

1. Select the **source** to which you want to listen by clicking its icon. Your computer will attempt to connect to that music source.

2. If the source is protected by a password, you will be prompted to enter the **password** for that source. Do so and click **OK**.

   After you have entered the correct password, or if no password is required, the source's music will be shown in the Content pane (see Figure 20.6).

3. If the shared source has one or more playlists, you can view the playlists for that source by clicking the expansion triangle next to the source's name. When it expands, you will see the playlists it contains.

If a music source requires that you provide a password to listen to it, you will see the padlock icon in the lower-right corner of the source's icon (for an example of this, look carefully at the iMac Music source's icon in Figure 20.5).

FIGURE 20.6

The iMac Music source is selected and its songs appear in the Content pane.

4. Select a playlist under the shared source, and its songs will be shown in the Content pane (see Figure 20.7).

5. Play **music** on the shared source just like music in your Library—by selecting **it** and clicking **Play**. Other playback tools, such as sorting the Content pane to change the order in which songs play, also work just as they do when you are listening to the music in your Library.

> **note**
>
> If only selected playlists on a source have been shared, when you select the source, you will see all the songs in the shared playlists rather than all the music in that machine's Library (which is what you see if the entire Library has been shared).

FIGURE 20.7
The shared
source iMac
Music has a
number of
playlists avail-
able; the Most
Frequently
Played playlist is
selected.

THE ABSOLUTE MINIMUM

The ability to share your music with other computers on your network and being able to listen to the music on other people's computers is pretty cool, don't you think? Following are some points to keep in mind to help your sharing:

- In order to share music, the computer sharing it must be turned on and cannot be in Standby (Windows) or Sleep (Mac) mode. If the computer goes to one of these modes or is turned off, the shared music will no longer be available.

- Similarly, iTunes must be running for music to be shared. If you quit iTunes while sharing music, the music you were sharing will no longer be available to others.

- When it comes to sharing, iTunes doesn't care whether a machine is a Windows computer or a Mac. You can share music or listen to shared music from either platform.

- When you access shared music, you can only listen to it. You can't add it your Library, put it in playlists, change its information, put in on a CD, or other tasks that you can do with the music in your own Library.

- You can share your music with up to five computers at the same time.

- If you access music that was purchased at the iTunes Music Store, you must validate that you have permission to listen to that music by authorizing it. Music that you purchase from the iTunes Music Store can only be used on three computers at a time, and someone sharing music you purchased counts as one of those three. To be able to listen to shared music at all, you must be able to provide the account and username under which it was purchased. You'll learn about this in more detail in Part III, "The iTunes Music Store."

IN THIS CHAPTER

- Take care of iTunes, and it will take care of you.

- Be safe, not sorry, by backing up your music.

- Get help with those very rare, but possibly annoying, iTunes problems.

21

MAINTAINING iTUNES AND SOLVING PROBLEMS

As an application, iTunes is so well designed that you aren't likely to have many problems with it. And that is a good thing because who wants problems? However, you can minimize iTunes problems by keeping the application updated to the current release. You should also keep your music collection backed up just in case something bad happens to your computer.

In the rare event that you do have troubles, you can usually solve them without too much effort.

Keeping iTunes Up to Date

iTunes is one of Apple's flagship applications, especially because it is the only current Apple application that runs on both Macintosh and Windows computers. Because of this, Apple is continuously refining the application to both make it even more trouble free and to enhance its features. You should keep your copy of iTunes current; fortunately, you can set up iTunes so it maintains itself.

Keeping iTunes Up to Date on Any Computer Automatically

Setting up iTunes so that it keeps itself current automatically is very simple. Open the **General** pane of the iTunes Preferences dialog box. Then check the **Check for iTunes Updates Automatically** check box (see Figure 21.1). Click **OK**.

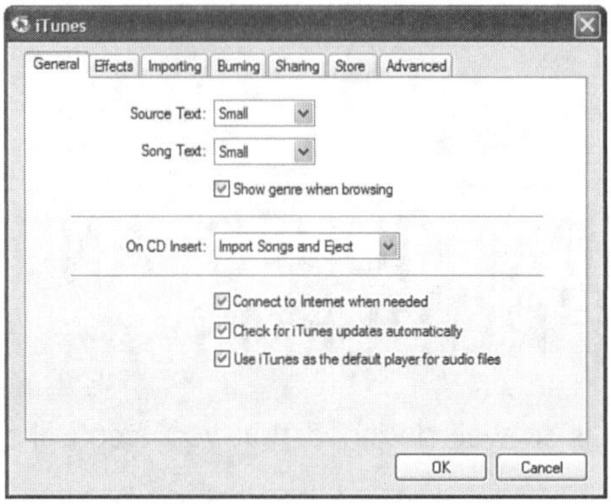

FIGURE 21.1

Using the General pane of the iTunes Preferences dialog box, you can have iTunes keep itself current.

Once per week, iTunes will connect to Apple's servers and check for updates. When it finds an update, you will be prompted to download and install it on your computer.

The benefit of this is that you don't have to remember to check for updates yourself. There isn't really a downside because you have the opportunity to decline to install the update if you don't want it installed. Also, you can always choose to do a manual update if that is your preference.

note

For automatic updates to work, you need to allow iTunes to connect to the Internet when it needs to. Check the **Connect to Internet When Needed** check box on the General tab of the iTunes Preferences dialog box to grant iTunes permission to do this.

Keeping iTunes Up to Date on a Windows PC Manually

You can check for an iTunes update manually any time you think one might be available or if you prefer to do manual updates for some reason. You can check for iTunes updates manually on a Windows computer by choosing **Help**, **Check for iTunes Updates**. iTunes will connect to the Internet and check for a newer version of the application. If a new version is available, you will be prompted to download and install it. If a newer version is not available, you will see a dialog box telling you so.

caution

In order for iTunes to perform this check, it must be stopped and started once during the week. In other words, if you never quit iTunes, it won't ever perform this check.

Keeping iTunes Up to Date on a Macintosh

Because both Mac OS X and iTunes are Apple products, iTunes is one of the applications tracked by Mac OS X's Software Update feature.

If you have set Software Update to check for updates automatically, it will check for iTunes updates according to the schedule you set. When it finds an update, you will be prompted to download and install it.

To manually check for updates, choose **Apple**, **Software Update** (see Figure 21.2). If an iTunes update is available, you will see it in the **Software Update** window. You can then select it and download it to your Mac.

note

If the computer you use doesn't have a consistent connection to the Internet (perhaps you use a laptop and only connect to the Internet occasionally), you'll need to use the manual update process to keep iTunes current because there is no way to make sure it checks for updates during the times you have an Internet connection.

FIGURE 21.2

On a Mac, you can use Software Update to keep your version of iTunes current.

Backing Up Your iTunes Music Library

Hopefully, you have and use a good backup system to protect all your files, including your iTunes Library. If so, you get extra points from me and can skip the rest of this section.

If you don't use a backup system to protect yourself, shame on you. However, you can earn some points back by at least backing up your music collection to CD or DVD. You can do this by creating a playlist containing the music you want to back up. Then, you burn that playlist to a CD or DVD. That will place a copy of your music on disc so that you can recover it should you ever need to. For detailed steps to burn discs, see Chapter 19, "Burning Your Own CDs or DVDs."

note

Unless you have a very limited music selection, backing up your music on CD isn't practical. However, if you only have a CD writer available, you should at least back up any music you purchase from the iTunes Music Store or download from the Internet. That will protect the music you get from those sources. You can always reimport music from the original audio CD sources if you have to.

If the playlist you select contains more songs than will fit on a single CD or DVD, you will be prompted to see whether you want iTunes to place the playlist on multiple discs. If you allow this, iTunes will keep burning discs until all the songs in the playlist have been placed on a disc.

Solving iTunes Problems

iTunes is about as trouble-free as any application gets; this is especially amazing because iTunes offers so many great features. However, even the best application is bound to run into a few hiccups.

Because the odds of me including in this book the specific problems you might experience are small, it is more profitable for you to learn where you can access help with problems you might experience. So, I've included the solution to one problem you are relatively likely to encounter here. Then, you'll learn how to get help for other problems should you experience them.

Solving the Missing Song File Problem

One problem you might encounter occasionally has nothing to do with iTunes not working properly. This problem occurs when something happens to the file for a song in your Library. When this happens, iTunes doesn't know what to do because it can't find the song's file. To show its confusion, iTunes displays an exclamation point next to any songs whose files it can't find when you try to play them or do anything else with them for that matter (see Figure 21.3).

To fix this problem, you have to reconnect iTunes to the missing file. Here are the steps to follow:

1. Double-click a song next to which the exclamation point icon is shown. You will see a prompt telling you that the original file can't be found and asking if you would like to locate it (see Figure 21.4).

tip

When you back up your music, make sure you use the MP3 or data format options, not the Audio CD format. If you choose Audio CD format, you won't be able to fit very many songs on a single disc.

caution

iTunes depends on QuickTime to work. If you remove QuickTime from your system, iTunes will stop working. You'll have to reinstall QuickTime or run the iTunes Installer to get it working again.

note

The most likely cause of the missing file problem is that a song's file has been moved or deleted outside of iTunes.

2. Click **Yes**. You will see the **Open** dialog box.

3. Move to the song's file, select it, and click **Open**. You'll return to the iTunes window, and the song will begin to play.

Missing file icon

FIGURE 21.3

The missing file icon means that iTunes can't find the file for a song.

FIGURE 21.4

When you see this dialog box, iTunes can't find a song's file.

If the problem was that the file had been moved, you might want to cause iTunes to place it back within the iTunes Music folder to keep your music files nicely organized. To do this, choose **Advanced**, **Consolidate Library**. In the resulting prompt, click **Consolidate**. iTunes will place a copy of any missing songs you have reconnected manually back into the proper location (within your iTunes Music folder).

note

If you can't find a song's file (probably because it has been deleted), you will have to reimport that song into your iTunes Library. (Because you have backed up your music, this isn't a problem. Right? Right!)

Getting Help with iTunes Problems

When you run into a problem that you can't solve yourself, the first place to go for help is Apple's Support Web site.

If you use iTunes on a Windows computer, go to `http://www.apple.com/support/itunes/windows/`. This page provides solutions to common problems, and you can search for specific problems you might experience (see Figure 21.5).

FIGURE 21.5

If you use iTunes on a Windows computer, check this Web site when you have problems.

Mac users are certainly not immune to problems either. For help with those, check out `http://www.apple.com/support/itunes/` (see Figure 21.6).

You can also access Apple's general support resources at `http://www.info.apple.com/`.

Of course, the usual Mac support sites, such as `macfixit.com`, are also good sources of information about iTunes problems.

You can also write to me with iTunes questions. My email address is `bradmacosx@mac.com`.

FIGURE 21.6

Mac users can get help here.

THE ABSOLUTE MINIMUM

Heck, who wants to spend time solving problems with a music application when the whole point is to spend time listening to and working with music? Not me, that's for sure. Fortunately, iTunes is designed and implemented so well that you aren't likely to experience any problems. If you do, help is available to you on the Web and from other sources.

- Of course, you can lower the chances that you will ever have problems with iTunes by keeping the application up to date. Fortunately, you can set iTunes to do this automatically.

- Just in case the worst happens, keep your music safe by keeping it backed up separately from your computer, such as on CD or DVD.

- You aren't likely to need to solve many problems. You might occasionally run into the "missing song file" problem. Fortunately, you learned how to solve that one.

- If you experience problems with iTunes, you can access the application's help system. You can also get help from the Apple Support Web page or by writing to me.

PART **III**

THE iTUNES MUSIC STORE

22

TOURING THE ITUNES MUSIC STORE

The iTunes Music Store might just be the best thing to happen to music, well, since iTunes and the iPod. The iTunes Music Store gives you online access to hundreds of thousands of songs and thousands of albums by thousands of artists (that's a lot of thousands!). You can search for or browse for music in many different ways. When you find music that interests you, you can preview it to see if it seems to be up your alley. If it is, you can immediately buy it and download it into your iTunes Library. This all works so well because access to the iTunes Music Store is built in to iTunes so that you can make the most of the store using the iTunes tools you already know so well.

Why the iTunes Music Store Rocks

There are many reasons the iTunes Music Store is great. To get you pumped up, here are a few:

- **The one hit wonder**—You know what I mean—that group or artist who put out one great song and that's it. Before the iTunes Music Store, if you wanted to own such a song, you usually had to buy a CD with 11 less-than-good songs to get the one you wanted. Not so with the iTunes Music Store. You can buy individual songs, so you only pay for the music you want.

- **Try before you buy**—You can preview any music in the store to make sure you know as much as possible about a song before you actually buy it.

- **It's legal**—Unlike many other sources of online music, the iTunes Music Store contains only music that is legal for you to buy and download.

- **It's convenient**—Because you access the iTunes Music Store through iTunes, shopping for music is very easy and convenient.

- **You can find the music you want**—You can search for specific songs or you can browse entire genres, artists, and more.

- **Immediate gratification**—Because music is immediately downloaded to your Mac, you don't have to wait for a CD to be delivered.

- **It's cheap**—Individual songs are only $.99. When you buy a CD's worth of songs, the price gets even lower and is usually less than you would pay elsewhere. Plus, there are no shipping costs.

Ever hear a song on a commercial or TV show you like? You can often find and buy such a song in just a few minutes.

- **Music allowances**—You can create music accounts that enable someone to purchase music up to a certain amount per period (such as per month). This is a great way to put a cap on the amount someone spends on music in the iTunes Music Store. Because it is so fun and simple to buy music this way, it is easy to get carried away. You might even want to put yourself on a music allowance.

- **Pick and choose**—Because you can buy individual songs, you can pick and choose among songs from a specific artist. Even when you like an artist, sometimes collections from that artist might have only a few songs you like. Rather than getting stuck with several you don't like, you can buy only those you do like.

How the iTunes Music Store Works

Through the rest of the chapters in this part of the book, you will learn how to use the iTunes Music Store in detail. For now, read through the following sections to get an overview of this amazing tool.

Getting an Account

In order to purchase music from the iTunes Music Store, you need an account (you don't need an account to browse the store or preview music). This account lets you charge music you purchase and prevents you from having to enter your information each time you visit the store. After you create and configure your iTunes Music Store account, you can sign in to the store automatically so that you don't need to think about it again.

tip

You can use your iTunes Music Store account to log in to the store from any iTunes-equipped computer.

Accessing the Store

Accessing the store is as easy as clicking the **Music Store** source in the iTunes **Source List** (see Figure 22.1). The iTunes Music Store fills the Content pane, and you can begin browsing or searching for music.

FIGURE 22.1
When you shop at this store, you don't need to worry about parking.

Browsing or Searching for Music

You can use the iTunes Music Store's tools to browse for music by genre, artist, or other attributes. This is a good way to explore the store to look for music you might be interested in but are not aware of. You can also search for music using the iTunes Search tool, which becomes the Search Music Store tool when the Music Store Source is selected (see Figure 22.2).

FIGURE 22.2

You can use the familiar iTunes Search tool to search for music in the iTunes Music Store.

Previewing Music

When you find a song in which you are interested, you can play a preview of it. The preview typically consists of 30 seconds of the song. This can help you decide if the song is really one you want.

Buying and Downloading Music

When you find songs you want to add to your iTunes Library, you can buy and download them with a few mouse clicks. The music you buy is automatically placed in a special playlist called **Purchased Music** (see Figure 22.3).

What Happens to Music You Buy

When you purchase music, it is automatically placed in your iTunes Library. From there, with a few minor exceptions, you can do the same things with iTunes Music Store music as you can with music from CDs you purchase.

FIGURE 22.3

As you can see, I have had no trouble finding music to purchase from the iTunes Music Store.

What Can You Do with Music You Buy from the iTunes Music Store?

The answer to this question is, just about anything you can do with any other music in your iTunes Library. Of course, "just about" means that there are some limitations on the music you get from the iTunes Music Store. However, you aren't likely to ever find these very limiting (unless you are trying to do something you shouldn't be doing anyway). So, following are the exceptions that make iTunes Music Store music slightly different from the music you import from a CD:

■ **You can listen to music you purchase from the iTunes Music Store on up to three computers at the same time**. For most people, this isn't a limitation because they don't have more than three computers anyway (maybe one at work and a couple at home). Even if you have more than three computers, it is easy to authorize and deauthorize computers to enable them to play iTunes Music Store music as needed.

note

Although the iTunes Music Store has an enormous amount of music available in it, it doesn't contain music from every artist. Some music companies have chosen not to place their music in the iTunes Music Store—for now. The inventory in the iTunes Music Store is continually increasing, and because of its dramatic success, my guess is that most of these holdouts will eventually join the party.

- **You can burn to disc the same playlist containing iTunes Music Store up to 10 times**. So, you can create up to 10 copies of the same CD or DVD. You aren't ever likely to really want to create that many copies of a disc, so this isn't really much of a limitation either. Besides, all you have to do is change one song in a playlist and then you can burn the changed playlist onto up to 10 more discs.

- **You are supposed to use the music you purchase for personal use only**. Of course, this is the same limitation for the audio CDs you buy, too.

That's it. You likely will never encounter one of these limits in your regular use of iTunes Music Store music.

THE ABSOLUTE MINIMUM

The iTunes Music Store is one of the best things to happen to music, ever. Personally, in the first few months the iTunes Music Store was available, I purchased more music than I did in several of the previous years. That's because I have fairly eclectic tastes and don't often want to purchase full CDs because I like only a few songs by some artists. That said, I have purchased a number of full CDs as well. Since the iTunes Music Store opened, I haven't ventured into any other online or brick-and-mortar music retailer. My guess is that once you start using the iTunes Music Store, you, too, might find it to be the only music store you need.

- When you shop in the iTunes Music Store, you can try any song before you buy it!

- To shop in the store, you need to set up an account. This can be done in just a few minutes, and you set up your account using iTunes.

- To visit the iTunes Music Store, simply click the **Music Store** source.

- You can browse and search the store for specific music that you want to hear.

- After you buy music and download it into your Library, you can do all sort of things with it, such as listening to it (duh), adding it to playlists, burning it to CD, and so on.

23

CONFIGURING iTUNES FOR THE MUSIC STORE

Before you bust through the iTunes Music Store's doors, it is a good idea to configure iTunes for the store so that when you do get there, you can focus on finding and buying cool tunes to add to your collection. And that is the point of this chapter—to help you understand your shopping options and then to create and configure your iTunes Music Store account.

Understanding Your Shopping Options

When it comes time to buy in the iTunes Music Store, you have two basic options: 1-Click or Shopping Cart. The 1-Click option works best when you have a broadband connection to the Internet. The Shopping Cart method works well for everyone but is primarily intended for people using a slow connection, such as a 56K dial-up account.

1-Click Shopping

This method is aptly named. When it's active, you can click the Buy Album button to purchase an album or the Buy Song button to purchase a song (see Figure 23.1). The item you elected to buy (a CD of songs or a single song) is immediately purchased and downloaded to your iTunes Library. The process requires literally one click (which is where the name came from, I suppose).

FIGURE 23.1

The Buy Album button enables you to purchase and download an album with a single mouse click.

If you have a broadband Internet connection, such as cable or DSL, this is a useful option because it makes buying music so fast and easy. You can click a button, and the purchase and download process will take place in the background while you do something else, such as look for more music.

If you have a slow connection, such as a dial-up account, this is probably not a good option for you. Because downloading songs will consume your connection's bandwidth, you won't be able to do anything else while music is being downloaded. So, you will have wait until the download process is complete before continuing to shop. Therefore, you should probably use the Shopping Cart method instead.

Shopping Cart Shopping

When you use this method, music you select to purchase is moved into a Shopping Cart, which serves as a holding area for the music you want to purchase. When you find music you want to buy, you click the Add Album or Add Song button. The item whose button you click is moved into your Shopping Cart, which appears on the Source List underneath the Music Store source. When you select the Shopping Cart, you will see the music you have added to it (see Figure 23.2). From there, you can purchase the music, at which point it is downloaded to your computer and placed in your Library.

FIGURE 23.2

The Shopping Cart holds the music you are interested in.

If you have a slow Internet connection, the Shopping Cart method is useful because you can place music in the cart and then continue shopping for music in the store without being hampered by the music being downloaded to your computer. When you are done shopping, you can pop back to the cart and purchase the music in which you are interested.

Although the Shopping Cart is designed for slow connections, you can use this method with a fast connection in the same way. The benefit of this is that you can gather a collection of music without actually purchasing it. When you are ready to check out, you can move to the cart and select the music you do actually want to buy.

Configuring Your iTunes Music Store Account

To purchase music in the iTunes Music Store, you need to have an account and configure that account on your computer.

Obtaining an iTunes Music Store Account

If you already have an account with AOL, the Apple online store, or .Mac, then you already have an account with the iTunes Music Store because it can use any of those accounts.

If you don't have one of these accounts, you can obtain an account in the iTunes Music Store by following these steps:

1. Select the **Music Store** source. The Music Store will fill the Content pane (see Figure 23.3).

FIGURE 23.3

To sign in to the iTunes Music Store, you click the Account button.

Account button

2. Click the **Account** button, which is labeled Sign In when you are not signed in to an account. You'll see the Account Login dialog box (see Figure 23.4).

3. Click the **Create New Account** button. You will return to the Content pane, which will be filled with the first of the three screens you use to create an account.

4. Read the **information** on the first screen and click the **Agree** button. (The information on the first screen contains the terms of service to which you must agree if you want to use the iTunes Music Store.)

FIGURE 23.4

The Account Login dialog box enables you to log in to an existing account or create a new one.

5. On the next screen, enter an **email address**, which will be your account's username (called an Apple ID), and password. Then enter a **security question**, **your birth date**, and select any **information** that you want to be emailed to you. Then click **Continue**.

6. On the third screen, enter your **credit card information** and **address** and then click **Done**.

7. If you are prompted to enter any additional information, do so and click the **Continue** or **Done** button. When the process is complete, you will see a completion screen. You will then be logged in to your new account (see Figure 23.5). Click **Done**. You will return to the iTunes Music Store and you can start shopping.

note

Apple uses extensive security measures to protect your credit card information. These measures are similar to those used by other online shopping sites. Information you provide via your iTunes Music Store account, such as your credit card number, is encrypted when it is communicated to Apple. It is highly unlikely that anyone would ever be able to obtain this information for nefarious purposes.

FIGURE 23.5

When you see
this screen, you
are ready to
shop.

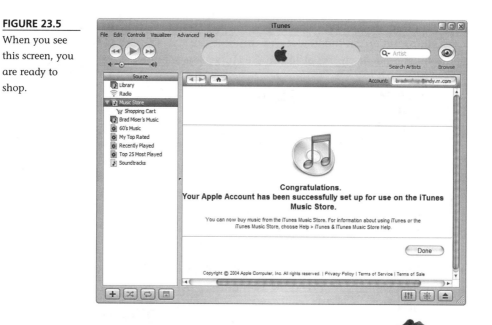

Logging In to Your iTunes Music Store Account

To be able to purchase music from the iTunes Music
Store, you must log in to your iTunes Music Store
account first. To log in to an existing iTunes Music
Store account, perform the following steps:

1. Click the **Account** button (this will be
   labeled **Sign In** when you aren't signed in
   to your account). You'll see the Sign In dialog box (see Figure 23.6).

If you just want to
browse for, search for, or
preview music, you don't have to
be logged in to your account.

FIGURE 23.6

You can sign in
to your iTunes
Music Store
account by
entering your
Apple ID or AOL
account infor-
mation in this
dialog box.

2. If you use an Apple ID to sign in to the store, click the **Apple** button. If you use an AOL account to sign in, click the **AOL** button.

3. Enter your Apple ID in the **Apple ID** field or your AOL screen name in the **AOL Screen Name** field.

4. Enter your password in the **Password** field.

5. Click **Sign In**. You will be logged in to your account. When you return to the iTunes window, you will see your Apple ID or AOL screen name in the Account field. After you are signed in, you can shop for tunes.

note

If a different account is currently logged in, you must log out of that account before you can sign in to another one.

When you click the AOL button, the Apple ID field becomes the AOL Screen Name field.

Logging Out of Your iTunes Music Store Account

To sign out of your account, click the **Account button**, which shows your Apple ID or AOL account name when you are logged in to your account. The Sign In dialog box will appear. Click **Sign Out**. You will return to the Music Store and the Account button will again be labeled Sign In.

Changing and Viewing Your iTunes Music Store Account

Times change and sometimes so does your personal information, such as your address or the credit card you want to use in the iTunes Music Store. If such changes occur in your life, you can change your Apple ID account information by using the following steps:

tip

If you can't remember your password, click the Forgot Password? button. You will move to a Web site that will help you retrieve your password.

1. Click your **iTunes Music Store account name**, shown in the Account button, as if you want to sign out. The Sign In dialog box will appear.

2. Enter your **password**. (Your account name will be filled in already.)

3. Click **View Account**. The Content pane will be replaced by the Account Information screen. On this screen, you will see various buttons that enable you to change your account information.

4. To change your account information (such as your address), click the **Edit Account Info** button and follow the onscreen instructions to change your information.

5. To change your credit card information, click **Edit Credit Card** and follow the onscreen instructions to change your credit card information.

6. To view your purchase history, click the **Purchase History** button. The screen will be filled with a detailed list of all the transactions for your account (see Figure 23.7). Review the **list** and click **Done**.

tip

A few other buttons appear on the View Account screen that you aren't likely to use. The Terms and Condition button displays the current terms and conditions for the store. The Privacy Policy enables you to view Apple's privacy policy, and the Reset Warnings button resets all the warning dialogs so that you see them again the next time they become relevant.

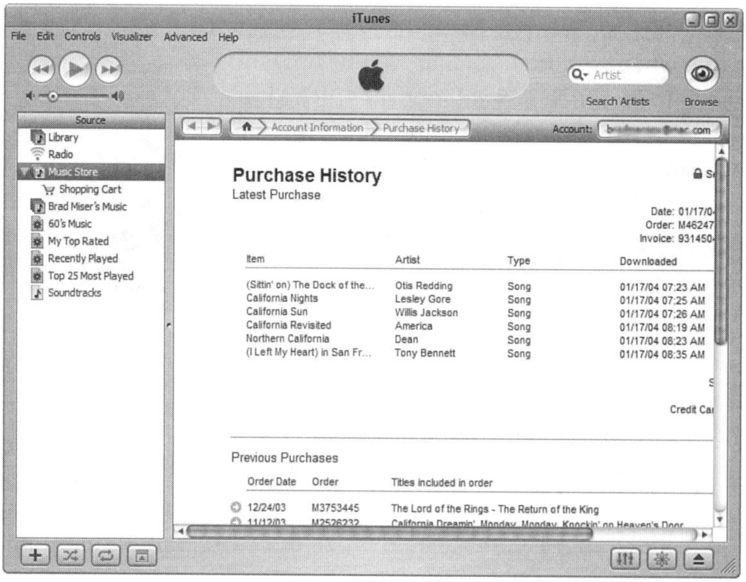

FIGURE 23.7

Yes, I do use the iTunes Music Store, as my purchase history shows.

7. When you are done making changes, click **Done**. You will return to the Music Store.

Setting Up a Music Allowance

You can create a music allowance for an iTunes Music Store account. This enables someone using that account to purchase a certain amount of music per month. This is really useful if you have kids who you want to be able to buy music at the store, and you want to provide a limited amount of credit for them to use. It can also be useful if you want to limit your own music purchases.

note

If you use an AOL account to access the store, you change your account information using the AOL software.

If the person to whom you are going to provide an allowance already has an Apple account, you will need his or her Apple ID and password. Alternatively, you can create an account for that person when you assign an allowance to him or her.

To create a music allowance, perform the following steps:

1. Access the **Account Information screen** for your account (see the previous section for the steps to do this).

2. Click **Setup Allowance**. You'll see the Set Up an iTunes Allowance screen.

3. Enter your **name** in the **Your Name** field.

4. Enter the **recipient's name** in the **Recipient's Name** field. If you are creating an allowance for yourself, enter your own information as the recipient's information.

5. Choose the **amount of money** the recipient will be able to spend each month in the **Monthly Allowance** menu—this amount will be applied to the recipient's account on the first day of each month. You can choose an amount from $10 to $200 per month, in $10 increments.

6. If the recipient already has an Apple ID, enter the Apple ID in the two **Apple ID** fields (one is a verification field). If the recipient does not have an Apple ID, click the **Create an Apple Account for Recipient** radio button and enter an **Apple ID** for that person in the two fields. Again, if you are creating an allowance for yourself, choose the existing account option and enter your account information.

note

If the recipient doesn't spend an entire month's allowance, it carries over to the next month.

7. If you want to provide a personal message about the allowance, write it in the **Personal Message** field.

8. Click **Buy Now**.

   If the recipient already has an Apple ID, you will see a screen that confirms that the allowance has been completed. Let the recipient know the good news—money is available in the iTunes Music Store!

   If you instructed iTunes to create an account for the recipient, you will see the Create an Apple Account screen. Complete the **information** on that screen and click **Create**. You will see an information screen. Read the information to make sure it is complete and then click **Buy**. You will see a screen that confirms that the allowance has been completed. Let the recipient know what his or her username and password are, and the shopping can begin!

   Click **Done** to complete the process or click **Set Up Another** if you want to set up another iTunes allowance. When you return to the Account Information screen, click Done to return to the iTunes Music Store.

The recipient will receive an email containing information about the allowance you set up, including the username and password (if you created one for this person). When recipient signs in, his or her current balance will be shown next to the username in the Account box. This balance always reflects the amount left for the current month. When the recipient has spent all of this, the account won't be able to purchase more music until the next month.

To manage your allowances, return to the Apple Account Information screen. This screen will now contain the Manage Allowance button, which enables you to change current allowances or to create new allowances.

Choosing Your Shopping Preferences

The final step in preparing to shop is to configure your shopping preferences. To do so, follow these steps:

1. Open the iTunes Preferences dialog box.

2. Click the **Store** tab to open the Store pane (see Figure 23.8).

FIGURE 23.8

You can customize your iTunes Music Store experience using the Store pane of the iTunes Preferences dialog box.

3. To show the iTunes Music Store source, which is the default condition, check the **Show iTunes Music Store** check box. If this box isn't checked, the Music Store won't appear in the Source List.

4. Choose your shopping method by clicking either the **Buy and download using 1-Click** radio button or the **Buy using a Shopping Cart** radio button.

5. If you want songs that you buy to play as soon as you download them, check the **Play songs after downloading** check box.

6. If you use a slow Internet connection and want song previews to download completely before they play, check the **Load complete preview before playing** check box. This will enable the preview to play without pauses that might be caused by your connection's speed (or lack thereof).

7. Click **OK**. If you select the Shopping Cart method, the Shopping Cart will appear inside the Music Store source. You are now ready to shop!

THE ABSOLUTE MINIMUM

Shopping at the iTunes Music Store is better than any music store I have ever seen. Here are some more shopping points to keep in mind:

- When you shop in the iTunes Music Store, you can choose the 1-Click or Shopping Cart method.

- To shop in the store, you need to obtain and configure an account.

- After you have an account, you configure iTunes to shop according to your preference.

- Almost all the music you buy from the iTunes Music Store has artwork associated with it. You can view the artwork by clicking the Show Artwork button.

- The music you buy from the iTunes Music Store is in the Protected AAC audio file format. This is the same AAC format in which you can import music into your Library, but it also includes some protections against copyright violations.

- The best thing about music you buy from the iTunes Music Store might be that you don't have to unwrap a CD. I hate trying to pry them out of their plastic wrapping!

Browsing for Tunes

Browsing for tunes can be a great way to discover music you might be interested in but don't know it. You click through the store to explore in various ways; when you aren't looking for something specific, browsing can result in lots of great music of which you might not have even been aware.

Browsing the iTunes Music Store Home Page

You have several different ways to browse for music from the iTunes Music Store Home page.

You will see several special sections titled **New Releases**, **Exclusives**, **Pre-Releases**, **Just Added**, and **Staff Favorites**; these categories of music are relatively self-explanatory (for example, Just Added contains music that is new to the iTunes Music Store). To scroll through the music available in these areas, click the scroll arrows or buttons (see Figure 24.2). When you do so, you will see the next set of albums in that category. If you see an album that interests you,

tip

Clicking the See All link in the upper right-hand corner of each category's window enables you to see all the albums in the respective category.

click it. You will see the details of the album on which you clicked (see Figure 24.3). Once you get to something that interests you, you can preview and purchase it.

FIGURE 24.2

You can browse the categories on the Home page by using the scroll tools.

Scroll buttons

Scroll arrows

FIGURE 24.3

Notice that browsing an album in the iTunes Music Store looks very similar to other iTunes sources; even better, it works in the same way too.

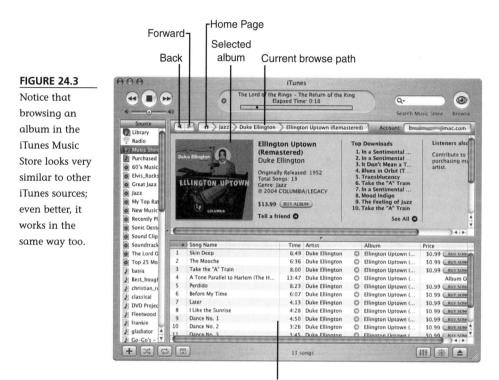

Content pane

You can also browse the iTunes Music Store Home page by using the various lists presented on the screen, such as the **Today's Top Songs**, **Today's Top Albums**, **Featured Artists**, **Celebrity Playlists**, and **iTunes Essentials**. To browse a list, you can click its title or on any of the songs or artists in the list. For example, to see the most downloaded albums on a given day, click the title text of the **Today's Top Album** list. You will see a screen that shows the albums that have been downloaded most on the day you visit the store (see Figure 24.4). You can click an album to view its contents.

In the upper-left area of the Home page, you will see a list that enables you to access special areas, including **New Releases**, **Just Added**, **Audiobooks**, **Music Charts**, and so on. Just click a link to move to the related area.

Also on the Home page are a number of ads that change over time. These ads feature specific artists, the current sales promotion, and so on. Just click an ad to move to its topic.

Browsing by Genre

Browsing by genre is a good way to find music by its style. Start from the Home page and choose a genre on the Genre menu. The Home page will be refreshed, presenting music only in that genre (see Figure 24.5). The tools on the Home page will be the same; the content of the music you see will be entirely focused on the genre of music you are browsing.

tip

You can browse the iTunes Music Store by clicking the iTunes Browse button. The Browser pane will appear above the Content pane just as it does when you are browsing your Library. You can browse the store in the same way too. For example, click a genre to see all the music of that genre in the store.

FIGURE 24.5

If you like jazz, as I do, browsing the Jazz genre is a great way to find new music.

Searching for Specific Tunes

Browsing for music is fun, but it can be time consuming and might not lead you to the music you want. When you want something specific, you can search for music using the iTunes Music Store Search tools. The two kinds of searches are basic search and power search.

When you do a basic search, you search by one search term. Basic searches are fast and easy, but can sometimes bring back a lot of songs that you aren't interested in. When you perform a power search, you can combine several search terms to make searching more precise.

note

When you browse by genre, think of the resulting page as the "Home page" for that genre.

Performing a Basic Search

Because you already learned how to search with iTunes, you already know how to perform a basic search in the iTunes Music Store because this type of search works in the same way. To perform a basic search, follow these steps:

1. Select **Music Store** as the source. You will see the iTunes Music Store Home page.

2. Click the **Magnifying Glass** icon in the iTunes Search tool and choose the **attribute** by which you want to search (see Figure 24.6). The options are All, Artists, Albums, Composers, Songs, or Power Search (you'll learn about that one in the next section).

FIGURE 24.6

You can use this menu to choose the attribute by which you want to search for music.

3. In the Search box, type the **text** or **numbers** for which you want to search.

4. Press **Return** or **Enter**. The search will be performed and you will be presented with the results window (see Figure 24.7). At the top of the window are the albums relevant to your search. At the top-right side are the top songs related to your search. At the bottom of the window, you will see that the Content pane lists the specific songs that meet your search criteria.

After you have performed a search, you can click the albums to view their contents, preview songs, purchase albums or songs, and so on.

tip

To clear a search, click the X button in the Search tool.

In this search, I found all the music in the store with "Basie" as the artist.

Performing a Power Search

Sometimes a basic search just doesn't cut it. Fortunately, you can use a power search if you want to find something very specific. With a power search, you can search by more than one attribute at the same time, such as by artist and composer. To search with power, do the following steps:

> **tip**
>
> You can also perform a power search by choosing Power Search on the Search By menu (open it by clicking the Magnifying Glass icon in the Search tool).

1. From the iTunes Music Store Home page, click the **Power Search** link located in the upper-left corner of the window. You'll see the Power Search window (see Figure 24.8).

2. For the first attribute for which you want to search, enter **text** or **numbers** in its box. For example, to search by artist, enter the artist's name in the Artist box.

3. Repeat **step 2** for each attribute for which you want to search.

4. If you want to limit the search to a specific genre, choose it on the **Genre** menu.

5. When you have configured the search, click **Search**. The window will be refreshed, and you will see the albums and songs that meet your search criteria (see Figure 24.9). Just under the search tools, you will see the albums that meet your search criteria. At the bottom of the window, you will see the songs that met your search.

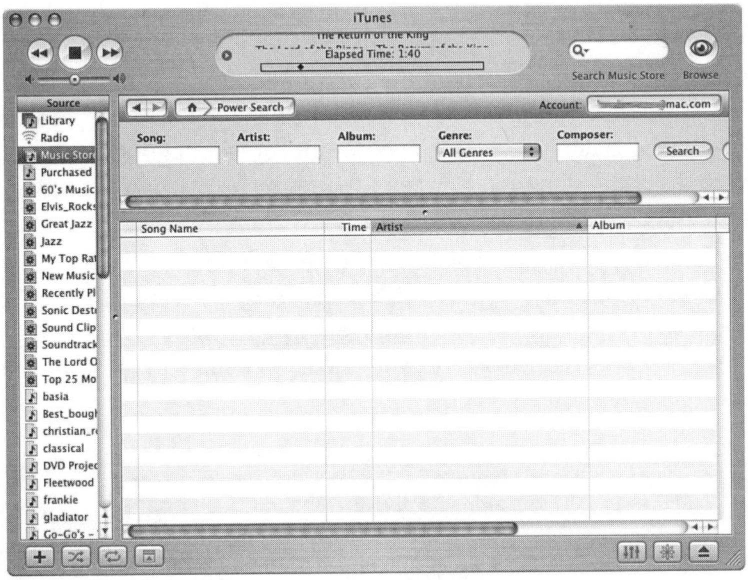

FIGURE 24.8

Using a power search, you can perform searches based on more than one attribute.

Just like a basic search, after you have performed a power search, you can click the albums to view their contents, preview songs, purchase albums or songs, and so on.

FIGURE 24.9

Here I have searched for music with the artist "Chapman" in the Inspirational genre.

Previewing Tunes

One of the great things about the iTunes Music Store is that you can preview music before you buy. These 30-second previews help you be more sure that the music you are buying is really something you want. For example, you can compare alternate versions of the same songs, listen to songs by artists who are new to you, or listen for any other reason.

To preview a song, you select it in the Content pane of the iTunes Music Store and click the **Play** button or double-click the **song** (see Figure 24.10). The preview will begin to play, again just like a song on another source, such as a CD or playlist. You can preview as many songs as you'd like, and you can preview the same song as much as you want.

FIGURE 24.10

When you browse an album or any other content on the iTunes Music Store, you can preview a song.

Buying Tunes

After you have found music that you want to add to your Library, you can purchase it. How you do this depends on which shopping method you selected: 1-Click Shopping or the Shopping Cart method (if you don't know what I am talking about, take a look at Chapter 23).

Buying Tunes with the 1-Click Method

The 1-Click method is aptly and literally named. It really does require only a single click. To purchase an album, you click the **Buy Album** button. To purchase a song, you click the **Buy Song** button. In either case, whatever you selected will be immediately purchased and downloaded to your Library (see Figure 24.11). (Because you entered credit card information when you configured your iTunes Music Store account, you don't need to provide any payment information—after you click the Buy button, the store automatically gets the information it needs to complete your purchase.) After the download process is complete, the music will be in your Library and it is now yours to listen to, put on a CD, and so on.

tip

When you log in to your account, you can indicate whether iTunes should remember your password for shopping purposes. If you allow this, you won't need to enter your password each time you purchase music. If you don't allow this, at some point in the process, you will be prompted to enter the password for the account you are currently signed on under to be able to complete a purchase.

FIGURE 24.11

In the Information area of the iTunes window, you can see that I am currently downloading the album shown because I clicked the Buy Album button.

Buying Tunes with the Shopping Cart Method

Whereas the 1-Click method requires a single click to purchase music, the Shopping Cart method requires all of two or three clicks to accomplish the same result—that being to add new music to your Library.

When you find music in which you are interested, click either the **Add Album** button or the **Add Song** button to add an album or song, respectively, to your Shopping Cart source. When you do so, you will see a message in the Information area telling you that the item you selected has been added to your Shopping Cart (see Figure 24.12). Continue adding music to the Shopping Cart as long as you'd like.

When you are ready to buy music, select the **Shopping Cart** source on the Source List. You will see the music you have added to the cart (see Figure 24.13). The total cost of all the items in your cart is shown at the bottom of the window. To remove an item from the cart, click its **Remove** button. The item will be deleted from the cart, and the cost information will be updated. When the cart contains only the music you want to buy, click the **Buy Now** button. The music in the cart will be downloaded to your Library. After the download process is complete, you can listen to it, put it in playlists, place it on CD, and so on. (Just like the 1-Click method, you don't need to enter payment information because that is stored as part of your iTunes Music Store account and is provided for you automatically.)

tip

If you don't see the Shopping Cart source, click the expansion triangle next to Music Store. Music Store will expand and you will see your Shopping Cart.

FIGURE 24.12
Here I have added an album to my Shopping Cart.

FIGURE 24.13
You can view the contents of your Shopping Cart and purchase the music it contains.

THE ABSOLUTE MINIMUM

You now have all the skills you need to find, preview, and buy music from the iTunes Music Store. If you are like me, you will be hooked after your first trip. Following are some pointers to help you shop like an iTunes Music Store master:

- When you search and iTunes can't find any music that matches your search, it will prompt you with its best guess about what you meant to search for. For example, if you were searching for music from the group Lynyrd Skynyrd and searched for "lynnrd" (who can ever spell that name right anyway!), iTunes would present a prompt in the search results asking you if you meant to search for "Lynyrd" because it can match that to its database. If you click the search text in the prompt, iTunes will search for that term instead.

- No matter which shopping method you use, the price for everything is listed next to the buttons you use to purchase the song or album or to add it to your Shopping Cart. Songs are $.99 each. The cost of albums varies, but in most cases, the price per song works out slightly less when you buy an album than when you buy the same music by the song.

- Some albums are available only as a partial album; this is indicated by the term "Partial Album" next to the album. This means that you can purchase one or more of the songs on the album, but not all the songs on the album or the album itself.

- Some songs are available only as part of an album. This means that you can only purchase the song by buying the album of which it is a part. Songs in this category are indicated by the text "Album Only" in the Price column of the Content pane.

- Even if you have a fast connection, you might prefer the Shopping Cart method because you can use the cart as a holding area for the music you might want to buy. This gives you a chance to think about it before you complete the purchase. When you use the 1-Click method, however, as soon as you click the Buy button, the deal is done.

25

Working with Purchased Music

The title of this chapter is somewhat misleading because it implies there is a lot different about working with music you have purchased than with other music in your Library, such as music you've imported from audio CDs. Although there are some unique aspects of music you purchased from the iTunes Music Store, mostly you can use it in the same way as any other music you have added to your own iTunes Library. But, there are just a few things of which you need to be aware, and that is where this chapter comes in.

The most important difference between music you purchase from the iTunes Music Store and other music in your Library is that a computer must be authorized to play music from the iTunes Music Store. You'll learn about this concept later in this chapter.

Understanding What Happens When You Buy Music from the iTunes Music Store

When you download music from the iTunes Music Store, whether you use 1-Click or the Shopping Cart, that music is added to your Library (see Figure 25.1). From there, you can listen to it, add it to playlists, burn it to disc, move it to an iPod, share it, and so on. In other words, it becomes mostly like music you have added to your Library from other sources.

note

Also, just like other music in your Library, if you define one or more smart playlists with live updating enabled and then purchase music from the iTunes Music Store that meets the criteria for those playlists, your purchased music will be added to the appropriate playlists automatically.

FIGURE 25.1

This music came from the iTunes Music Store; it doesn't look any different than other music in the Library and acts only a bit different.

Using the Purchased Music Playlist

Immediately after your first purchase from the iTunes Music Store, the Purchased Music source becomes available on your Source List (see Figure 25.2). This source is actually a special smart playlist that will capture all the music you purchase from the iTunes Music Store. You can always return to your purchased music by using the Purchased Music source.

You can use the Purchased Music playlist like other playlists. To see its contents, select **Purchased Music** on the Source list. The first time you select it, you will see a dialog box explaining the function of the playlist (see Figure 25.3). Read the information and click **OK** to move to the Purchased Music playlist.

note

One thing you can't do with the Purchased Music smart playlist that you can do with others is to edit its criteria. The Purchased Music playlist is what it is; you can't change it (not that you'd ever want to anyway).

FIGURE 25.2

The Purchased Music source is actually a special playlist that always contains all the music you have purchased from the iTunes Music Store.

FIGURE 25.3

I suggest you check the check box so you don't see this dialog box each time you use the Purchased Music playlist.

You can then browse the Purchased Music playlist, search in it, play it, and so on. Of course, you can also configure view options for it, sort it, and do the other playlist tasks with which you are hopefully familiar by now.

You can also move music from your Library that you didn't purchase from the iTunes Music Store into the Purchased Music playlist, but I don't recommend that you do so because that will dilute its purpose.

Understanding Authorization

The music you purchase from the iTunes Music Store is protected in the sense that it has certain limitations on what you can do with it. Fortunately, these limitations are not very limiting!

One of these limits is that you can only play iTunes Music Store music on up to three computers at the same time. To implement this limit, the computer on which you play iTunes Music Store music must be *authorized*. When you authorize a computer, iTunes will connect to the Internet and register that computer with the iTunes Music Store to play the music purchased under the user account you used to buy it.

To state this another way, you actually authorize the music for a specific user account on up to three computers at a time. When you authorize a computer, you authorize all the songs you have purchased under an iTunes Music Store account; you can't authorize some of the songs you buy on one machine and a different set on another computer. When a

note

You can store the music you purchase on as many computers as you'd like. Then you can easily authorize the machines on which you want to play the music and deauthorize the ones you aren't using at the moment.

computer is authorized, it can play all the music that has been purchased under an iTunes Music Store account. If it isn't authorized, you won't be able to play any of the music you purchased.

Fortunately, it is quite easy to authorize or deauthorize a computer, as you will see in the next sections.

Authorizing a Computer

The first time you purchase music on a computer, you must authorize that computer before you can play the music you purchase. After that, the computer remains authorized until you deauthorize it.

To authorize a computer to play purchased music, try to play the music you have purchased from the iTunes Music Store. If the current computer has been authorized, the music will begin to play. If it hasn't been authorized, you will see the Authorize Computer dialog box. Enter the username and password that was used to purchase the music and click **Authorize**. iTunes will connect to the Internet and authorize the computer. When that process is complete, the music will play.

If you attempt to authorize more than three computers under the same user account, you will see a warning prompt explaining that you can have only three computers authorized at the same time (see Figure 25.4). You must deauthorize one of the computers to be able to authorize the current one.

caution

You must be able to connect to the Internet to be able to authorize a computer. This can bite you if you want to play purchased music on a laptop while you are on the road and can't connect. If you didn't purchase music while using that computer, make sure you authorize the machine before you remove it from its Internet connection. If you don't, the purchased music on its hard drive will be only so much dead digital weight until you can authorize that computer.

FIGURE 25.4

If you see this warning, you must deauthorize another computer before you can authorize the current one.

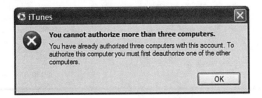

Deauthorizing a Computer

To deauthorize a computer, choose **Advanced**, **Deauthorize Computer**. You will see the Deauthorize Computer dialog box (see Figure 25.5). Click the **Deauthorize for Music Store Account** radio button and click **Finish**. You will see another Deauthorize Computer dialog box. Enter the username (Apple ID or AOL screen name) and password for the account that you want to deauthorize on the machine and click **OK**. iTunes will connect to the Internet and deauthorize the computer. When the process is complete, you will see a dialog box telling you so. Click **OK**. The computer will no longer count against the three-computer limit for the user account. (It won't be able to play music purchased under that iTunes Music Store account either.)

> **note**
>
> Just because you are signed into your iTunes Music Store user account on a computer, it doesn't mean that computer is authorized. In fact, you can purchase music using the same user account on a computer that isn't authorized. You won't be able to play that music until you authorize your computer.

You can authorize a computer again by attempting to play purchased music and providing the user account and password for which you want to authorize the machine. As you can see, it is quite simple to authorize and deauthorize computers.

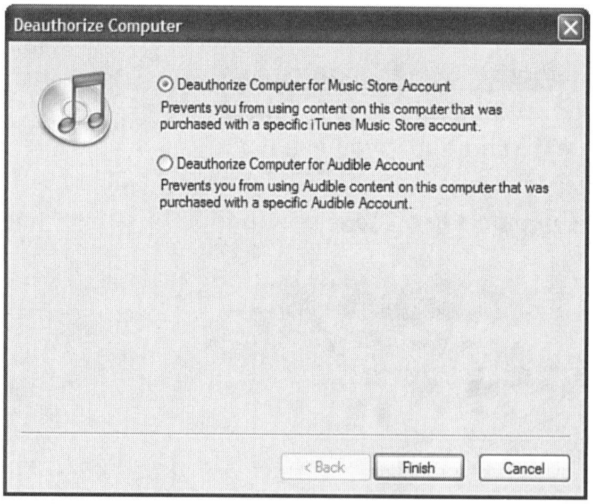

FIGURE 25.5

You use this dialog box to deauthorize a computer.

Deauthorize Computer

○ Deauthorize Computer for Music Store Account
Prevents you from using content on this computer that was purchased with a specific iTunes Music Store account.

○ Deauthorize Computer for Audible Account
Prevents you from using Audible content on this computer that was purchased with a specific Audible Account.

< Back | Finish | Cancel

In order to authorize or deauthorize a computer, you must provide the username and password for the account under which music was purchased. This information also enables you to buy music from the iTunes Music Store. If you don't trust others who will be playing music you purchased, you should authorize their computers directly rather than providing your username and password to them.

Moving Purchased Music to Other Computers

You can move any music between computers, but usually it is just as easy to import music from audio CDs to each computer on which you want to create a Library. However, if you have more than one computer, you might want to move music you purchased from the iTunes Music Store to the other computers so you can play it from there.

Understanding the Ways You Can Move Your Tunes

> **note**
>
> You can purchase music on a machine that isn't authorized to play it. If you do this, you will see a warning dialog box that will explain that you won't be able to play the music on the machine you are using to purchase it until you authorize that computer. You can also store music purchased under different iTunes Music Store accounts on the same computer. To authorize the computer to play that music, you must authorize it for the iTunes Music Store account under which the music you want to play was purchased.

First, you need to move the song files from the computer on which they are stored (the machine from which you purchased the music) onto the machine you want to be able to play that music on.

In order to move files to another computer, you need to know where those files are located. From Part II, "iTunes," you know that iTunes keeps all the files in the Library organized in the iTunes Music folder (assuming you followed my recommendations and set the preferences to allow this). You can move to this folder to find the files you want to move.

You can also find the location of song files by selecting them and choosing **File**, **Show Song File** or pressing **Ctrl+R** (Windows) or ⌘**+R** (Mac). iTunes will open a window showing the location of the files for the songs you have selected (see Figure 25.6).

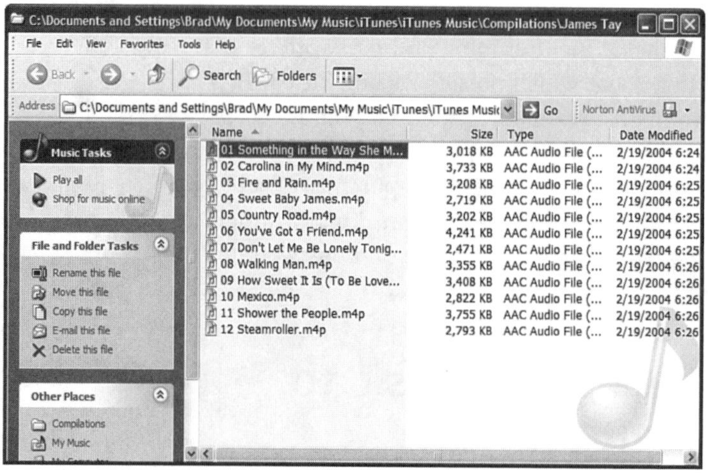

FIGURE 25.6

When you use the Show Song File command, iTunes opens a window to show you where the song's file is located on your computer.

After you have located the song files, you need to make them available to the computer to which you want to move them. There are many ways to do this, including the following:

- Create a data CD or DVD containing the music you want to move. You can do this from within iTunes by changing the Burning preferences to use the Data CD or Data DVD format and then burning a disc. This process is very easy to do and works regardless of there being a network connection between the computers. The primary limitation is the size of the discs you use and the time it takes to burn the discs.

- Use a network to share files on the computer from which you bought music with the one to which you want to move the files. This method is simple and doesn't place a limit on the sizes of the files you move. You also don't need to spend time or money to burn discs. The downside is that you have to have the computers connected via a network.

> **tip**
>
> You can share music you have purchased with other computers on your network. However, for other machines to be able to play your purchased music, they must be authorized to do so and therefore count against the three-computer limit. Fortunately, as you have seen, it is simple to authorize and deauthorize computers, so you can keep up to three authorized quite easily.

- Create an audio CD of purchased music and import that into the other computer's iTunes Library. This is also an easy process, but you are limited to the amount of music that can fit onto an Audio CD.

- Move the song files onto a networked drive, such as a server. For example, if you use a .Mac account, you can use your iDisk to transfer files by copying them to your iDisk. This has the same pros and cons as moving files directly across a network.

- Copy the files onto a portable hard drive, such as a FireWire or USB drive. This is faster than and doesn't have the same space limitations as using a CD or DVD. Of course, the con is that you have to have such a drive available to you.

Lastly, you need to add the files that you are moving into the Library. This involves using the Add to Library command and then moving to and selecting the files you want to add.

Moving Purchased Music Files Over a Network

The following steps provide an example of how to move files that are shared over a network and add them to the Library:

1. Share the files on the original machine with the network.

2. From within iTunes on the computer to which you want to move the songs, choose **File**, **Add to Library**. You will see the Add to Library dialog box.

3. Move to and select the files or the folder containing the files you want to add to the Library (see Figure 25.7).

FIGURE 25.7

Here, I am accessing song files that are stored on a computer on the network.

Add To Library

James Taylor_ Greatest Hits

Brad Miser's C...	James Tay...atest Hits	01 Somethi...Moves.m4p
iDisk		02 Carolin...y Mind.m4p
Network		03 Fire and Rain.m4p
Panther		04 Sweet B... James.m4p
Mac OS X		05 Country Road.m4p
FW_800		06 You've ... Friend.m4p
FW_400_disk		07 Don't Le...onight.m4p
DDRIVE		08 Walking Man.m4p
CDRIVE		09 How Sw...d By Y.m4p
		10 Mexico.m4p
abg_ipod_itunes		11 Shower ...People.m4p
page_ct.xls		12 Steamroller.m4p
abg_ipod_itun...		
Favorites		
Desktop		
bmiser		

New Folder   Cancel   Open

4. Click **Open**. The songs you selected will be copied into your Library (see Figure 25.8). If the music you moved into the Library was purchased on a different computer, you need to authorize the current computer to play that music (see the next section).

tip

The keyboard shortcut for the Add to Library command is **Ctrl+O** (Windows) or ⌘**+O** (Mac).

FIGURE 25.8

You can see that the files I selected in the previous figure are now in the Library.

iTunes

The Grey Havens
Elapsed Time: 0:39

Q⁃ taylor

12 of 1867   Browse

| Source |
| Library |
| Radio |
| Music Store |
| Purchased Music |
| 60's Music |
| Elvis_Rocks |
| Great Jazz |
| Jazz |
| My Top Rated |
| New Music |
| Recently Played |
| Sonic Destop Music |
| Sound Clips |
| Soundtracks |
| The Lord Of The Rings |
| Top 25 Most Played |
| basia |
| Best_bought |
| christian_rock |
| classical |
| DVD Project Sound |
| Fleetwood |
| frankie |
| gladiator |
| Go-Go's - VH-1 Behind |

Genre	Artist	Album
All (24 Genres)	All (175 Artists)	All (157 Albums)
Alternative	101 Strings	1
Blues	Al Green	16 Biggest Hits
Blues/R&B	The Alan Parsons Project	20th Century Masters – The Mille
Business & Finance	America	20th Century Masters – The Mille
Classical	Amistad	A Fresh Aire Christmas
Country	Amy Grand/Sandi Patti	A Legendary Performer
Dance	Andy Williams	Acoustic Sketches
Easy Listening	Antonio Vivaldi	America

Song Name	Track #▲	Time	Artist	Album
Something in the Way She Moves	1 of 12	3:13	James Taylor	James Taylor: Grea...
Carolina in My Mind	2 of 12	4:00	James Taylor	James Taylor: Grea...
Fire and Rain	3 of 12	3:26	James Taylor	James Taylor: Grea...
Sweet Baby James	4 of 12	2:54	James Taylor	James Taylor: Grea...
Country Road	5 of 12	3:25	James Taylor	James Taylor: Grea...
You've Got a Friend	6 of 12	4:32	James Taylor	James Taylor: Grea...
Don't Let Me Be Lonely Tonight	7 of 12	2:38	James Taylor	James Taylor: Grea...
Walking Man	8 of 12	3:35	James Taylor	James Taylor: Grea...
How Sweet It Is (To Be Loved By You)	9 of 12	3:39	James Taylor	James Taylor: Grea...
Mexico	10 of 12	3:01	James Taylor	James Taylor: Grea...
Shower the People	11 of 12	4:01	James Taylor	James Taylor: Grea...
Steamroller	12 of 12	2:59	James Taylor	James Taylor: Grea...

12 songs, 41.3 minutes, 37.9 MB

You can create an audio CD from music you purchase from the iTunes Music Store and then import that music into a Library on another computer. Because the music is converted into the Audio CD format when you do this, it doesn't count against the three-computer limit for music you purchase from the iTunes Music Store. However, if you use this technique to play music you have purchased on more than three computers at the same time, you will violate the spirit and letter of the license agreement that you accept when you purchase music from the store. I recommend that you only use this method

tip

Purchased songs that you move to a different computer won't be added to the Purchased Music playlist automatically. You can drag them onto that playlist from the Library if you want to put them there.

if this won't result in more than three computers playing this music at the same time. This can be particularly useful if one of the machines on which you will be playing music can't connect to the Internet, which is required for authorization to take place.

Viewing the Music You Have Purchased

You have a couple ways to see the music you have purchased.

The first way you have already read about. Select the **Purchased Music** source and you will see all the music you have obtained from the iTunes Music Store. (This assumes you haven't removed any songs from this playlist.)

The second way is to view the entire purchase history for a user account. To do so, perform the following steps:

1. While signed in under the user account whose history you want to see, click the **Account** button (you need to select the Music Store source to see this button). You will be prompted to enter the password for that account.

2. Enter the account's password and click **View Account**. The Content pane will be filled with the Apple Account Information window, which provides, amazingly enough, information about the user account.

3. Click the **Purchase History** button. The data will be retrieved, and the Content pane will show the music purchased during each shopping session (see Figure 25.9).

4. To view the detail for a shopping session, click its **Detail** button. The screen will be refreshed, and you will see a detailed list of all the music purchased during that session (see Figure 25.10).

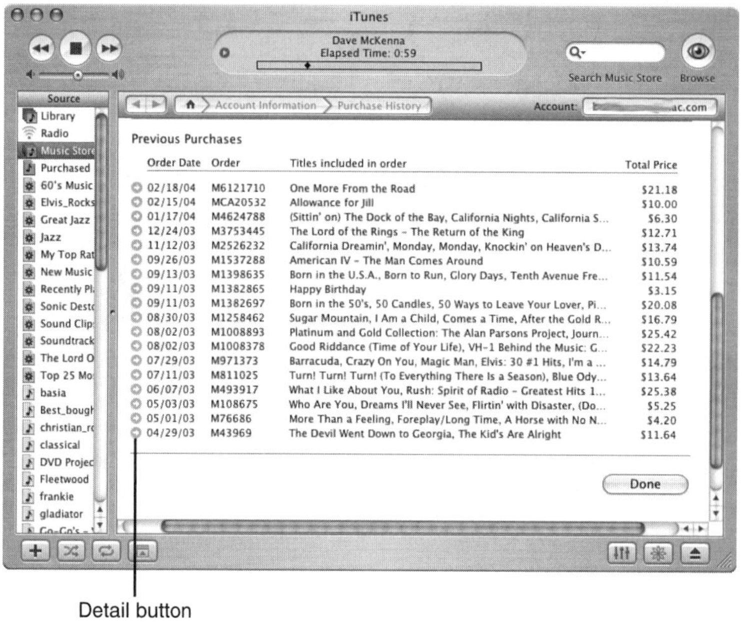

FIGURE 25.9

Your purchase history will be organized by shopping sessions.

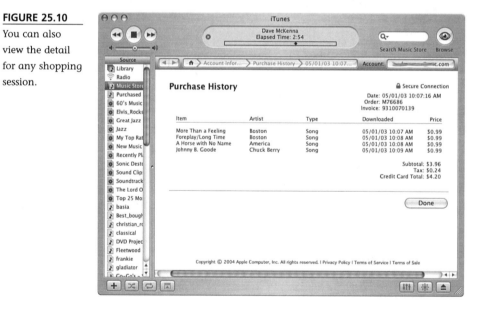

Detail button

FIGURE 25.10

You can also view the detail for any shopping session.

5. When you are done viewing the history of your purchases, click the **Done** button; you'll need to click it twice if you are viewing a detail screen. You'll return to the Apple Account Information screen.

6. Click **Done**. You'll move back to the iTunes Music Store.

Backing Up Purchased Music

Because you don't have music that you purchase from the iTunes Music Store "backed up" on a disc (like you do for the music you have on audio CD), you should make sure you back up the music you buy. The easiest way to do this is to burn a disc from the Purchased Music playlist. Of course, if you have purchased more than can fit on a single CD or DVD, you will need to use multiple discs to back up the entire collection.

Consider creating a smart playlist whose criteria is based on the date you added music to your Library and for which live updating is enabled. When you purchase new music, update the criteria so that the added date is just before you made your most recent purchase. Then, all the music you purchased since that date will be added to the playlist. Burn that playlist to disc, and you will have backed up your new music that you purchased since the last time you did this.

THE ABSOLUTE MINIMUM

The iTunes Music Store is very well designed and makes it quite easy to find and buy music—from individual songs from your favorite one-hit wonder to complete collections of classic artists. As you work with the tunes you buy, remember the following musical morsels:

- When you purchase music from the iTunes Music Store, it is downloaded into your Library.
- By default, all the music you purchased from the iTunes Music Store is stored in the Purchased Music playlist.
- To play purchased music on a computer, that computer must be authorized. You can have up to three computers authorized at the same time. You can deauthorize a computer by choosing the Deauthorize Computer command.
- To play purchased music on a computer that is different from the one on which you purchased it, you can move the purchased music to another computer. There are several ways to do this.
- There are a couple of ways to see the music you have purchased. One is to use the Purchased Music playlist. You can also use the Purchase History information for your iTunes account to see a list of all the music you have purchased from the iTunes Music Store.
- You should back up the music you purchase from the iTunes Music Store. The easiest way is to do this is to burn a CD or DVD of the Purchased Music playlist.

26

SOLVING iTUNES MUSIC STORE PROBLEMS

You will see that this is a short chapter. The reason is simple: You just aren't likely to encounter that many problems when working with the iTunes Music Store. The store, just like iTunes and the iPod, is well designed and works flawlessly most of the time. If you do encounter a problem, this chapter will help you find the solution.

Recovering Music That Wasn't Downloaded Successfully

If the download process for music you purchased wasn't completed for some reason (for example, you lost your Internet connection in the middle of the process), you can restart the download process to recover music you have purchased but weren't able to download successfully.

To do this, choose **Advanced**, **Check for Purchased Music** (see Figure 26.1). You will be prompted to enter the user account and password for the account under which the music was purchased. Do so and then click Check.

The music you have purchased will be checked against the music that has been successfully downloaded. If music is found that hasn't been downloaded successfully, you will be able to download it again. If you have successfully downloaded all the music you have purchased, you will see a message stating so (see Figure 26.2).

note

No, you can't use this technique to download music you have purchased to more than one computer. When you successfully download music, that music is marked as having been downloaded. The iTunes Music Store doesn't care to which computer you have downloaded it. When you buy music, you are entitled to download it once and only once.

FIGURE 26.1

You use the **Check for Purchased Music** command to recover music you have purchased but weren't able to download for some reason.

FIGURE 26.2

When you see this message, you have downloaded all the music you have purchased.

Solving the "Not Authorized to Play" Problem

As you learned in the previous chapter, you can play music you have purchased on up to three computers at the same time. If you try to play purchased music and see the "This Computer Is Not Authorized to Play This Music" message, you need to authorize the computer before you can play the purchased music. If you already have three computers authorized, you will need to deauthorize one before you can authorize another. (If you need help doing these tasks, see Chapter 25, "Working with Purchased Music.")

The challenge can sometimes be remembering how many and which computers you have authorized. The "how many" part is easy. Just access the **Apple Account Information** screen for your account. The Computer Authorizations section will tell you how many computers are currently authorized to play music for the account (to learn how to access this screen, see "Viewing the Music You Have Purchased" on page **355**).

The "which ones" part is a bit more difficult. The easiest way to tell is to try playing purchased music from each computer you might have authorized. If it plays, the computer is authorized.

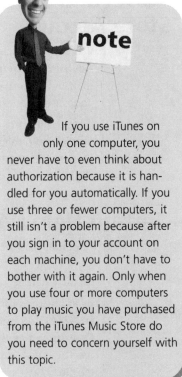

note

If you use iTunes on only one computer, you never have to even think about authorization because it is handled for you automatically. If you use three or fewer computers, it still isn't a problem because after you sign in to your account on each machine, you don't have to bother with it again. Only when you use four or more computers to play music you have purchased from the iTunes Music Store do you need to concern yourself with this topic.

caution

If you sell a computer or stop using it, make sure you deauthorize it first. Even if you wipe the machine's hard drive, it still counts as an authorized computer. If you no longer have access to an authorized computer, you will need to contact iTunes Music Store Customer Service to have that machine deauthorized.

Correcting Problems with Your iTunes Music Store Account

You can change information for your iTunes Music Store by accessing the **Apple Account Information** page and using its tools to make changes to your account, such as to change the credit card you use to purchase music. (For help using this page, see "Changing and Viewing Your iTunes Music Store Account" on page **325**.)

If something has changed from the iTunes Music Store side of the equation, you will be prompted to change your account information. The dialog box that appears will also enable you to access your Account Information page to make the required changes.

Getting Help with iTunes Music Store Problems

Hopefully you won't ever have any problems with the iTunes Music Store, and if you do, the information in this chapter should help you solve them. If not, don't despair because help is just a few clicks away.

To access the iTunes Customer Service page, choose **Help**, **Music Store Customer Service**. Your default Web browser will open and you will move to the **iTunes Customer Service** page for the type of computer you are using (see Figure 26.3). Use the links and information on this page to get help. For example, you can click the **Get Help with Computer Authorization** link to get help deauthorizing a computer to which you no longer have access.

FIGURE 26.3

This is the iTunes Customer Service page for Windows users.

Reporting Music You Can't Find in the Store

Although the iTunes Music Store is great, it isn't perfect. Its major flaw, which is a perfectly understandable one, is that it doesn't contain every song ever produced (as if that is even possible). The good news is that Apple is continually adding music to the store, especially as music producers and record companies see what a great way it is for them to distribute their music.

If you can't find the music you want to buy in the store, you can let Apple know about it. (Who knows, your contact may be the one that causes some specific artist or music to be added to the store!)

To request music, perform the following steps:

1. Open the iTunes Music Store's home page.

2. Click the **Requests & Feedback** link located in the upper-left corner of the screen.

3. In the Make a Request section, choose the type of request you want to make, such as **Song** or **Artist**, on the **My Request Is for A** menu.

4. Type what you want to request in the **Your Request** box.

5. Click **Send**. Your request will be submitted, and you will see a confirmation screen that explains that you won't get a personal response to your request. Hopefully, at some point, the music you requested will be added to the store.

THE ABSOLUTE MINIMUM

The iTunes Music Store is a great tool to search for and add music to your iTunes Library. In fact, you might never purchase a CD again (okay, that's a bit dramatic, but you get the idea). Fortunately, the iTunes Music Store works very well, and you aren't likely to have any problems using it, which is a good thing.

Just in case, in this chapter, you learned how to do the following tasks:

- Recover music you didn't download successfully.
- Solve the "Not Authorized to Play" issue.
- Fix problems with your iTunes Music Store account.
- Get help from Apple.
- Request music you can't find in the store.

If you do have problems and none of the information in this chapter helps you, you can always write to me at bradmacosx@mac.com, and I will do my best to help you get back into your best shopping form.

Index

How can we make this index more useful? Email us at indexes@quepublishing.com

How can we make this index more useful? Email us at indexes@quepublishing.com

How can we make this index more useful? Email us at indexes@quepublishing.com

How can we make this index more useful? Email us at indexes@quepublishing.com

How can we make this index more useful? Email us at indexes@quepublishing.com

How can we make this index more useful? Email us at indexes@quepublishing.com

How can we make this index more useful? Email us at indexes@quepublishing.com

Q - R

How can we make this index more useful? Email us at indexes@quepublishing.com

How can we make this index more useful? Email us at indexes@quepublishing.com

How can we make this index more useful? Email us at indexes@quepublishing.com

W

X - Y - Z